W9-BLF-701

SKILLS AND
STRATEGIES
TO IMPROVE
MOTHER-DAUGHTER
RELATIONSHIPS

SIMON & SCHUSTER
New York   London   Toronto
Sydney   Tokyo   Singapore

HOW TO MANAGE YOUR MOTHER

Nancy Wasserman Cocola

Arlene Modica Matthews

SIMON & SCHUSTER
Simon & Schuster Building
Rockefeller Center
1230 Avenue of the Americas
New York, New York 10020

Designed by Nina D'Amario / Levavi & Levavi
Manufactured in the United States of America

10 9 8 7 6 5 4 3 2 1

Library of Congress Cataloging in Publication Data

Cocola, Nancy Wasserman
    How to manage your mother : skills and strategies to improve
mother-daughter relationships / Nancy Wasserman Cocola,
Arlene Modica Matthews.
        p.   m.
    1. Parent and adult child. 2. Mothers and daughters.
I. Matthews, Arlene Modica.   II. Title.
HQ755.86.C63   1992
306.874'3—dc20   91-48204
                                                    CIP

ISBN: 0-671-74216-7

The excerpt from *Love You Forever*
is reprinted with the permission of
Firefly Books Ltd.

Acknowledgments

We thank Carla Glasser, Nancy's agent, for her faith in this project, for her matchmaking, and for her unfailing encouragement at every stage of this book's evolution. Thanks also to Bob Tabian, Arlene's agent, for his part in bringing this project to life.

Our deepest gratitude and admiration goes also to our editor, Laura Yorke, for her invaluable suggestions, her scrupulous efforts to ensure that our visions are realized, and her tireless commitment to this project, which in every way exceeded the usual "call of duty."

Thanks to everyone at Simon & Schuster who helped to bring this book to fruition. Special thanks to Bob Asahina, Wendy Nicholson, and Sarah Pinckney.

We would like to thank the vast community of women who have shared with us their experiences, hopes, and disappointments in their relationships with their mothers. They were our greatest advocates in writing this book . . . a testament to how every woman forever longs to make the most of her maternal bond.

We would specifically like to recognize the many women whom we have treated over the years. They have all shared their mothers with us. We wish to acknowledge them and express our profound sense of privilege at being the recipients of their trust.

From Nancy: I would like to thank my dear friends Fran, Nadine, and Ann. It was years ago, amid the warmth and trust I shared with each of them, that the mother-daughter conundrum was first spoken of and explored. It was at the heart of everything we talked about, even if we didn't know it at the time. We are all mothers now, with a greater appreciation of how hard it is to *express* perfectly this perfect love we feel for our children. We are walking a mile in our mothers' shoes and are humbled by the experience. Today our talks are more complex, for we live our lives as both daughters and mothers. But we are more peaceful, for we have reached common ground with our mothers at last.

Words cannot convey the deep sense of gratitude I feel toward John and Matthew for their boundless good cheer. Their cooperation always made it possible for me to focus on my work. They offered words of encouragement when I was at my most puzzled. They celebrated when I reached a milestone and they comforted when I was weary. I am indeed a fortunate woman.

From Arlene: I would like to thank my father, Vincent Modica, who, along with my mother, gave me the gifts of life and love. As always, I would like to thank my intrepid husband, "Clark Kent."

To my husband, John, whose constant love and genuine support mean everything to me. He is my greatest champion and always invites me to reach beyond myself

To my son, Matthew, whose joyful presence gives shape to my world and illuminates my way

To my mother, Evelyn, who gives me two priceless gifts: her love and her firm belief that I can do anything

—NWC

For my mother, Frances Piccione Modica,
who has given me so much:
life, love, and an enduring faith in the power of books

—AMM

Contents

PART I

THE MOTHER MAZE

INTRODUCTION:
Can I Possibly Manage *My* Mother?

She is slower than a speeding bullet, unable to leap tall buildings in a single bound. Yet she has the power to wound you with words and to stop you in your tracks with a disapproving glance. A recent frustrating exchange with her may have dampened your mood for days on end, and conflicts the two of you had long ago may still echo inside your head. She is your mother and, as such, the one person on earth most likely to relegate you—yes, you, a grown-up, competent, capable woman; perhaps a working woman, a corporate executive or respected professional; perhaps a busy student off on your own for the first time; perhaps a wife and mother yourself; perhaps a woman whose own children are grown—to the temporary status of raving lunatic.

It is true that you love your mother and doubtless true that she loves you. But if you are like most grown daughters in our society, it is also likely true that no matter how many difficult people and how many daunting tasks you manage, you have never learned to manage the situations in which you interact with her. It is probably true that you have never learned to manage the "maternal voice" that resonates loud and clear inside your psyche, whether or not your mother is actually around.

You *can* learn to manage these things.

The title of this book is not meant to imply that there is a way to "manage" one's mother—at least not in the sense that "to manage" means "to be in charge of." Rather, it is meant to suggest that there are ways to manage your response to your mother and to master situations where you and she have traditionally encountered roadblocks to constructive relations.

In these pages you will find a systematic and easy-to-follow program of skills and strategies designed to help you foster a wider, richer, healthier repertoire of interactions between you and your mother; to disrupt old patterns and erode the barriers that prevent mutual understanding and appreciation; and to distinguish between your mother as she is and your mother as you imagine her to be. You will learn how to get what you need from your mother and ultimately to give to your mother what she needs from you.

As psychotherapists we have worked with women of all ages and all generations who are navigating their way through what we call the Mother Maze—the labyrinth of emotional pathways that determines what goes on between daughters and mothers, both at conscious levels and at levels beneath conscious awareness. We have worked with young adults just beginning to form their adult relationship with their mothers, struggling with issues of identification and seeking ways to overcome alienation. We have worked with women who are about to give birth and who, in contemplating their own imminent motherhood, are seeking to reevaluate their relationships with their mothers and beginning to see themselves as part of a greater whole, a generational link in a chain, with its particular set of strengths and weaknesses. And we have worked with other women who are grappling with decisions about caring for their own aging mothers and who are reinvolving themselves with mothers from whom they have been apart, sometimes for many years.

We have seen these women struggle, but we have also seen many of them grow as they come to terms with the natural embrace in which mother and daughter are forever enveloped. We have learned that it is possible to make the most of the comforting aspects of our bonds with our mothers and to minimize the limiting and uncomfortable aspects of those same bonds. We have learned, too, that it is possible to negotiate an optimum distance between oneself and one's mother, a space in which one feels neither smothered nor estranged and in which one neither gives in nor gives up. It is a space filled with empathy and awareness, a space free of capitulation and manipulation, and a place for transformation.

But many of you may read this and shake your heads. Well, that's all very nice, you may say, but *my* mother makes me *crazy*. She misunderstands me, she hurts my feelings, all under the aegis of "mother love." Perhaps so. Perhaps you are one of the many grown daughters who have been known to throw up their hands after yet another exasperating, disappointing conversation with their mothers, crying, "If I never see or speak to her again, it will be too soon." But no matter how common such protestations may be, very few of us actually take the step of completely estranging ourselves from our mothers. And even those who resort to such drastic measures find that, in many significant ways, their mothers are with them still, an integral part of the fabric of their daily lives.

What choice is there, really, but to deal with the issues that loom between you and your mother? What choice is there but to begin to effect change?

We are optimistic that change can be effectuated in both a subtle and a positive manner, without causing earthquakes of disruption and anxiety. Indeed, we encourage honing one's sense of humor and playfulness as among the skills needed in building better working relationships. We are confident that feelings of anger and frustration can be lessened—and feelings of objectivity and calm heightened—as each of us takes responsibility for managing *all* of our relationships more productively. Many aspects of this book will address how an improved relationship with one's mother will, by extension, result in enhanced relationships with other members of the family, that is, one's father, siblings, grandparents, children, and spouse.

We recognize that undoing lifelong patterns is a challenging endeavor. Striking forth into new territory generally offers profound rewards, but a certain amount of trepidation and resistance to change goes with that territory, which is only natural. Change requires that certain realities be acknowledged, yet it also requires that certain fantasies and fallacies be renounced. The acceptance of *what is* and the relinquishing of certain prevalent myths and fantasies are among the premises that inform this book and are among the themes to which we will be returning again and again.

In her novel, *The Joy Luck Club*, Amy Tan writes that mothers and daughters are doomed—and blessed—to live like stairs, "one step after another, going up and down but all going the same way." None of us wants to trip and fall on those stairs. Most of us want to change what no longer makes us feel good about our relationships with our mothers without alienating them and without depriving ourselves or our children or children-to-be.

This is a delicate task. It must be started slowly, with small, almost imperceptible shifts in behavior, responses, and communications. Yet it must persist in spite of any natural resistance encountered. For as it persists—and as *you* persist—deeper self-awareness and empathy will evolve, and those qualities will take you where you most want to go.

How to Manage Your Mother is structured with this sort of emotional progression in mind. Part I, The Mother Maze, is devoted to explaining and exploding some fundamental myths that keep daughters trapped in unsatisfying patterns when interacting with their mothers. It also examines some predominant types of Maternal Styles and in doing so begins to illuminate just how and where so many common mother-daughter difficulties are wont to begin.

Part II of this book, Basic Skills and Strategies, focuses on helping you become acquainted with the way cause and effect operate in your relationship with your mother. It offers ways of breaking any destructive emotional habits you and she have built up over the years. It suggests ways of setting limits and strengthening interpersonal boundaries, of developing objectivity and discovering your own motives, of validating your mother's best impulses and tolerating her most frustrating gambits. And, finally, it offers tools for understanding and influencing the roles other family members play in creating the kind of rapport you and your mother share.

The techniques prescribed in Basic Skills and Strategies serve a dual purpose. They are meant to act as emotional stopgap measures, designed to curb nonconstructive emotional patterns, and they also lay the foundation for Part III, Advanced Skills and Strategies, which focuses on more complex, multilayered issues. In Advanced Skills and Strategies you will learn much more about managing the "maternal voice" that rattles around in your psyche, regardless of your mother's physical whereabouts, and about how you can actually use that voice to become a better "mother" to yourself. You will discover the emotional implications of watershed events in your life and in your mother's life—your marriage, her retirement, and the like. And you will discover the many ways in which a woman's own transition to motherhood impacts on her identity as a daughter. As a result of all this, you will learn how to care for and nurture the woman who nurtured you, to "mother your mother" as the two of you grow older and—we hope—wiser together.

CHAPTER 1

TRAILBLAZING:
New Solutions to Old Problems

We shall not cease from exploration
And the end of all our exploring
Will be to arrive where we started
And know the place for the first time.
　　　　T. S. Eliot, *the Quartet*

To begin to blaze new, productive trails in the Mother Maze, we must gaze from the vantage point of adulthood at the realities that exist. We must take heart and acknowledge that we have to give up previously held misguided notions in order to let new realities light the way.

Three of the fundamental new realities we will stress throughout this book are these:

In order to manage our relationships with our mothers, we must relinquish the myth of the "ideal" mother.

We must give up the idea that we can avoid, ignore, or "tune out" our mothers—no matter how much we say we desire to do so in moments of anger.

We must recognize that mother-daughter relationships do not occur in a vacuum but rather are the result of historical and contemporary forces at work within the family matrix.

This chapter is devoted to clarifying these three basic precepts.

THE MYTH OF THE IDEAL MOTHER

All of us look to our mothers for approval, comfort, and reassurance. As we grow we require them to provide these supports on a routine, day-to-day basis, adding extra doses in times of great stress. Depending on our mother's capacity to provide and on the degree of our ever-changing level of need, we come away from interactions with our mothers feeling either full and satisfied or empty and wanting. No matter which of these two things we feel, we are compelled by our incredibly intense biological and psychological bond with Mother to return to her for reinforcement, for encouragement, for her blessing on our endeavors.

We all know the flush of good feeling when we have met Mother's expectations and won her praise. We all know the sense of desolation when we have failed to do so. The drive to obtain maternal accolades is so much a "given" in our emotional makeup that advertisers have cleverly appropriated it for the selling of goods and services. Floor waxes and dishwashing liquids are marketed on the strength of their ostensible capacity for sparing us embarrassment when Mother drops in unannounced. Furniture emporiums coax shoppers to save on floor samples so that "Mother will be proud of you." The U.S. Postal Service scores an emotional bull's-eye with a pre-Mother's Day pitch for Express Mail, headlined: THERE'S STILL TIME TO WIN MOM'S APPROVAL.

Why do we crave this approval so badly? In part it is because we have always wanted—and still want—our mothers to be happy and comfortable. As small children we were keenly attuned to what made our mothers happy. We had to be, for when things went well for Mother, life tended to be quite pleasant for us. This knowledge of what pleases Mother remains with us always.

In part, too, it is because the need for Mother's approval, even as we take independent steps away from her protection and authority, is essential for developing a positive sense of self. If we meet with disapproval, either as children or as adults, our sense of ourselves as being capable and generally "all right" is tarnished.

Of course, these ingrained habits of approval-seeking present problems. Let us say, for example, that a mother *dis*approves when her little girl engages in bold, adventurous behavior—exploring new things, asking probing and perhaps embarrasing questions, taking what Mother perceives as unwarranted risks. The daughter will be left with the distinct impression that the way to keep Mother happy and earn praise for herself is to be calm rather than rambunctious and to keep herself "out of harm's way." Her bold and brave qualities may not vanish, but they are likely to go underground.

As the daughter gets older and becomes less outwardly dependent on her mother's day-to-day reinforcement and approval, she may dust off those unappreciated qualities and, all decked out as her more intrepid self, explore the world once more. Indeed, she may garner a certain satisfaction in reacting *against* Mother's cautionary dictums. But what happens next? In many cases, something like this:

Lydia, at twenty-eight, was about to embark on a dream vacation—a long-awaited trip to Africa. She never shared this dream with her wary, somewhat overprotective mother, not even during the period in which she happily made all her travel plans. Once her itinerary was complete, however, Lydia's excitement was palpable, and her desire to infuse everyone around her with enthusiasm mounted. Ultimately, she called her mother to talk of her impending journey. "*What?*" said her mother. "*Africa?* Why that's impossible. Girls can't travel alone there. It's so primitive. It's so filthy. Who will look after you?" Lydia was taken aback by her mother's response. After their conversation came to its somewhat tense conclusion, she stood staring at the phone receiver in her hand. Feeling deflated and depressed, she shook her head and muttered, "Why did I even bother? I should have known better than to think Mom would be different this time."

Lydia's question to herself is certainly a good one. Why *was* she so unnerved by her mother's response? After all, hadn't she been getting this response in one form or another her entire life? One might have been able to predict this reaction, and, in fact, on an unconscious level Lydia herself predicted it. Why else would she have waited until all her plans were in place before breathing a word of them to her mother? She was not prepared to encounter disapproval until after she was relatively comfortable with her own choice and until it was too late to alter her arrangements.

So why did she call her mother in hopes of approval at all? Why did she traverse this well-worn pathway through the Mother Maze in search of an elusive Ideal Mother? Because to take a new trail would have required certain emotional skills that Lydia, like so many grown daughters, had never mastered, skills she may not even have been aware *could* be mastered.

Quite frankly, most of us can't even see that there are other paths available when it comes to dealing with our mothers. We repeat what is familiar, no matter how unsatisfactory the results may be.

Why do we repeat such unsatisfying behaviors and engage in such disappointing interactions? Behavioral psychologists see repetitive behavior as learned responses to conditioning experiences that remain imprinted in our biological and psychological selves. Like mice in a laboratory maze who are trained either by reward (such as cheese) or aversive treatment (such as electric shock), humans, too, they say, turn the same corners, burrow through the same tunnels, and perform the same maneuvers that bring us to the "prize at the center."

But what if there is no prize? What if, like Lydia, our *hope* that repeated forays into the Mother Maze will earn us the reward, the cheese, the ideal sought-after response from Mother repeatedly proves unfounded? Why do it again? Even mice are savvier than that!

Sigmund Freud would have explained such behavior by a concept he called "the repetition compulsion," which he characterized as a need to reenact certain frustrating experiences no matter how painful. He believed that individuals unconsciously sought out and re-created in the present situations that echoed past conflicts they had not resolved or overcome. The act of repetition, he posited, was a way of trying to master these lingering conflicts. Obviously enough, when it comes to the Mother Maze, true mastery does not this way lie. It lies instead in adopting new ways of thinking, of understanding, and of accepting the mother *who is*, not the ideal fantasy mother for whom you pine.

But how so?

Let's say you call your mother with the good news that there is a strong possibility you will be getting a much-desired promotion and raise at the office. You tell her you heard the news unofficially from someone in management who is fairly reliable, adding that you hope he is not mistaken. You go on to say that this person told you how highly regarded you are by the company and how he feels your future is happily assured. Now the cheese, or ideal prize, might be a response from Mother along the lines of, "Well, dear, I hope this person is right, too. I'm so happy the company realizes how wonderful and capable you are. I already knew that! And, you know, even if it doesn't come through this time, the fact that they recognize your extraordinary qualities means there will certainly be a next time." You can walk away from this exchange with your mother feeling supported and nurtured. She acknowledged your good qualities and offered you a sense of hope even if your promotion doesn't come through.

But suppose you get a less ideal response, such as, "Who is this person in management? How high up is he? Does he know what he's talking about? Don't count your chickens before they hatch. You can get in lots of trouble that way. You shouldn't be talking to so many people about this anyhow. How do you know whom you can trust?" Needless to say, this is not the reaction for which you'd hoped. Suddenly, you find yourself testily defending the person who told you the news. You end up pointing out to your mother, with ever-increasing frustration, that you are aware there is a chance you will not get the promotion and that you can handle it. You end by hanging up abruptly, in a state of unblunted chagrin. You entered the Maze and got the usual upsetting response from your mother, and now you have to spend time calming yourself down. Ten minutes ago you were on top of the world, now you are sullen and pessimistic. This flip-flop of feelings is not new to you. You have walked this trail before.

But in your own repetition lies a glimmer of salvation. Think about it.

Precisely because you have walked this path before, you can empower yourself to avoid its pitfalls. The truth is your mother always responds with anxiety and dread when anything new may be about to happen to you. She responds with anxiety every time anything new happens to *herself*. Her anxiety causes her to be dubious, even downright suspicious, and it appears to you as if she is withholding that all-important stamp of acceptance and approval. Yet her reaction is not unloving or uncaring. It is simply a reflection of the way she is.

This time, the prize, the cheese, may be less than completely satisfying, and perhaps not the most well balanced of meals. But although you were unable to elicit from your mother the type of emotional sustenance you desired, you received something of value nevertheless. You received what your mother could give, given her predilections. You received her concern. You received advice—which you are not obliged to follow but which was nonetheless well meant.

So what are your options? You can wallow in disappointment and confine yourself to a prison of longing. You can blame your mother for her inability to live up to your fantasy— until it is time for another "doomed" foray into the Mother Maze, at which point, once again, you will repeat the past, hoping in vain for a breathtakingly new outcome. Or for a change you can accept what your mother has offered and begin to pave the way for the best possible realistic relationship between two women whose deep and genuine connection to each other can—indeed must—be strong enough to weather human failings and imperfections.

We opt for the latter course, for only in it do new possibilities lie. Caught up in repetitive cycles, you and your mother seek only to reconfirm what you know or think you know about each other. "My daughter counts her chickens." "My mother never gives me enough credit." Your perception of what is happening in the moment is wholly colored by your relentless accumulation of what has happened in the past. Fresh observation is impossible. Spontaneity is impossible. And this is a shame because when we were little, it was through the avenues of experimentation and play that we learned so many positive things from our mothers.

In this book we hope to be able to help you find new kinds of "prizes" from your frequent expeditions into the Mother Maze, for these sojourns will never cease. This leads us to examine the second fallacy we must relinquish:

THE FALLACY OF "EMANCIPATION PROCLAMATIONS"

The more tempestuous a daughter's relationship with her mother, the more likely she will fall prey to the aforementioned "If I never see or speak to her again, it will be too soon" type of thinking. Where rapport is especially stormy, a daughter may come to view looming watershed events in her own life— say, heading off to college or heading down the marriage aisle—as potential opportunities for "liberation" from Mother. She may fantasize about the many ways in which she will thrive and flourish once she is "released" from the bond she perceives as a bind.

But in the vast majority of instances, although leaving for

school, getting married, taking a job in another state, or signing up for field work in Papua, New Guinea, will very likely introduce some shifts and variations into the mother-daughter matrix (more about this in a later chapter), the relationship itself—complete with bonds and binds—will persist despite the twists on life's road. Regardless of where they go or what they do, most grown daughters will inevitably find themselves touching base with their mothers periodically, and they will find that a phone call from across town or a letter from across the world can pack as big an emotional wallop as a communication offered face-to-face.

That is but one reality that speaks *against* the fantasy of utter emancipation and *for* the necessity of coming to terms with the ins and outs of the Mother Maze. Another reality is this: For more of us than ever before, there is every likelihood that, no matter how far away we have lived from our mothers, we may well end up caring for them in their elder years, face-to-face once more but with roles reversed (more about this in later chapters as well). We are all living longer, and studies show that as a result the average contemporary woman will spend approximately eighteen years taking care of her mother, a full year longer than the years estimated she will care for her own children.[1] There seems little point in spending a good part of a lifetime attenuating contact with one's mother if there is a strong possibility that one will, at a certain juncture, be faced with the prospect of helping her cope with the aging process and the many changes that process brings.

Of course, for most of us there will come a day when Mother really is no longer around—not on the other end of a telephone wire, not at a retirement home, not upstairs in the spare bedroom vacated by our grown daughters or sons. Yet she will be with us in spirit as she was with us in spirit in the moments of our lives when we heard her "maternal voice" echo in the chambers of our psyche. That internalized maternal voice— the psychological term for which is the *introject*—is yet another manifestation of the bond that never breaks.

Throughout this book we'll be stressing the significance of

the Internal or Introjected Mother. We will explore how the introject comes into being, how to recognize it in ourselves, when to embrace it, and when to try to quiet it down. But since it is so key a concept, let us begin by saying a little about it here. Many of you may be wondering what this Introjected Mother is, anyhow. A new weapon designed by the defense department? A billion-dollar daughter-seeking missile?

In truth, one could liken the process of acquiring an introject to swallowing, in whole or in part, someone else's value system. Every one of us carries within us an Introjected or Internalized Mother, for all of us first learn about the world by absorbing what is around us. To a certain degree a mother's view of the world becomes an integral part of her child's view of it. This process occurs naturally. It happens without any conscious effort or acknowledgment on the part of either person. As Gestalt therapists Erving and Miriam Polster have written, "The child simply experiences many aspects of living in a that's-how-it-is manner and learning is like blood flowing through veins or like breathing."[2]

Men and women retain many traits, attitudes, and habits originally engendered by their mothers, which is not surprising, since all babies begin life in symbiotic union with their mothers, a kind of psychological continuance of the magnificent and mysterious connection that began in utero. When D. W. Winnicott, the renowned pediatrician and psychoanalyst, commented that there was "no such thing as a baby," he was referring to the fact that an infant is truly unable to exist without a nurturing caregiver to tend it. Even after the initial months of infancy are past, it generally takes years for the baby's psychological "hatching" process to stabilize and for anyone else to come close to being as powerful a figure in the baby's life as Mother.

Yet by and large the Internalized Mother that daughters retain remains a more potent force than the one retained by sons, for as little boys start to toddle away from their caregiving mothers, they find they have their fathers to imitate and to identify with, to walk like, talk like, and toss a baseball like.

On the other hand, mothers tend to be not only primary caregivers to daughters, but primary role models as well. A little girl learns from a mother not only what it means to be a person but what it means to be a female.

Obviously, such a profound dual influence can lead a daughter to embrace and act out her mother's value system to a significant extent. Such an arrangement may prove very comfortable and workable as long as mother and daughter remain in agreement on life's fundamentals. If a mother values, say, good grades above all, and a daughter willingly forgoes other things in order to study, all will be harmonious, at least on the surface. But as the daughter grows older and as her own needs and preferences unfold, this arrangement may flounder. A sudden, intense interest in boys may preclude the value system of getting good grades. The local teen hangout—the place where the class "hunk" reigns after school—may prove far more appealing than the lure of books waiting at home. The daughter may begin to resist the maternal voice, and a lifelong struggle begins. Should she or shouldn't she? Will she or won't she? Whom should she heed, whom should she please, herself or her mother? And what will be the psychic cost of choosing one over the other?

The Introjected Mother has many subtleties, takes many forms, and can lead to sundry emotional scenarios. Because of our residual propensity to emulate our mothers' most salient characteristics, we sometimes imitate the maternal behaviors that frustrated and annoyed us the most. ("I can't believe it," we lament in the aftermath of a thirty-minute diatribe on why our children should never wipe their hands with the guest towels. "I heard my mother's words coming out of my mouth.") Because we cleave to the refrains of the maternal voice, we sometimes censure ourselves ("You can't do that, you're not cut out for it") or disparage others ("He's a nice guy, but not good enough for you") the way our mothers might have.

In some cases, ironically enough, the desire to defy the maternal voice is so great that it overshadows all other desires until we can no longer tell what we do because we want to and what we do because she doesn't want us to. (Do we really want ruby red nails or thrice-pierced ears, or is it because our mother deems them tasteless that we have them?) Though much of the behavior our mothers rewarded was doubtless of a constructive nature, we may cast aside self-benefitting tendencies simply because she condoned them. (Brought up by a mother who stressed thrift, for example, we may splurge to excess as a kind of rebuttal.)

Like it or not, our Internal Mother is with us to stay even if our External Mother is not. Our so-called introject is a part of us. Why should we strive to deny it when we can manage it instead? We have all been wired by a kind of "Mother Electrician." Yes, we can do some rewiring, and this book will explore how. But we can never turn off the current, nor should that be our goal.

THE FAMILY CONTEXT

Finally, some elaboration on the third of our basic precepts—the one that reminds us mother-daughter relationships do not occur in a vacuum. No one can navigate successfully through the Mother Maze who does not heed the signposts that read: FATHER AHEAD; SIBLINGS TO YOUR LEFT AND RIGHT, and, of course, GRANDMA AND GREAT-GRANDMA SLEPT HERE.

The first two signposts draw attention to the dynamics of the nuclear family. The ways in which mothers and daughters learn to relate to each other is, in most cases, profoundly affected by transactional patterns that are established within their larger family constellation. They are affected by family rules that dictate the parameters of "acceptable" behavior in the household. (It's okay to play with Mom's pots and pans, but don't touch Dad's tools. It's okay to cry when you're sad but not to yell when you're angry.) They are affected by the ways in which those rules are communicated, that is, whether family dictums are verbalized or unspoken, whether they are communicated by a shrug of the shoulder, a nod, a wink, or by signals so subtle even the sender of those signals would deny their existence. They are affected, too, by the formation of subgroups or subsystems within the family unit.

Within every family, conscious or unconscious emotional pacts serve to create various alliances between members. These alliances can exist between two, three, four, or more people. They can be formed along generational lines—for example, mother-father, brother-sister. Or they can be formed along transgenerational lines—all the males in one family, for example, may form a subsystem, a kind of executive club for men within the family.

More than likely each of us has at times belonged to several subsystems within our family. In each of these involvements we learned to play certain roles. We may have become brother's protector, sister's tormentor, or Daddy's little girl. Needless to say, we may also have taken on any number of roles that compelled us to behave in certain ways with regard to our mothers. Yet it is important to remember that *it was not through interaction with Mother alone that we learned to act out our parts.*

How, for example, do we learn to be Mother's Confidante? We might sense a kind of "breakdown" in the parental subsystem. We might perceive a coldness or distance between our parents. We might overhear arguing or notice Mother alluding to the fact that Father is difficult to talk to, that he simply doesn't understand her. We may well experience concern for our mother's lonely predicament. And what if, say, big brother, seems to spend a lot of time with Dad, leaving us out of that "subgroup"? That, too, may serve to propel us in Mother's direction. Suddenly, we may find ourselves picking up the gauntlet and stepping in for Father. We may ask Mom what's bothering her and inquire whether she's okay. Soon, Mom may begin sharing with us disclosures that in a more smoothly functioning family would be recognized as inappropriate information with which to burden a youngster. ("Your father doesn't make enough money." "He flirts with Lulu, the next-door neighbor.")

In return for our ministrations we earn a dual sense of satisfaction. First, we have done a good turn by offering Mother a proverbial shoulder on which to cry, and second, we helped get Father off the hook. We may experience quite palpably her gratitude and his relief.

We learned this role and its attendant behavior by being exquisitely sensitive to family communications; to all sorts of overt and subliminal exchanges that not only imparted family law and lore but prescribed specific action. We did not make a considered choice to evolve into Mother's Confidante. Instead, we were recruited through a cluster of messages. Could we have ignored the messages? Not likely. As children most of us are intently dependent on—and thus emotionally loyal toward—our parents. Very few of us are seriously tempted to or capable of packing our belongings in a bandanna, tying them to a stick, and hopping a freight train. Instead, we simply learn to adapt to the conditions laid down for us by the adults in our lives and to respond to them.

The impact of fathers and siblings on mother-daughter interactions is a fascinating subject, one that we will hve a great deal more to say about in the course of this book. As you will see, the wise daughter seeking to improve her maternal relations ought never to ignore those *father* and *sibling* roadsigns, lest she wind up lost in an emotional cul-de-sac.

Let us now turn our attention to the third signpost mentioned at the start of this section: GRANDMA AND GREAT-GRANDMA SLEPT HERE. The impact of generations gone by adds yet another dimension to the intricacies of the Mother Maze. Messages are relayed not only between family members in the present but are also handed down across time. They may be relayed via word, deed, or emotional attitude. And homage may be paid them through compliance or through defiance. Either way, their influence is bound to be resurrected in some form sooner or later, just as real as the nose on your face or the color of your eyes or hair.

Everyone's mother is also someone's daughter. You may deem your mother's behavior frustrating, just as she might deem her mother's behavior daunting and your behavior incomprehensible. Yet they are all connected, in ways this book will continue to investigate, all part of a patchwork family quilt that has been in the making countless lifetimes and endless heartbeats, sewn of threads so fine they can't be seen, only felt.

The knowledge of how you and your mother are products of the generations of mothers and daughters who have preceded you is a crucial part of the knowledge you will need to redirect the course of the future. The piece of the quilt that will portray our lives and the lives of our mothers has not yet been woven in final form. Here is an opportunity to make your relationship more of what you want it to be, not just a replica of all the pieces that came before.

So now you know what new realities await your personal discovery. Beginning with chapter 3, it will be revealed how these tie into the learning of new skills and strategies that will help you respond to your mother in a more constructive fashion. But before we delve into specific skills we will devote this next chapter to an exploration of maternal styles. Chapter 2 will help you understand just how and why you and your mother developed your particular patterns of interaction in the first place.

CHAPTER 2

MATERNAL STYLES

I'll love you forever,
I'll like you for always,
As long as I'm living
My baby you'll be.

Robert Munsch, "I'll Love You Forever"

The foregoing refrain is from a children's book that tenderly describes the abiding nature of a mother's love. The sentiment it conveys rings familiar to most of us, for it would probably be impossible to count the ways in which the vast majority of mothers let their daughters know that, no matter how far along in adulthood they are, they will always be their mothers' babies.

But alas, more frequently than not, "As long as I'm living, my baby you'll be" reflects not just the way mothers love their grown daughters but the manner in which they treat them.

Over and over we hear highly competent and knowledgeable women complain: Why can't my mother adjust to me as I am? Why can't she see me as others do? They may ask: Why must she meddle? Or: Why won't she give me credit? Or perhaps: Why must she always worry? Or: Why can't she seem to figure out where she ends and I begin?

Why, indeed?

At times it may be very difficult to understand what drives

and motivates your mother's actions and attitudes. This chapter is meant to provide you with the means of comprehending her complex behaviors as well as your complex set of responses to them.

Though most mother-daughter relationships have their rough spots, some duos seem to chafe and grind more than others. The discomforting undertone in their interactions seems always to be present. That discomfort is somewhat like having a stone in one's shoe. Complaining about it is of little use. The irritation can't be alleviated until the source of the pain is discovered and attended to.

Understanding your mother's Maternal Style is much like locating the stone in the shoe, the *why* of so much of your frustration. Subsequent chapters will help you remove it and walk toward or alongside your mother with smoother strides. For now, let us look at how the stone got there in the first place.

THE SHAPING OF MATERNAL STYLES

As we already know, most mothers and daughters seem stuck in certain patterns. It can be difficult to step off the well-worn paths of your particular Mother Maze and ascertain how you got to this point. Did the disharmony begin with her or with you?

Certainly, any negative patterns to which you and your mother have become habituated have a chicken-and-egg emotional quality, but you ought to know, too, that some of the foundations of these patterns may have been laid even before you were an egg, before you were conceived let alone born. Likewise, some were formed while you were an egg, during the months you nestled inside your mother's womb. And some were formed during your earliest years of babyhood, years when every incremental gain of independence and autonomy of yours may have been registered as a kind of parallel loss by your mother. Naturally, Maternal Styles are also shaped by extenuating circumstances you aren't directly the cause of, such as marital discord between your mother and father that fosters various maternal tensions which are never alleviated, even when the crisis is over.

Among the many determinants of Maternal Style that exist are voices from the past. Long before a woman has a child or even contemplates having one she has certain ideas about mothering, whether she is actively aware of them or not. As we've said, everyone's mother is somebody's daughter. Within one family, generation after generation of women may have mothered in much the same fashion. If your grandmother used criticism as the currency of exchange to get your mother to do what she thought was appropriate, your mother may well have been predisposed to develop what we call a Hypercritical Maternal Style. If your grandmother was a champion guilt-invoker, your mother may have learned by emotional osmosis to wield guilt as skillfully as Arthur wielded Excalibur. And guilt, as we shall see, is a hallmark of numerous frustrating styles of mothering.

TEMPERAMENTAL MATCHES AND MISMATCHES

No sooner does a woman become pregnant than conscious musings about motherhood begin to occupy her mind. At this point the hand-me-down generational edicts may become crystallized, and she may form certain ideas and opinions about her baby-to-be based on them—for example, "All the babies in our family are quiet and sleep through the night" or "All the baby girls on our side are so smart, they talk before they are one." Other factors enter into an expectant mother's anticipatory thoughts as well. What a woman has read about parenting, what she has heard from numerous sources, including her friends and peers, her doctor, her Lamaze coach, and so on, along with what her own private fantasies of the "perfect" mother-child relationship might consist of, all combine to prompt her to imagine and plan for the arrival of a certain kind of child.

If, once the newborn debuts, the mother gets more or less what she has bargained for, the budding relationship is wont to begin on a harmonious note. If the mother's expectations and the child's behavior do not mesh, however, the child enters life with its mother already disconcerted—perhaps even somewhat disappointed.

If a calm, robust baby is anticipated and a fussy or sickly one arrives, a Chronically Worried Maternal Style may take root at life's start, with the baby's mother continually fretting that something is wrong and that her child requires constant vigilance. Likewise, if a highly alert, ever-burbling future debate team captain is anticipated (perhaps by a new mother whose older sister has given birth to three such paragons) and a docile late-bloomer shows up, a mother may develop an insistently Controlling Style or Hypercritical Style in an attempt to "correct" what she perceives as her child's shortcomings.

Perhaps the most generic sort of expectation that mothers have when it comes to infant daughters is that they will be similar to themselves. Yet, as fate would have it, many methodical mothers with a passion for routine have been paired with unpredictable babies whose whimsical sleeping and eating habits refuse to fit into anything resembling a schedule. And any number of fast-moving dynamos have given birth to infants with comparatively relaxed dispositions. These temperamental mismatches can themselves help mold Maternal Styles. Rather than appreciating the vicissitudes of their daughters' temperaments, some mothers may seek to obliterate the differences by developing a Merged Maternal Style. They blur the boundaries between mother and child and treat their daughters not as unique individuals but as split-off parts of themselves, which they continually strive to attract back to them as if by magnetic force.

BABY MOVES AWAY

For many new mothers, of course, the earliest months of their baby's life—the "lap baby" phase—though a period of many changes and challenges, is experienced not as problematical but as blissful. Wrapped up in their critical role as nurturer and protector, many women glean particular pleasure in being such an important figure to another human being. This may be the first time in their lives that they feel needed and loved with the exquisite, exclusive devotion only a newborn can provide.

During this period mother and baby can be envisioned as suspended in a kind of enveloping bubble, remaining almost as unified as they were during the months of the pregnancy itself. Not surprisingly, as child development expert Margaret S. Mahler notes, this is a phase when the mother experiences her infant's body as "part of the representation of her 'self.' "[1] It is also a phase when the infant experiences herself and her mother as part of a single self-contained system. This "dual unity" is relatively short-lived, however. Sooner than many mothers may recognize, their child begins the multistaged process of developing its own sense of self and of slowly but surely separating from them.

The signs are small at first. Instead of molding itself to Mother's body, the baby lifts its head, squirms about, and sizes up the outside world. There is a strong sense of mother but also an emerging sense of "other." The *differentiation* phase, as Mahler calls it, has begun. Soon, at around ten months of age, in a phase Mahler refers to as *practicing*, the baby begins to crawl and climb. Next, it stands upright and walks, exhilarated with its achievement and, as Mahler speculates, with its "escape" from the confines of mother-child symbiosis. Though the toddling baby returns frequently to Mother for "refueling," it also seems periodically oblivious toward Mother, wholly absorbed in new discoveries and with the logistics of getting around.

As these stages proceed along their natural course, a mother may be dismayed at each subsequent achievement by her daughter. Though on some level she may be intrigued and delighted when her baby girl averts her rhapsodic gaze to ogle a visitor's shiny shoe buckle or a stuffed giraffe, she may also feel rejected. And when her daughter wriggles off her lap and ventures forth into the world—or at least into the living room—a mother may feel at once proud and bereft. No longer will she routinely experience the joy of having her baby languish for hours in her loving arms.

Just as babies must master a series of developmental tasks throughout these phases of childhood, so, ideally, should mothers. During the differentiation and practicing phases, a mother needs to relinquish possession of her baby's body. In a second-year stage, which Mahler terms *rapprochement* and which is typified by a child's sometimes confounding alternation between a dramatically needy and demanding nature and equally dramatic contrariness, a mother faces additional tasks. She must give up the idea that her child should be *all one way*. She must be flexible enough to accommodate her daughter's inconsistencies, and tolerant enough to weather her increasing self-assertion and intermittent fretfulness. She must be emotionally available to assist in her child's quest for both freedom and protection, and she must be willing and able to respond to her actual daughter rather than to her preconceived ideas of how her daughter ought to be.

For many mothers, scaling these emotional hurdles is a tall order. Indeed, only in textbooks do mothers manage to offer the perfect blend of encouragement, acceptance, flexibility, patience, and unconditional support theoretically required to mold a child into a paragon of psychological maturity. Most mothers seem to have days when they wish their two-year-old would either grow up quickly and get a high-paying job or revert once more to a lap baby, stop this endless challenging, and resume gurgling and cooing again.

Nevertheless, a mother who experiences extreme loss and frustration in the face of a child's individuation may, throughout a daughter's life, offer up words, gestures, facial expressions, and overall attitudes that convey the message "stay with me" just as surely as did her sighs and admonitions when her daughter first attempted to propel herself out of Mother's orbit. Her messages may instill in her daughter a sense of hesitancy and trepidation.

Conversely, mothers who place inordinately high value on their child's rapid and unremitting progress through the developmental stages and are preoccupied with and rewarding of "advanced" behavior, putting extreme pressure on the child to "get on with it," may be sowing the seeds of an ongoing maternal message which conveys the overall sentiment that "needing is no good." Such a mother's commands may engender in a daughter a false self that feigns independence and bravado in order to prevent inner vulnerability from showing through and to retain Mother's approval. Though the daughter may feel flooded with unmet needs, she may also feel badly about herself for having needs in the first place.

"UNACCEPTABLE" FEELINGS

To make matters even more complex, though a Maternal Style may develop as a relatively straightforward extension of a mother's feelings, it may also grow out of *defenses against those feelings.* In the course of having and raising a child, especially a child of the same gender, a mother who is reasonably well attuned to her own varied emotional agenda is bound to acknowledge that she experiences an entire spectrum of emotions. Giving birth and rearing children, for all the fulfillment they provide, can also offer occasions for anxiety, sadness, guilt, anger, jealousy, and fear of one's own inadequacy, yet many women deem such wholly natural feelings unacceptable.

Rather than acknowledging that it is utterly human to experience, say, envy of one's young and beautiful daughter, they may label such an emotion shameful and undesirable. This is especially true of women of older generations who came of age in a time when social expectations were high and psychological understanding was low. The harder they try to deny a feeling's existence and banish it from their consciousness, however, the more they may be doomed to act out the feeling rather than face it and express it appropriately. If jealous, they may develop a Competitive Maternal Style while outwardly insisting to themselves and others that they have no desire to outshine their child. If they fear they are inadequate mothers and if they also suffer from unmet needs, they may develop what we call a Pseudoperfect Maternal Style, behaving as if they were ideal mothers (in short, the stuff of fantasy), yet withholding from their daughters the precious gift of genuine warmth.

In the remainder of this chapter we will take a closer look at the six Maternal Styles that we have found to engender the most frustration in daughters and create the most chafing in mother-daughter dyads. We will look, too, at what grown daughters unwittingly do to perpetuate and contribute to problematical styles that have long been in place. (Though we have encountered countless daughters who complain, say, of phone calls from their Chronically Worried Mothers reminding them to carry their umbrellas on a rainy day, we have not failed to notice that an inordinate number may unconsciously do things to keep those phone calls coming, such as plaintively informing their mothers, "I got soaked the other day on my way to the bank.") Along these lines, we will also introduce the concept of *compliant* and *defiant* daughters. Although we will amplify this important concept in later chapters, we will begin to see how and why some daughters tend to cooperate with Mother and others tend to rebel against her.

Of course, no mother is one-dimensional in her approach to mothering, and you may find traces of your mother in more than one of these capsules. Most mothers don't fall cleanly under the heading of just one style, just as most mothers don't fall cleanly under the heading *good mother* or *bad mother*.

(*Most* mothers operate out of heartfelt love. *Most* mothers struggle to be good mothers. Most mothers are "good-enough" and produce daughters who blossom into reasonably mature, curious, hopeful, resourceful and multi-faceted women—albeit women who at times count among their very human troubles a relationship with their mother that is not quite as satisfying and positive as they would wish.) Recognizing aspects of your mother as you read through these descriptions and recognizing aspects of your contribution to your mutually frustrating interactions are both integral parts of sorting out and improving your relationship.

THE MERGED STYLE

"I think the incident that best sums up my Mom's approach to mothering," says Janet, a twenty-nine-year-old computer technician, "happened when I was in the sixth grade. I remember I was riding my new bicycle, and just as I passed our house I fell off and chipped my tooth. My mother, who I didn't know was watching for me, bolted out the front door, ran up to me, and scooped me up in her arms for what I thought would be a comforting hug. What she said to me, though, was 'Look what you've done to my beautiful teeth.' To this day my mother can't seem to tell us apart."

If this scenario rings a bell, if—like Janet—your mother cannot seem to distinguish exactly who is who and what belongs to *you*, chances are your mother employs what we call a Merged Maternal Style. Exactly who is the Merged Mother, and what does she want from your relationship?

   She is the mother who manifests a deep concern about the people and events in your life. She wants to know where you go, what you do, and who you see. She wants to hear intimate details, perhaps on a daily basis. She has been known to insist boastfully, "My daughter is my life." Sadly, she's not exaggerating. Indeed, she seems not to enjoy a full life of her own and requires too much of yours to feel complete herself.

This is a mother who never came to terms with the stages of separation and individuation. While you were struggling to distinguish yourself from her, she was striving to remain undifferentiated, to hang on to that oceanic feeling of oneness that defines the psychic atmosphere inside a mother and newborn's early bubble of bliss.

Perhaps when you were young your Merged Mother dressed the two of you alike. Looking back over your family album, you may see pictures of the two of you costumed in identical gingham pinafores. Perhaps, if you now have a daughter of your own, you can recall a moment early in your child's life when your Merged Mother jubilantly clutched your baby in her arms and exclaimed, "Isn't she beautiful, and she's *ours!*" There's "no room for Daddy" in an exclusive sorority such as this!

Chances are high, if your mother has a Merged Style, that one of the earliest messages you received from her was that *she was always available to you.* Indeed, she lived for you. Perhaps she declined to go away weekends with your father because she didn't want to leave you. Perhaps she revolved all her social engagements around your friends and your hobbies. Most likely she saw your successes as her own and your setbacks as hers as well. Her reactions to your defeats may have seemed more dramatic than your own so that whenever you were feeling blue, you had to stop and comfort her.

In many ways all of this placed a heavy burden on you, for if you were determined to be a "good daughter," it became imperative never to do anything that upset Mother. Alas, your very growing up upset her. She said she would do anything for you, but when you wanted to do something that took you away, she used martyrdom as a technique to reel you back in. The look on her face when you were all dressed up and ready to go to a party was ridden with dread more suited to a wartime farewell. You could laugh about it if it wasn't such a potent catalyst for stirring up your guilt and such a poignant testament to just how merged she is.

Failure upset Mother as well, so you simply couldn't fail. But perhaps you didn't dare attempt anything too difficult, lest such a possibility loom. Like many daughters of Merged Mothers you may have developed a stance of "cautious perfection"— always reaching, but never beyond what you were certain was your grasp.

On the face of things, it is the daughter who looks powerful in a merged relationship. After all, it is her existence around which Mother ostensibly revolves. In actuality, however, the daughter of a Merged Mother is disempowered. She is not free to make her own decisions because she must always take into account how her Mother will "enjoy" her choice. She feels immense pressure not to make a mistake because a mistake means not only her own suffering but the aggravated suffering of her mother. She experiences troubling, recurring resentments toward her self-sacrificing mother who makes her feel like an ingrate. She may feel continually overwrought—as well she might, for living life for two people is no small task. She feels obligated to provide her mother with details on the minutae of her life, because keeping Mother informed seems tantamount to keeping her alive. Yet telling a Merged Mother too much about one's existence apart from her can backfire. Why didn't you tell her sooner, she wants to know? Why didn't you consult her? Why is she left in the dark?

Let us say right here that just about all mothers want to be kept abreast of their daughters' lives to some degree. What's more, virtually all mothers revel to some extent in their children's successes and feel their disappointments. The Merged Mother, however, takes such natural inclinations to extremes. If your mother has a Merged Style, you will know it by your responses to her cues. If you continually feel that you are walking on eggshells when imparting news to your mother, waiting with a constricting sensation in your chest for her reaction, you will know. If you seem unable to feel angry at your mother without feeling sorry for her at the same time, you will know. If you experience a constant self-imposed nagging that says you should do more for and with your mother, though you already fear you may be doing too much, you will also know.

Another way of telling whether your mother had an inordinate urge to merge is by assessing how your relationship with Mother affects your relationships with others. The daughter of a relentlessly Merged Mother may never be able to develop an allegiance to her own husband that surpasses her filial loyalty. She may find it hard to make the types of private decisions (private from Mother, that is) that abound in marriage. In such cases her inability to truly "team up" with the man in her life can take much of the potential joy and satisfaction out of their union.

In a slightly different vein, a Merged Mother's daughter may feel compelled to make the welfare of others her paramount concern. Unaccustomed to the true intimacy that comes from the interdependency of two self-reliant human beings, this daughter may attempt in her romantic relationships to repeatedly conjure up bonds of pseudointimacy, becoming her partner's overseer, attuning her emotions to his, and losing herself in the process of making sure he is all right.

Now that you know whether or not your relationship with your mother is a merged one, what remains is to ask yourself what's in it for you. Why suffer all the Sturm und Drang inherent in this merger? Why not pull away? An ancient Greek myth, the tale of Demeter and Persphone, offers some insight into these issues. It is perhaps the first recorded chronicle of a classic Merged Mother–daughter collusion.

In this myth the lovely young Persephone, daughter of Demeter, goddess of agriculture, was merrily gathering flowers when Hades, god of the underworld, spirited her to his domain, where he intended her to be his bride. Upon learning what had befallen her daughter, Demeter grew wild with despair. She vowed to her fellow gods never again to set foot on Mount Olympus until her child was returned. She vowed, too, that no crops would grow on the earth until Zeus commanded

Hades to deliver Persephone back to her mother. So Zeus intervened, and Hades complied, more or less. Ultimately, a compromise was reached whereby Persephone would be allowed to spend two-thirds of each year with her mother in the upper world and one-third with her husband in the netherworld, from which she would return each spring.

Clearly, Demeter held the bulk of the power in determining her daughter's fate. Hades had some power, but even the lord of the underworld was obliged to appease his mother-in-law or else, quite literally, "all hell would break loose." But one may well wonder where Persephone was in all of this. What did she want? We don't really know. Perhaps she didn't, either.

Persephone is what we would call a compliant daughter of a Merged Mother who seemed all too willing to let others make decisions on her behalf. More passive than passionate in nature, her chief desire seemed to be to make everyone happy except herself. For to be passionate means to take a stand, a stand that may cause Mother to suffer.

The unnaturally prolonged "bubble" state in which Merged Mothers and their compliant daughters find themselves suspended sounds oppressive, and oftentimes it is. But it has its attractions and its rewards. In return for Mother's many sacrifices, she gets herself a daughter who is a devoted companion. She also gets a chance to experience vicariously some facets of life she would never have known on her own. (One can almost hear Demeter querying her daughter, upon her annual returns, "What's it really like in the underworld? Tell me everything, darling!") In return for her compliant allegiance and guilt, the daughter gets a measure of safety and calm. She can abdicate responsibility for her own life and be assured that she will not upset her mother. Choices can be anxiety-provoking. To defer them indefinitely or to allow onself only such choices as will not burst the mother-daughter bubble can forestall anxiety.

The appeal of protracted "oneness" can be remarkably compelling, remarkably comforting. Its limits may go unnoticed for many years, in some cases forever, but some Persephone-type daughters realize one day that something is amiss. Perhaps their privacy is invaded once too often (Mother is caught rummaging through their purse or reading their diary). Perhaps, one time too many, Mother forbids them to participate in activities that exclude her. Suddenly, their mothering seems too smothering. They rebel, becoming defiant daughters.

These defiant daughters find their mother's style so invasive and enraging that they overtly seek to sever their merger with her, no matter what the emotional expense to themselves. If the defiance takes root in early childhood, they may create a fantasy world, complete with imaginary playmates, that excludes Mother, thus limiting her participation in their lives. As adolescents they may live in disgruntled silence, unwilling to offer their mothers the remotest piece of information about themselves. As adults they may find themselves creating psychical and physical distance from Mother at every opportunity.

Make no mistake, however: These defiant daughters still long for connection with their mothers even as they deem such connection too enervating. Alas, their sense of being thwarted in their wish for a healthier bond will never diminish as long as defiance predominates. The truth is that between compliance and defiance there is a middle ground that is desirable and attainable. In order to manage the Merged Maternal Style most effectively, the daughter must begin to step outside the confines of the symbiotic bubble, but she must do so gently. The object of managing one's response to the Merged Mother is to dissolve the bubble with care, not to burst it with a pinprick of rage.

THE CHRONICALLY WORRIED STYLE

"When I signed my first book contract years ago," says Louise, a forty-one-year-old novelist, "I decided to celebrate by buying myself a computer for word processing. I told my mother I was going computer shopping, and she became distraught. She warned me: 'With your bad eyesight you'll go blind staring at

a computer screen.' Of course this had no bearing on reality whatsoever, but it sent me off the deep end nonetheless. I was furious at her. She'd reminded me of all the times in my childhood when she used my 'poor eyesight' as an excuse not to let me do the perfectly routine things all the other kids did. It took much of the fun out of my computer purchase, too. No matter how ridiculous my mother's contention, a little voice inside my head kept wondering, 'Could she possibly be right?' "

If you have spent much of your life with the words *don't, can't,* and *watch out!* reverberating in your ears, if the sight of your mother's knitted brow is indelibly printed in your mind's eye, if you have never had to pick up a newspaper to be informed of the latest disaster anywhere on the globe, your mother may have what we call a Chronically Worried maternal style.

What is the Chronic Worrier's agenda? She would say, Only to protect you. And she would wonder, What's so wrong with that? After all, in ancient times people who made a habit of predicting disaster were revered as oracles. How fortunate you are, she might insist, to have your own personal soothsayer—someone to remind you not to run your hairdryer in the bathtub; someone to call you in the middle of your vacation, just wondering whether you'd remembered to shut the patio door before you left; someone to conclude you have jaundice when you switch to a new shade of face makeup.

But most likely the Chronically Worried Mother has a hidden agenda as well, perhaps even hidden from herself. Just as the Merged Mother has difficulty with separation-individuation issues, so may a mother with an apprehensive bent. Yet a Worrier would not so much insist that her daughter is her life as she would contend that she fears *for* her daughter's life. She does not perceive her daughter's independence as threatening to her but rather as threatening to her daughter. This mother's drive to "play it safe" may be exacerbated if she herself had an overprotective mother with a nervous disposition, if she felt neglected in her family and became determined to watch fiercely over her own child so that such a situation would not be re-created, or if threatening behavior abounded in her own family.

Early on, your Worried Mother probably expressed her distress at your new ventures via anxious exclamations. Standing sentry in the playground as you negotiated the high rungs of a jungle gym, she called out a string of cautionary phrases: "Be careful! . . . Now don't fall. . . . Are you crazy? . . . You'll kill yourself!" Later, as you moved out of her immediate purview, she administered more detailed and elaborate precautions: "Don't sit next to Betsy on the bus. I heard her coughing, and I don't want you to catch a cold"; or "I don't want you swapping food with any of the kids in the lunchroom. You never know what has germs. You just never know."

Alas, though such communications explicitly convey well-intentioned concern, their implicit message is: Trust no one, least of all yourself. The exception to that unspoken rule and its implied corollary is, of course: The only one you dare trust is your mother.

But where did all these admonitions lead you? Suddenly, sitting next to Betsy, whom you liked, and trading half your bologna sandwich for Melissa's delicious turkey seemed fraught with jeopardy. Your options had been nipped in the bud, and so had naturally blossoming relationships with your peers. By curtailing your relationships with people outside the family, you may have been deprived of maturational social experiences. You may have become skittish and come to doubt your judgment, beginning to envision the world not so much as a fascinating place but as a dangerous one.

Some daughters of mothers with Chronically Worried Styles may comply with the maternal program to varying degrees, adopting a shy, tremulous stance when young and retaining it for life. If a Chronically Worried Mother has the "good fortune" to have a compliant daughter, she has someone with whom she speaks a common language and who gives her a sense of importance and purpose. After all, what could be a more exalted job than oracle and protector?

But other daughters of Chronic Worriers may go in a completely opposite direction, defying Mother's cautious prescriptions for living. Their defiant mode often kicks in during adolescence.

After years of tentatively living under mother's anxious rule, a teenage daughter, in the grips of psychological and physiological forces that are wont to "stir the pot" at this juncture in life, may start to spend as much time apart from an overprotective mother as she possibly can. The more determined she is to defy her mother, the more she may bait her by seeking the most "unsafe" element she can find. Allying herself with precisely the sort of friends her mother would be most likely to deem "a bad influence," perhaps experimenting with the very things most likely to cause Mother the greatest alarm, the rebellious daughter may quite willfully test the limits of her mother's power and authority. In later years such reactive trends may be tempered, but a daughter who gains satisfaction from antagonizing a Chronically Worried Mother may frequently engage in behavior crafted to provoke her.

Ironically, Chronically Worried Mothers may secretly take pride in their "contrary" daughters' daring and adventuresomeness. Courage, even once removed, satisfies a need in them. Having opted for safety and familiarity in their own lives, they obtain a thrill of sorts in observing their children trying new things, even while widening their eyes and clutching their chests in alleged horror.

For daughters in this situation, however, their Chronically Worried Mothers' clandestine pride can have little redeeming value. For it is Mother's often and openly stated fear that seems to have the most psychic salience. Faced with challenge and change, such daughters may forge ahead resolutely. Nevertheless, they may have done such a good job of internalizing a Chronically Worried maternal "commentator" in their own minds that, despite outward calm, they are rarely able to face the unknown without nagging dread. Moreover, some of these defiant daughters may take on challenges they would just as soon defer, simply to prove to themselves and to their mothers that they can.

Though living one's life in opposition to an overprotective mother generally affords one more latitude than living within the narrow perimeters a Chronically Worried Mother prescribes, in neither scenario is a daughter truly free. The insular world characteristic of this Maternal Style provides the compliant daughter with the ability to avoid choices and decisions in her life. By avoiding options that fly in the face of her Chronically Worried Mother's preferences, she avoids distressing her mother and, in turn, herself. As for the defiant daughter, even her most daring and "dangerous" decisions can be, ironically enough, based on a kind of nondecision, for often they are born out of a reaction to Mother rather than a positive and active choice to venture forth.

Nevertheless, both defiers of and compliers with Chronically Worried Mothers may stand to gain something from surrendering to the dynamics of this Maternal Style. Why else would so many of them take pains to persuade their mothers that their day-to-day lives are indeed risky business, fraught with sudden downpours (their umbrellas, you'll recall, were inadvertently left at home) and with mysterious aches and pains ("Gee, Mother, I have that crick in my elbow again. I *hope* it's nothing serious.) What is the point of so many daughters going out of their way to convince Mother of their vulnerability if her worry is such an anathema to them? Perhaps it is because focusing on Mother's fears is a way of disavowing fears and concerns of one's own. If Mother is in charge of worrying, you don't have to be. And it may prove far easier to avoid facing your demons if Mother can be counted on to detect demons *everywhere.*

In the end, of course, neither total compliance nor defiance is satisfying. True courage consists of recognizing one's own fears and facing them squarely while still recognizing one's power to effect change. When that sort of courage is achieved, a Chronically Worried Mother won't seem such a burden anymore. And one's response to her can be adjusted so as to hear the care behind her constant concern.

THE HYPERCRITICAL STYLE

"My mother loves to point out the hair in my shower drain and the spoiled milk in my refrigerator," says Cynthia, a thirty-five-year-old attorney. "I can't seem to do anything right as far as she's concerned, and that always puts me on edge. Not long ago I raced straight from the hairdresser to a lunch date with Mother, petrified that she would scold me for keeping her waiting. She didn't mention my lateness, but she did mention my new haircut. She said, "Oh, my, what have you done to your hair? You look like a boy."

Though as a well-established lawyer Cynthia has learned to plead her clients' cases with admirable skill, she finds herself in a filial relationship in which her mother is judge and jury and she is a defendant without benefit of legal counsel. If, like her, you live in a continual state of tension, aware that there is little you can do to gain your mother's approval and if, like Cynthia's mother, the valence of your mother's attention is constantly focused on what you did wrong rather than on what you did right, then chances are your mother has a Hypercritical Style.

What does the Hypercritical Mother want? In most cases she wants her daughter to do well, to excel, to make Mother proud. The goal in and of itself is difficult to fault. Certainly, most mothers want this for their daughters. Alas, this mother's way of "inspiring" her daughter is not through positive reinforcement but through negativity.

A Hypercritical Maternal Style is wont to manifest itself early on in the life of a child. If a mother wants her daughter to pick up her toys, she has two choices: She can say, "Let's see how quick you can pick up those toys. My, you're so speedy. I'm always amazed at what a good little cleaner-upper you are!" This will enable the daughter to feel capable and admired. Or she can also say, "Look at this mess! Can't you be tidy? I don't know what I'm going to do with you! Pick up these toys right now, missy!" To this latter barrage she may append unfavorable comparisons ("Your cousin Eugenia always picks up her toys!") and perhaps even threats ("If you don't change your ways, I'll never buy you another toy!"). This response engenders a feeling of shame and self-ridicule. Quite an enormous difference in outcome for such a "minor" event.

As a daughter grows, a Hypercritical Mother's tactics are not likely to change. Whatever new threshold her daughter crosses will afford her another opportunity to find fault. Your small part in the school play is never good enough for this mother; only leads will suffice. Your boyfriends are never good enough, either, and certainly your husband won't be.

Advanced age may not mellow a mother with a Hypercritical Style. Should she end up in her daughter's care when she is getting on in years, she may well continue to grumble and gripe even as her daughter struggles to capitalize on her dwindling opportunities to make Mother happy. Returning to her elderly Hypercritical Mother's apartment with a bagful of groceries, a daughter may be subjected to an all-too-familiar refrain: "Why did you buy that kind of tuna? It's so expensive? . . . I wanted yellow paper towels, not white!"

Perhaps what is most problematical of all about a Hypercritical Mother is that her daughter's behavior and judgment are not the only things she criticizes. Most likely, if your mother has a Hypercritical Style, you will have noticed that you were sometimes reproached for having certain *emotions*. When feeling upset or distressed, for example, about an accident that had befallen a close friend, your mother may have given short shrift to your expressions of kind empathy. "Well, it's not *your* problem," she may have told you. "She's the one who should be upset. Who do you think you are?" When you were feeling rejected by a man, she may have hastened to drive home the point that "there were other fish in the sea" and that you shouldn't "waste your time" feeling bad.

This negation of your feelings may have left you unable to determine for yourself what exactly *was* appropriate in a given situation. Like many daughters of Hypercritical Mothers, you may have come to doubt the validity of your emotions. Most especially, you may have come to doubt whether or not you were justified in feeling what you were certainly entitled to feel toward your mother, at least every now and then: anger.

Faced with a mother who, however well meaning, questions the way you act, look, think, and experience the world, it is only natural that one might occasionally get good and mad. Unfortunately, where Hypercritical Mothers are concerned, anger presents a Catch-22. You may be mad at your mother, but if you show it or even allow yourself to feel that anger fully, you imagine—with good cause—that she will get mad at you and criticize you for misinterpreting her motives. You fear her anger and disapproval, yet the ire you experience has to get expressed somehow. Consequently, you may turn that anger against yourself, perhaps suffering recurrent depressions, perhaps incorporating an Introjected Mother who chastises you more severely than your real mother ever could.

Perhaps, too, at that introject's behest, you sabotage yourself, behaving in ways that further bear out criticism. You meet her historic expectations of you and end up feeling worthless.

In what may be the most severe of scenarios resulting from this type of Maternal Style, daughters of Hypercritical Mothers may become addictive personalities, assaulting their own psyches and bodies with an overabundance of substances that serve both to temporarily salve their wounds *and* to protect their mothers from the intensity of their upset. For example, though often not consciously aware of it, many beleaguered daughters have fixed themselves an extra-large helping of fudge-drenched ice cream rather than stand up to an habitually faultfinding mother and admit, "You make me furious when you pick on me the way you do." They would rather swallow their anger, along with unnecessary calories, and risk the self-inflicted shame that follows a binge rather than risk hurting Mother and devastating themselves with the awareness of the strength of their true feelings.

Some daughters of Hypercritical Mothers tend to become

"addicted" to the very act of approval-seeking. They turn into habitual people-pleasers, longing for someone's nod of confirmation to fill the hollow where their own self-acceptance ought to be and feeling despondent when unconditional acceptance is lacking. Yet even when the opinions of others are replete with praise, these women may not hear the compliments. What good is it if fifty people tell you your new haircut is fabulous if your mother has already told you it makes you look like a boot camp recruit?

Hypercritical Mothers, too, may have compliant or defiant daughters. The compliant daughter may reinforce her mother's bent for reproachfulness by denigrating herself whenever Mother is within earshot. "I don't know what it is, Mother," she may plaintively insist, "I just can't seem to do anything right." Why does she deliberately reveal "failures" to her mother, knowing with certainty they will net disapproval? Because if she sets herself up, she knows what to expect and can thus attempt to ameliorate her pain. In addition to this, another gain of sorts emanates from compliance. A daughter who cooperates with a Hypercritical Mother may be using her mother's persistent negativity to justify her own reluctance to persevere in the face of obstacles. What's the point of trying, she may tell herself, when she can never win anyhow?

As for the defiant daughter, she tends to withhold a great deal from her Hypercritical Mother. She may grow wary of sharing not only her anger but her other emotions, and she may hesitate to offer not only news of her failures but of her accomplishments as well. Such accomplishments are often hard-won, of course, because the daughter is often handicapped by her mother's style and must pursue her goals without benefit of maternal cheerleading. Defiance, therefore, tends to occur only when the daughter has had her self-esteem nurtured by other significant people in her life.

Why does the defier "clam up" when her Hypercritical Mother is around? For one thing, of course, she wants to protect herself. For another thing, she may consciously or unconsciously wish to keep Mother off-balance. Oftentimes, a Hypercritical Mother may defend against her own insecurities by focusing on her daughters' "flaws." When that is no longer easy to do, this Mother can be notably rattled.

Key to coming to terms with a Hypercritical Mother without capitulating or retaliating is realizing that the source of one's confidence should not lie outside oneself but rather within. Giving yourself permission to be you—however you look, however you act—is the first step on the journey toward gathering "evidence" and "making a case" for yourself that will hold up in the "courts" presided over by both your actual and your Internal Mother. Giving yourself permission to feel your feelings is the next step. Your anger need not damage you or your mother, nor should your love make you your mother's silent victim. The more awareness you gain of the powerful emotions that fuel your relationship, the less likely they will careen out of your command.

THE CONTROLLING STYLE

"My mother's favorite maxim is 'It's not enough to vacuum,' " says twenty-seven-year-old Marianne, a travel agent. "Last week she learned I was going out of town on business and called to ask whether it would be all right if she came to my apartment while I was gone and had my rugs cleaned. Why? 'Because it's not enough to vacuum.' The funny thing is, the apartment was getting a little messier than usual because I'd been too busy with work to houseclean. I think Mother has a sixth sense about when that happens—and nothing can deter her from doing something about it. Did I let her come? Well, sure. It would have taken more energy to fight her than to acquiesce. And at least I'll have the cleanest rugs on the block."

Does your mother seem to be everywhere, know everything, and anticipate your unspoken needs in the most uncanny way? Is she such a whiz at taking care of things that people shake their heads and wonder how she does it? Is she the sort of mother who tiptoes into your kitchen after you've loaded the dishwasher to arrange the plates "correctly"? Did she take charge of your two-hundred-guest wedding so completely that you were left wondering just whose wedding it was? If shocks of recognition are causing you to nod, then there is little doubt your mother has a Controlling Style.

What does the Controlling Mother want? Well, control. Her driven nature and dramatic personality serve to give her the feeling that she is the master of all she surveys. Though often a false sense, that feeling helps her keep anxiety at bay. By continually scanning the environment for potential threats and disruptions that might affect her or her daughter, by planning ahead for worst-case scenarios and bearing contingency schemes firmly in mind, a Controlling Mother preserves the illusion that her vigilance can stave off the vagaries of fate. No harm will befall her child or herself while this mother is around. She's a virtual human amulet. And for that her daughter had best be grateful.

By always "knowing best," this mother staves off her own fears of uncertainty, incompetence, or futility. Those feelings all end up residing in her daughter.

The Controlling Mother, in her most exaggerated form, is the butt of many comedians' jokes. Her relentless manipulations are indeed quite hilarious to others, but not to you. Guilt is the Stealth Bomber in this mother's arsenal of emotional munitions, and histrionics is her secret weapon. If you don't do what she wants—say, call her at 6 P.M. each day though it may be the most inconvenient hour for you to stop and phone—she will not only make you feel bad ("I was up all night worrying about you") but rapidly segue into a high-pitched, tear-laden litany of all the torments she suffered at your hands ("I called all the hospitals, I saw you lying dead on the highway, then I called all your friends, and they said you were on a date. When I found out you were all right, I felt like a fool").

Mothers with Controlling Styles are so proficient at generating emotional storms that many of their daughters opt for giving in rather than weathering those tempests. Even daughters who register overt objections to their mothers' machinations, protesting through gritted teeth, "Mother, please don't tell me what to do," often end up doing exactly what Mother wants. Fighting her is so exhausting and laden with anxiety, it seems futile to try.

Besides, there is always a "logical" reason why a Controlling Mother does what she does. She still deposits your paycheck because: (1) her bank is closer, (2) you have no time to bank, and (3) it's safer if she knows where your money is.

Compliant daughters routinely take the path of least resistance, capitulating to the vast majority of Mother's edicts, letting her take charge. These daughters get the peace of mind that comes from imagining they have a foolproof talisman to shield them from catastrophe and strife. The peace is, of course, a false peace. For the unexpected is bound to happen, by definition, when it's least expected.

Alas, in the long run compliant daughters of Controlling Mothers may find they have acquired few skills of their own when it comes to thinking on their feet, planning ahead, or even—because the Controlling Mother is often adept at financial bailouts—saving money for a proverbial rainy day. They assume they will never have to face the unexpected, let alone an out-and-out crisis. After all, they have never had to. Mother has always been there either to forestall crisis or, at the very least, to minimize its impact. Furthermore, where rigidity prevails—and rigidity always prevails where total control is in effect—there is no room for inspiration or improvisation or for the joys of discovery and the delights of serendipity.

What do compliant daughters do when Mother is not around to fend off or alleviate trouble? Some turn to their Internalized Mothers for solutions to their problems. Certainly the answer to the query, "What would Mother do in a case like this?" will likely be readily forthcoming. But what if "a case like this" never occurred before? Faced with new situations and unanticipated snags, a daughter who has habitually acquiesced to a Controlling Mother may feel hopeless and helpless. She may cast about hurriedly for someone else—*anyone*—to tell her what to do. In some cases she will forfeit control of her life to an overbearing mate. In extreme scenarios she may even surrender her autonomy to a religious or social group that offers righteous prescriptions for behavior and thought.

Of course, some compliant daughters of Controlling Mothers may come to realize that having "the cleanest rugs in town" is a poor substitute for the pleasures of one day exclaiming, "Eureka! I've figured something out for myself. And it feels good." Ultimately, they may choose to break free and defy their mothers.

Since Controlling Mothers have a dramatic bent, defiance may require upping the histrionic ante. In order to jettison herself from her Controlling Mother's orbit, the defier often participates in a major fireworks display. Consequently, these mother-daughter relationships often wind up as constant battles. And even though the daughter might from time to time actually long to solicit *some* maternal counsel, she cannot do so, she fears, without potentially surrendering body and soul. The result for this daughter is often excessive self-reliance. She may have difficulty letting others get close to her for fear that they, too, will want to control her.

The key to skillfully managing one's response to the Controlling Mother, obviously enough, does not lie in full-fledged firework defiance. Rather, it lies in a gradual diminishment of one's obedience and subjugation. When this is handled with skill by the daughter, some Controlling Mothers may eventually find themselves exclaiming with pleasure, "My daughter did that. I'd never have thought of it. It sure makes me feel proud."

THE COMPETITIVE STYLE

"Let me tell you about my mother," says Lillian, *a twenty-two-year-old psychology graduate student. "She was an unu-*

sual mother of the bride at my wedding last month. I was very proud to fit into a size 8 wedding dress after having dieted for months. I couldn't wait to show off my new, streamlined figure. My mother, who has always been a knockout, kept her dress a secret and surprised us all when she arrived wearing a low-cut gown that was bright, bright red. All eyes were on her—some in appreciation and some in shock. But the net result was the same: Mother stole the show, as usual."

Whatever you have done, she has done it, too—only better and more often. Whatever you wear, she can wear—sometimes a size smaller. When you buy something for yourself, she muses aloud about how good it would look on her. And when you are upset, she reassures you that she has shed her share of tears—bigger, saltier tears than yours. If this describes your mother, she has a Competitive Style.

This type of mother sends an overt message to her daughter that she is loved and cherished, though subliminally her daughter picks up a silent message that she is either unimportant (Mother never seems to hear what she is saying) or unlovable (Mother is so much better at wooing her friends and boyfriends than she is).

What many competitive people want is simply attention. Being in the limelight helps them maintain a sense of well-being. The motivation of Competitive Mothers is explained, in part, by this dynamic.

Some Competitive Mothers derive self-esteem from being firmly in the center of the nuclear family orbit. To this end they may arrange things so that everyone in the household must communicate through them. They may "channel" messages between siblings, isolating them from one another and assuring that they themselves remain the pivotal focus.

In addition, they may overtly interfere with or subtly undermine a daughter's relationship with her father. When you have a private moment with Dad, you sense she seems somewhat angry with you or she immediately finds a reason why she has to draw Dad's attention away. (Is she really so helpless? Must he open that jar of pickles in the kitchen at this particular moment?)

Mothers like this may never have come to terms with their part in the quintessential Oedipal battle in which young children "fall in love" with the parent of the opposite sex and experience rivalrous feelings toward the same-sex parent. Long after the days when her three-and-a-half-year-old daughter coquettishly snuggled up to Dad and snubbed Mom on a fairly routine basis, a Competitive Mother clings intently to the notion that family life is a tournament, with Father as the prize. She cannot step back to see her small daughter's innocent flirtations as normal, rather than a personal threat. In some cases this is a result of her own father never having afforded her the recognition she craved when she was young.

But in many cases Competitive Mothers aim to shine even outside the family arena. They strive to be the hub in the wheel that encompasses a daughter's peers and pals. If you grew up with this sort of mother, she may have been popular with your girlfriends, always up on the latest preteen heartthrobs and schoolyard slang. When you were an adolescent, you may have come home from a babysitting stint to find her and your boyfriend huddled amicably in the kitchen over a sprightly game of Scrabble—a game you detest. If his attention strayed, she wooed him back with frothy cocoa and chewy brownies.

Where mother-daughter relationships are concerned, however, attention is not the only thing that is gained by a Competitive Maternal Style. What Competitive Mothers may achieve through their behavior is denial of the fact that they are growing older. In the natural order of things, a mother may begin to require a higher level of cosmetic maintenance at around the time her daughter comes into full bloom. Mother's hair may require coloring just as her little girl abandons pigtails for a coif that flatters her alarmingly wrinkle-free visage. Mother's body may begin to show signs of sagging as her daughter transits from gawky to gorgeous. But a mother who dresses and grooms herself so as to outsparkle her daughter may succeed, albeit only temporarily, in blocking out of her consciousness the inevitable laws of gravity.

Moreover, a Competitive Mother may perceive her daughter's options as expanding even as she imagines her own are narrowing. As Shirley MacLaine, playing a maturing show biz diva in *Postcards from the Edge,* said to Meryl Streep, who plays her actress-singer daughter, "You are at the beginning, and I am coming to the end." If a woman views the future as her daughter's domain, she may contrive all manner of strategies to prolong her own "day in the sun." And the more uneasy a mother is with the aging process, the more likely she will be to take competitive tactics to uncomfortable extremes.

Whether the Competitive Style emerges out of a need to be the center of attention, win Father, or woo your friends, or whether it emerges out of fear of aging and ebbing opportunities, these mothers experience their daughters—and possibly all women—as potentially usurping their place in the world.

For daughters whose mothers employ a Competitive Style, life is a constant double bind. On the one hand, they long to be like the woman who raised them—she is so popular, so pretty, so charismatic. They want to paint themselves in her image, but they also long to be their own woman. What happens if the woman they become turns out to be painted of colors even more resplendent than those of Mother herself? For many daughters that's when the stone in the shoe seems crippling because to outdo Mother may be to *undo* her.

Rather than fragment a Competitive Mother's fragile ego and risk experiencing herself as cruel, a compliant daughter may choose to mute and subdue herself so that all eyes will remain on her staunchest rival. Even when she is outside her mother's immediate sphere of influence, such a daughter may tone herself down. She may be loathe to compete for a job or to vie with other women for the affections of a man. She may repeatedly bring herself to the brink of success and then undermine her own efforts. For this daughter the Internalized

Mother serves as a nagging reminder of all she herself cannot or dare not do.

Defiant daughters, on the other hand, often perceive their mothers as having "thrown down the gauntlet." They find themselves competing *back* by striving diligently to seek their own place in the sun. But their triumphs are often hollow, for, as we'll see in later chapters, it's not unusual for such high-achieving wowen to feel like imposters. Deep down they may not believe they are entitled to the prizes and accolades after which they have chased.

Life with a Competitive Mother sounds almost as grueling as an Olympic marathon. The ability to endure and develop in spite of Mother's agreed-upon place as front-runner is a challenge, to be sure. Many a daughter alternates between frantically sprinting full-out and competing avidly against her mother, then dropping back to applaud her at the finish line. Learning to run your own race and leave Mother to win at hers is a goal worth training for.

THE PSEUDOPERFECT STYLE

"My cousins hosted a family reunion last summer at their home in a Chicago suburb," says forty-five-year-old Allison, an interior designer. I still live near Chicago and I happily attended, as did many of my relatives who live far and wide. My mother, who is retired and living in northern California, declined to come because she said Chicago is too hot in the summer. But she called during the party to say hello to everyone. For fifteen minutes my aunts, uncles, and cousins passed the phone around until, finally, Mother asked to speak to me. Someone handed me the receiver and laughingly whispered I was 'last but not least.' But when I picked up the phone, I did feel I was 'least,' because Mom said abruptly, 'Hi, honey. I didn't really want to talk to you because this is costing a lot of money. But how would it look if I didn't say hello to my own daughter?' Ob-

viously, I felt her primary concern was—as always—how things appeared to others."

Allison's mother has what we call a Pseudoperfect Style. The last of the Maternal Styles we will be focusing on, this one may be harder to recognize than the others because the key to it is not so much in how a mother behaves but in how she makes her daughter feel. Indeed, on the surface, a Pseudoperfect Mother may behave close to perfectly.

If you have a Pseudoperfect Mother, she may appear to your friends and relatives as the quintessence of the ideal fantasy mother for whom so many women pine. She always says the right things about you ("My wonderful daughter just did thus and such") and *to* you when others are around ("Aunt Hattie, look at my baby. Isn't she the loveliest, smartest girl you've ever seen?"). Yet you may have the uneasy sense that her relationship to you is achieved through smoke and mirrors. Not surprising, for this mother is a bit of a magician. She seems able to conjure up sentiments and actions that society deems appropriate at the veritable drop of a hat. But what are her genuine emotions? Often, it is hard to tell.

These mothers show their affection by offering things *they* would want to receive—emotionally or, more likely, materially. They think in terms of their needs and have difficulty grasping those of their daughters. And they tend to define themselves primarily through the admiration of others.

Helene Deutsch, one of the first female psychoanalysts, might well have viewed these Pseudoperfect Mothers as analogous to what she termed *as-if* personalities. These chameleonlike individuals, she maintained, are characterized by a "readiness to pick up signals from the outer world and to mold oneself and one's behavior accordingly."[2] In keeping with this definition, Pseudoperfect Mothers seem to feel that they should affect toward their daughters the kind of love the world would like to see. This, of course, is a large bill to fill. Our world glorifies motherhood, and our language deifies it (Mother Earth, we say, and Mother Church). Consequently, we wish mothers to be bountiful fountains of sustenance, generous to the point of selflessness, intuitive to the point of clairvoyancy. No mother can be all this in actuality, but Pseudoperfect Mothers may pretend to be.

Many women who mother with Pseudoperfect Styles do so out of a keen deprivation in their own upbringing. Many never felt their strong need to be loved was sated. Many were, it seems, deprived of the right to be dependent in childhood. The lingering evidence is that so many of them manage to communicate to their daughters that they *still* need to be taken care of.

In order to defend against low self-esteem or unacknowledged neediness, a Pseudoperfect Mother may relate to her daughter *as if* she never had a droplet of anger or frustration or a single ounce of self-interest. But the way she thinks about herself does not jibe with the way she wants others to think about her. Never feeling quite "real," she becomes a master of mixed messages, engendering a fundamental mistrust in her daughter and perpetuating a cycle of self-doubt.

If you had a Pseudoperfect Mother, she probably gave you lots of attention in your childhood, but rather than being tender, that attention may have felt forced and overstimulating ("Wake up, baby, so Mother can play with you and show your cute face to Uncle Fred"). Throughout your life this mother may have lavished you with money and material gifts as if to place a dollar value on her devotion. In adulthood this mother may still spend a remarkable amount of time with you, using the frequency of your contact—as opposed to feelings of real closeness—as a measure of her interest and loyalty. Yet she's somehow absent even as she sits beside you. Everything goes well when you two are together, but somehow something is very wrong. Mother's false self strikes a false note.

It is not easy for daughters of Pseudoperfect Mothers to have faith in the genuineness of Mother's communications to them. Nevertheless, many daughters feel they have little choice but to comply and assist in preserving Mother's image and taking care of her at the same time. When Mother says, "Dad wants to take me to his company conference in Maui next week, but of course I said I had to stay in town and take you to dinner for your birthday," the compliant daughter knows the socially appropriate reply is, "Don't be silly, Mother. Of course you must go to Maui. We can have dinner anytime." And being raised by a flawlessly socially appropriate mother predisposes one to do the "proper" thing.

But what about feeling as opposed to doing? For many daughters of Pseudoperfect Mothers, real feelings toward Mother are not to be divulged. Making a heartfelt emotional communication to her (for example, "I feel hurt when you change our plans") seems unthinkable. Because of this you may find very few daughters in this category who openly defy or challenge their mothers. They may even feel uncomfortable offering the slightest complaint about their mothers to others. After all, these women are so "perfect," who would believe them?

As long as these dynamics are in force, the mother-daughter relationship is doomed to be limited and superficial. What's more, the daughter is in danger of avoiding intimacy in all her relationships. The chameleonlike quality of this mother leaves the daughter without a requisite stable role model to react to, learn from, and even rebel against. Consequently, the daughter adopts the same malleable ways of relating to situations and people that are the hallmarks of her mother's style. With a Pseudoperfect Internal Mother as her guide, she may fine-tune strategies that ensure true closeness is artfully dodged.

As always, there is something for the daughter as well as the mother in perpetuating the style to which they both have become accustomed. There is no arguing that true intimacy has the potential to make one feel vulnerable, so avoiding it has its own gratifications. Gratification may also be gleaned by a compliant daughter's preserving her mother's fragile facade, lest she feel responsible for inflicting pain.

Unlike Controlling Mothers, Pseudoperfect Mothers are

rarely the butt of "mother humor." Their modus operandi is too subtle and elusive to inspire caricature. Yet in many ways Pseudoperfect mothering comes closest to formula mothering. A mother hits upon what she imagines is the fitting and proper way to "do her job" and plays the role for which she thinks she has been cast. That formula is the mother's armor, and it gives her relationship with her daughter a tinny quality. Nevertheless, behind the suit of mail, this mother probably has seomthing valuable to offer. What prevents her from offering it is fear and neediness.

Perhaps the saddest aspect of Pseudoperfect Mothers is that, deep down, they are women who suspect that it is what they do that makes them worthy of love, rather than who they are. Because they feel they are not deserving of love without strings attached, they cause their daughters to feel undeserving, too. The natural, wholehearted love these daughters experienced toward their mothers as tiny, helpless creatures is not allowed to blossom into a mature, abiding affection that is welcomed and valued simply because it is what it is. There are always conditions attached, bargains struck, dances danced.

It is challenging indeed to manage one's response to the Pseudoperfect Mother so that one is not compelled to play along with her "Everything's fine" script. Nevertheless, in finally coming to terms with the fact that relations with this mother are not perfect, those relations can improve in the sense that daughters can feel more grounded and have more realistic expectations.

This chapter began with a refrain from a children's book of a mother cooing to her child: "I'll love you forever,/I'll like you for always,/As long as I'm living/my baby you'll be." At the end of that book the tables are turned. The child holds its frail, aging mother in its arms and slightly alters the verse, "I'll love you forever,/I'll like you for always,/As long as I'm living/my Mommy you'll be."

Wouldn't it be nice if mothers and daughters could simply enjoy and cherish one another? But as we already know, for many mother-daughter duos this is not so simple.

Part II of this book is meant, as you'll recall, to pave the way toward mutual enjoyment by promoting tolerance and understanding. It will examine many of the specific practices your mother employs—probably unwittingly—to keep the irritating stone of disharmony firmly lodged in your shoe. More important, it will show you how to develop skills and strategies for beginning to minimize the impact of these practices.

You'll learn, among other things, how to bring frustrating exchanges with Mother to a timely and amicable close, how to find avenues toward common ground, how to appreciate the lighter side of mother-daughter interactions, and how to recognize the importance and complexity of family influence in mother-daughter relationships.

Our next chapter is called Setting Limits. Its title is pretty much self-explanatory. As we've said, all mothers have something to offer their daughters, and that's good. But what happens when a mother offers too much, too often, or too insistently, threatening her daughter's autonomy in the process? Chapter 3 will focus on how to construct healthy boundaries in your relationship—not brick walls but permeable membranes through which love can flow.

PART II

BASIC
SKILLS AND
STRATEGIES

CHAPTER 3

❦

SETTING LIMITS

Wherever and whenever a boundary comes into existence, it is felt both as contact and as isolation.
　　　　　　　　　Fritz Perls, Ego, Hunger and Isolation

Good fences make good neighbors.
　　　　　　　　　Robert Frost, "Mending Wall"

Caroline, a thirty-year-old freelance photographer, lives in a small apartment not far from her mother's home. Caroline's mother, who displays elements of both Merged and Hypercritical Maternal Styles, has a tendancy to drop in on her daughter whenever the whim strikes. Like many mothers in whom such a habit is ingrained, her impromptu visits usually take place when her daughter's apartment is at its most disorganized. It seems to Caroline as though each time her doorman alerts her that her mother is on her way up, there is a week's worth of potential dry cleaning stacked on her bedroom chair, several meals' worth of dishes cluttering the kitchen sink, and an array of negatives, contact sheets, and other telltale signs of impending work deadlines scattered across the living room floor. As her mother approaches her door, Caroline—helpless, vulnerable, clad only in her bathrobe—briefly whirls around looking for something to tidy, something to hide. But it's hopeless. Resignedly, this grown daughter awaits the doorbell with a sense of unparalleled foreboding. Soon her mother will begin inspection, hunting that which, ostensibly, she least wishes to see: disarray, dirty dishes, and concrete evidence of her daughter's busy life apart from her. Within minutes she will be scrutinizing Caroline's heap of clothing for stains, and waxing eloquent about the number of dangerous microorganisms that can fester in a single unwashed casserole pan. Soon she will lament the fact that Caroline seems unable to take care of herself. Chances are that many of you have experienced similar episodes of maternal infiltration into your domestic terrain and subsequent disturbance of your emotional equilibrium. In fact, some of you may have had incidents such as this occur with such frequency that you can predict exactly what your mother will say to you and exactly how you will respond to her in an attempt to defend yourself. Or perhaps you can predict exactly what you *won't* say because her matter-of-fact reprimands, coupled with the liberties she takes in your home, leave you believing that her behavior is justified. She *must* be entitled to drop in and say whatever she feels whenever she feels like it. Perhaps she confirms the nagging suspicion you harbor that you *can't* take care of yourself.

Or perhaps you have a mother who takes liberties in slightly different ways. Perhaps she routinely reaches over to adjust the collar of your blouse as a roomful of relatives looks on. Perhaps she awakens you at 7 A. M. to hear every detail of the party you attended the night before ("Any nice men?") Perhaps she continually offers advice when you don't want it or proffers gifts that come with a plethora of emotional strings attached. If any such intrusions have become recurring themes in your relationship and if you repeatedly allow your mother to overstep the bounds of appropriate behavior only to resent it later, you may well ask, How can this ever be different?

Before she learned how to set limits, Caroline used to wonder the same thing. From time to time she would allow herself to imagine that her mother would miraculously change one day and that instead of popping by to straighten up and chastise her daughter, she would call ahead, arrive at an appointed hour, sit down on the sofa, and, idly brushing yesterday's newspaper aside, inquire, "How are you?" and "What's new?" That fantasy lasted about two minutes, until Caroline remembered it was her real mother she was dealing with, not some idealized fantasy incarnation of Donna Reed. (Remember our first basic tenet—the myth of the ideal mother must be relinquished!)

Ultimately, Caroline realized that it was possible to gain a measure of control over the redundant scenario that strained her liaison with her mother by introducing a new scenario into their repertoire of interactions. The next time her mother dropped in unannounced, Caroline took a different tack. She instructed her doorman to tell her mother she was just on her way downstairs and to please wait for her in the lobby. She donned a sweatsuit and jacket, greeted her mother warmly, and explained that she was on her way out to do some errands but that she would love to take her for a cup of coffee and a chat before going on her way. She did not make a big issue of her plan but presented it as matter-of-factly as her mother habitually presented *her* plans and point of view.

Caroline's mother was a bit startled but acquiescent, and even a bit pleased. Together the two women adjourned to a coffee shop and had an agreeable interlude, discussing objective topics toward which Caroline skillfully steered the conversation. ("Look at that woman over there, Mother. Do you think that dress is the right color for her?")

Amazingly, Caroline had succeeded in going *out* for coffee instead of staying *in* for criticism. She managed to view old behavior and old results from a new framework and to change her behavior accordingly. You can learn to do this, too. And that's what this chapter is all about.

BORDERS AND BOUNDARIES: ACHIEVING OPTIMUM DISTANCE FROM MOTHER

In our first chapter we maintained that it was possible to negotiate a range of optimum distance between oneself and one's mother, a space in which one feels neither too close for comfort nor too far for meaningful contact. Yet it is difficult for many grown daughters to imagine relating to their mothers from a place where both connection and independence are feasible. What, they wonder, would that place even feel like?

To begin to conceptualize that very viable area wherein daughters cannot just survive but also thrive, let's turn for a moment from the human realm and extract an analogy from the plant kingdom. Ecologists have discovered that in a forest, seeds which have the best chance of sprouting and surviving are those that land neither too near to the parent tree nor too far. When they fall too close to the mother tree, the seeds don't get enough sunlight. What's more, they may be exposed to toxins that wash off "maternal" leaves or exude from "maternal" roots. On the other hand, seeds that fall too far from the mother tree lack the sanctuary of shade. They are more likely to suffer from exposure and from other dangers brought about by virtue of their distance. Unprotected and vulnerable, they are more likely, for example, to get trod upon by passersby.

Out in the forest the greatest potential for healthy development exists when filial seeds settle somewhere in the middle. The same holds true back in the family drama of our own lives. Like new saplings, daughters can suffer when overshadowed by their mothers, but like saplings, too, they tend not to fare well when deprived of the shelter and security a mother can provide.

There is a point, however, where such similarities end. Plants are immobile, and seeds, buffeted by the wind, have no choice in the matter of where they wind up. We, of course, are not solely at the mercy of random forces. We can find the right range of space from which to relate comfortably to our mothers, and we can remain within the periphery of that space by setting limits and observing appropriate boundaries.

Boundaries have to do with borders that define one's territory, whether actual or emotional. Geographic boundary zones, as military leaders of any sovereign nation can attest, tend to be politically sensitive areas. Emotionally, they are sensitive areas, too. As the epigraph for this chapter indicates, Fritz Perls, the founder of Gestalt therapy, has noted that boundaries may be experienced both as contact and as isolation—*isolation* because they prevent limitless, habitual merging and because they constitute a barrier to trespassing, but *contact* because they define an area of mutual restraint and mutual respect. The observance of a boundary by two parties signifies an agreement of sorts. I won't tread on your turf unless invited, and vice versa. We may give and take but not encroach. We may share but not spill over.

Boundaries are delicate places of proximity. When people cross them carelessly, they are potential friction zones. When they are approached properly, as when citizens of one country present passports and visas at various checkpoints so they may visit another country for a limited duration, there is little cause for border skirmishes.

Having a natural ally at its border can give a country strength and a sense of security. Having a hostile entity at its edge can sap much of a nation's energy and assets. Anxiety is pervasive, and constant vigilance is demanded. Things are much the same in relationships between individuals. If a daughter wants to coexist peacefully with her mother, she must do what she can to enlist her as an ally even while defining the bounds of her private territory.

But hold on here, you may be thinking. You've obviously never met my mother. Since junior high school I begged and pleaded with her to leave my things alone and keep her hands out of my dresser drawers. I insisted she stop reading mail that was addressed to me, and stop putting her ear to my door. But nothing worked. Why, years ago I moved from Virginia to Texas just to get some breathing room. There are six states between us as the crow flies, not to mention the Mississippi! How many borders and boundaries is that? Yet she still manages to impose herself in a million ways.

Well, what with the legacies of Alexander Graham Bell and the Wright brothers, not to mention Federal Express, fax, and the rest, the truth is that fleeing looks less and less like a solution. The key to establishing optimum distance lies in your own backyard, that is, in your own attitude. It does not lie in begging, pleading, or insisting that your mother do anything. Those sorts of communications, as you already know, are likely to go in one ear, out the other, and on into the stratosphere.

The key to optimum distance lies instead in taking subtle yet positive action toward preserving your autonomy. It lies in defining the limits of what you'll allow yourself to give to your mother. What access will she have to your space, your time, and to knowledge of your affairs? And it lies in deciding what you'll allow yourself to take from her. How much free advice will you solicit? How many presents will you accept, and what will her gifts actually cost you? It lies in employing alternatives to unsuccessful negotiating and to armed conflicts at your physical and psychical border zones, whether your mother lives around the corner or thousands of miles away.

SETTING SPACE LIMITS

Of course, the nearer a mother actually lives to her daughter, the more likely that actual physical border zones will intermingle with psychical ones. In Caroline's case, for example, we see a grown daughter who experienced her mother's extemporaneous sojourns into her apartment not just as physical disruptions but as emotional intrusions. But for Caroline to correct what became an intolerable pattern, she needed to tackle the physical side of the matter as a means of getting at the issues beneath its surface. If, like Caroline, your routine face-to-face contact with your mother presents you with emotional quandaries, it will be especially useful for you to set what we call "space limits."

Unlike the way this term sounds, establishing space limits with your mother has nothing to do with wishing she would take a pleasant, extended holiday on, say, the moon. It has to do with letting Mother know what your terrain is and under what conditions it is permissible to enter it.

Managing Mother's Border Crossings

Caroline's mother had grown used to entering her daughter's dominion virtually anytime. She assumed that her status as mother served as a permanent passport. In the new way Caroline dealt with the situation, she in effect told her, "You do have a passport, but your visa is not valid today." By prohibiting entry into her apartment, she communicated—not in so many words, but through attitude and action—that a border existed. Yet she did not turn her mother away. She offered a sensible and caring alternative: that they meet on neutral ground (where, by extension, they would be likely to discuss more neutral things.)

What was involved on Caroline's behalf was a small shift in the way she viewed her options and entitlements. Before she envisioned herself as being entitled to set limits, she could imagine doing only the following: (1) letting her uninvited mother continue to invade her space impulsively and criticize her as well, or (2) waiting for a spontaneous, miraculous epiphany to alter her mother's attitude. When at her angriest, Caroline sometimes fantasized another scenario: lashing out at her mother and ordering her to simply go away. But none of these options was truly reasonable. Perpetuating habitual patterns ultimately became far too damaging to Caroline's self-esteem. And while miracles should never be ruled out, few would argue that celestial intervention is rarely a certainty. As for unleashing a tirade at Mother, that would have done little except exacerbate the chronic sense of blameworthiness which in part made Caroline so tolerant of her mother's liberties to begin with.

So Caroline broadened her horizons. She reminded herself that virtually any list of options also contains the following choice: none of the above. She decided not to tolerate poor treatment any longer, but she did not dwell on fantasies of perfect mothers nor estrange herself from her mother. Instead, she blazed a new trail, steering herself and her mother clear of the "friction zone."

You may argue, of course, that this business of small shifts leading to change is all very nice, but that such things are more easily said than done. Indeed, just as small shifts on the earth's surface may reflect major rumblings below ground, small shifts in behavior may correspond to rumblings deep in one's psyche. Whenever a new behavior is put into effect where one's mother is concerned, one may well expect to encounter resistances. Remember, what we are doing here is *undoing* lifelong patterns. It is only natural for oppositional forces to exert a tug.

Managing Your Resistances to Change

Upon self-reflection, Caroline became aware of a cluster of feelings that seemed to be conspiring to keep her from blazing a trail, that is, of finding a new repertoire of interactions with her mother. As the routinely compliant daughter of a Merged Mother who contended *my daughter is my life*, Caroline felt guilt at the prospect of drawing a line. She felt sadness, too, for the potential loss of the comforting aspects of such a symbiotic bond. And she felt anxiety. For if Mother was no longer going to come over and "help" her get organized, she would have to take more responsibility for herself.

Moreover, because her mother also displayed aspects of the Hypercritical Style, Caroline had never been trained to trust the validity of her own preferences and priorities. She felt self-doubt and wondered if perhaps she was wrong to think her mother was mistreating her. Yet deep down her anger felt so powerful and genuine that it induced in her a sense of dread. What if, once she broke out of the habit of enduring her mother's criticism, she lost control? The thought of a confrontation of world war proportions frightened her so thoroughly that she was sorely tempted to continue her policy of appeasement.

Guilt, sadness, anxiety, self-doubt, and fear—that was quite a quintet of resistances for Caroline, or anyone, to grapple with. Yet to some extent all daughters in the process of redefining their relationships with their mothers will experience at least some of those emotions some of the time.

What served Caroline well and what will serve anyone well is not to ignore those emotions but to give them their due. It was because Caroline was willing to acknowledge and tolerate *all* her feelings without falling prey to them that she was able to proceed with successful action. Had she not been willing to remind herself, "These are only feelings. They need not prevent me from acting in my best interests," she might have undermined herself. Perhaps she would have presented her plan to her mother in a way that was almost certain to provoke a quarrel ("You're not coming up today, Mother. If you must see me, let's go out!") or evoke a waterfall of tears and guilt-invoking rebuttals ("Mother, why do you come over and pick on me? Don't you love me?").

Awareness of Mother's Resistances

Of course, along with a willingness to have her own feelings, Caroline had to be willing to let her mother have her own feelings, too. Since she did such a successful job of making her alternative to apartment-invasion an appealing prospect, her mother did not feel angry or hurt. But let's be realistic. Some mothers would have taken umbrage at any suggestion that threatened old familiar patterns of relating, and some would have manifested ingenious spontaneous counterstrategies to reinstate the old order of things. ("But I must come in, darling. I have to go to the bathroom.")

If your mother does not take well initially to new limits, regardless of how delicately and diplomatically you introduce them, it will help you to remember that while it is your responsibility to be sensitive to your mother's feelings, it is not in your power to control them. As for the "bathroom" issue or others like it, we'll leave that up to you. We'd like to suggest, however, that while boundaries should be clear, they should not be inflexible. Mother's use of your facilities should not be viewed as a backward step in your progression, provided you do not let that hamper you from following through with your overall intent.

Too Many Cooks: Using Realism, Prioritization, and Generosity

Now let's look at some other means of setting space limits, and let us look, too, at how a daughter's resistances to change may manifest themselves.

Paula, a thirty-nine-year-old office manager with a husband and twin sons, lives in Seattle, Washington. Her widowed mother, sixty-year-old Alice, lives in Santa Barbara, California. Though this mother and daughter live far apart, for quite some time they have reunited annually to reenact the same border skirmish.

Each year Paula likes to have friends and relatives gather at her house for Thanksgiving, as her mother did while she was growing up. Since the first year she prepared the traditional holiday feast in her own home, she invited her mother as a guest. And since the first time she attended, Alice, who has a decidedly Controlling Maternal Style, has managed, as Paula says, to "take over."

"I know that everything from the menu to the choice of table settings to the timing of the meal to where people hang their coats is fair game for Mother," Paula complains. "She seems to be everywhere all at once. How in the world do you set limits on someone who has no limits?"

This is a good question. As a Controlling Mother, Alice is determined to run the show in what is rightfully her daughter's arena. Indeed, she probably believes on some level that if she does not do so, disaster might ensue. Her modus operandi is to leave nothing to chance. Paula is obviously frustrated. The "assistance" her mother provides makes her feel infringed upon, yet she cannot imagine tackling a problem that seems so immense.

For a moment, put yourself in Paula's shoes. (For many of you, we suspect, this will be easy.) What can she possibly do?

What can any grown daughter do when, literally or figuratively, she finds there are too many cooks in her kitchen?

First and foremost, it is necessary to *be realistic*. If your mother is long used to taking over your Thanksgiving dinner, recognize that you will not be able to stop her from attempting to take over in some fashion. But recognize, too, that in truth she isn't everywhere at once. It just seems that way. By setting space limits you can help keep her controlling behavior confined.

Second, *prioritize*. Decide for yourself what is most important for you to control. Do you make delicious cranberry sauce and chestnut dressing (at least according to everyone else except your mother)? Then perhaps it is the cooking you wish to preside over rather than, say, the decorating. If so, your task will be to keep your mother away from the stove.

Third, *be generous* and give credit where credit is due. Does your mother make exquisite flower arrangements and set a beautiful table? Encouraging her to focus on those chores—in the dining room and away from your pots and pans—may turn a Thanksgiving trial into a triumph.

Once you are clear as to your own desired boundaries and your own intentions, it will be your job to articulate them as calmly and clearly as possible. Weeks before the dinner you may try saying, "Mother, I've decided that the kitchen is off-limits to everyone at the party. I'm going to do all the work in there myself. I'm really looking forward to it, and I have it all planned in my mind." And, being generous, you may add, "You are such an expert at arranging flowers, and I know absolutely nothing about it. Would you do me the biggest favor and plan on arranging them for me? Oh, and also . . . would you mind being in charge of setting the table? You make a table look so elegant, it almost seems a shame to put food on it!"

On the big day itself you may even consider reinforcing your border regulations with the written word. You might hang a good-humored sign on the kitchen door reading: NO ADMITTANCE IF YOU HOPE TO EAT IN THIS CENTURY! And when your mother protests, as doubtless she will, you can point laughingly at your placard and remind her that her expertise is required elsewhere.

Will you experience resistances to setting these limits? Of course. As the daughter of a Controlling Mother you will almost certainly experience self-doubt and anxiety as you claim an autonomous role for yourself. Suppose the turkey burns to a crisp? Suppose you prove yourself incompetent? You will likely experience a sense of futility as well. Your mother is so demanding that even the thought of revising her agenda has always made you feel exhausted in advance.

But the key word here is *always*. Your Controlling Mother has always induced in you feelings of helplessness, hopelessness, and anxiety. In the past these induced feelings have caused you to circle obediently round and round in the same loop of the Mother Maze—or perhaps to lose your temper and behave in the most *un*diplomatic fashion. Now, however, neither of these reactive behaviors need result. Your conscious awareness and acceptance of your feelings empower you to behave differently.

Without such awareness and acceptance you may undermine yourself in all kinds of unconscious ways. You may, for instance, forget to post your NO ADMITTANCE sign on the kitchen door. Or you may forget to pile all the silverware on the dining room table before your mother arrives so that she has to come into the kitchen to get it. Or you may buy too few flowers to occupy Mother. (The point of having her arrange the flowers is to keep her busy for a long time, especially since you know she will arrive well before the agreed-upon hour.)

Becoming aware of your resistances by owning up to your feelings and your fears and acknowledging the part of you that longs to put things back the way they were before will help prevent your unconscious from taking over. With your feelings as your servants rather than your master, you will be free to blaze a trail and improvise. Then, even in the unlikely event that your worst fear comes true—the turkey incinerates and the stuffing coagulates—you can order a pizza and spice it up with the satisfaction of knowing you did things your way. And if your mother says, "I told you so," you can be generous and agree with her. "Why yes, Mom," you can say pleasantly, "you certainly did!"

Elbowroom: Employing Creative Non Sequiturs

Before moving off the subject of space limits, it is necessary to address another, more subtle type of space that certain mothers are wont to invade: your distinct personal physical space, the inches or feet that define the elbowroom you need to function comfortably.

Some of you have encountered variations in elbowroom space when traveling in other countries. In Scandinavian cultures, for example, people usually stand farther away from one another and speak to one another across a greater distance than they do in Mediterranean climes, where people tend to communicate nearly toe-to-toe. For some mothers, regardless of cultural background, being toe-to-toe or nose-to-nose with their daughters seems the most natural way to be.

Mother-daughter physical contact is among the most natural phenomena in the world, and realistically speaking, mothers do have an interesting dilemma, having raised us very tactilely. Indeed, if we see a mother who shuns physical contact with her child, we are alerted to a problem immediately. But as we evolve from totally dependent beings into more independent ones, it is also quite natural that we take on more and more control of how much physical contact we have with Mother. As growing infants we wriggle and squirm until Mother lets us go. As adolescents we shut our bedroom doors with a loud bang to let them know there are moments we simply don't want them near. Though we may be clumsy at first in conveying our messages about what degree of contact we desire, our methods are often effective.

But surprisingly enough, many of us, as grown adults, can do little else but sigh with exasperation when Mother reaches over to straighten one of our earrings or smooth the bangs on our foreheads. We cannot find the means of expressing what we want, and as a result we may get less of what we want than do wriggling babies.

If you are among the adult daughters faced with this conundrum, we would like to suggest a technique we call the Creative Non Sequitur. What this term refers to is simply a method of curtailing an uncomfortable pattern or habitual exchange by inserting a benign topic.

Earlier we saw how Caroline, seated in a coffee shop with her Merged and Hypercritical Mother, diverted the conversation from its usual collision course by focusing on objective topics ("Look at that woman over there, Mother. Do you think that dress is the right color for her?") This was a clever use of a Creative Non Sequitur. The unsuspecting woman had virtually nothing to do with Caroline and her mother. Neither of them was invested in the shade of her outfit, and her appearance could be praised or damned without creating a conflict between the two. When physical elbowroom is at stake, Creative Non Sequiturs should contain a decidedly physical element.

The next time your mother invades your personal space by adjusting your collar, dabbing at your lipstick with a tissue, or correcting your posture with a firm squeeze to your shoulders, you can subtly set a limit by implementing a Creative Non Sequitur that necessitates your moving away. You might get up to change the tape in your stereo, check your answering machine, or fetch your mother a cup of tea. You might discover a smudge on a mirror across the room, or you might simply choose that moment to answer a call of nature. Excusing yourself politely and with a credible explanation, you can remove yourself from the range of your mother's reach until her immediate impulse to repair or realign you has abated.

Again it is important to remember your three steps to setting space limits: (1) *Be realistic.* For reasons already mentioned, your mother is bound to feel entitled to take a hands-on approach to you at least some of the time; (2) *Prioritize.* Decide which of her "love taps" are tolerable to you and which are not; (3) *Be generous.* Just as children rightfully feel unhappy when deprived of physical contact, so do we all. And give credit where credit is due because maybe, just maybe, being alerted to the occasional lipstick smear wouldn't do you any harm.

But do keep the technique of Creative Non Sequiturs in mind, for it will serve you well in many instances. We shall soon see how it can be used in setting the next category of limits we will address—time limits.

TIME LIMITS: HOW MANY MINUTES FOR MOTHER?

The idea of setting time limits with one's mother may conjure up visions of turning over a sand-filled egg timer each time your mother telephones and talking for precisely three minutes. Nothing quite so drastic is required. There are, however, a number of difficult situations we engage in with our mothers in which the limiting of time can help to increase the comfort level in our relationship.

One way you may wish to set time limits is limiting the frequency with which you and your mother get together. Some women who feel obliged to see their mothers each and every time their mothers express a desire to see *them* end up feeling resentful and drained. If that describes you, your relationship would doubtless prosper by arranging to see your mother at times that are convenient for you and on occasions when you are at your most relaxed rather than your most fragile.

You may also wish to limit exasperating, redundant conversations in which your mother goes on and on about a subject that "pushes your buttons." If marathon conversations with recurring themes are a source of frustration in your interactions, you need to learn to discontinue them gracefully before you explode outwardly at your mother or turn your frustration inward on yourself—feeling restless or glum but powerless to prevent a tirade.

Limiting the Frequency of Interactions with Mother

Let's look at the first of these situations.

Here is the case of one grown daughter who needed to come to terms with scheduling dates with her mother.

Madeline, a twenty-six-year-old magazine editor, has a mother with a Pseudoperfect Maternal Style. Inwardly needy and demanding yet outwardly vibrant and giving, Madeline's mother is most comfortable displaying her affection for her daughter in very public settings. She likes to spend a great deal of time being out and about with Madeline and calls several times a week to suggest joint activities, from tennis matches to bargain hunting to theater matinees.

For a long time Madeline complied with all the requests it was within her power to meet—and then some. Occasionally, she even left her office on a hectic day to grant her mother some time, though she regretted it sorely later as she worked far into the night.

Madeline long had the impression that her mother craved their meeting, yet her cravings never seemed sated when her daughter arrived. Indeed, like most people with Pseudoperfect personalities, Madeline's mother was more at ease with the *idea* of a relationship than with the actuality of one. She had difficulty experiencing her daughter's presence even when they were side by side. Instead, she focused on reassuring both of them—and all within hearing range—what a good time they were having.

Because her and her mother's meetings never involved a true sense of camaraderie or intimacy, Madeline never felt they brought the two of them closer together. Indeed, after each outing she felt disappointed, frustrated, and vaguely angry, though she could not put her finger on exactly why. Ultimately things reached a point where Madeline felt she had to set a limit. She recognized that her frequent get-togethers with her mother were not only dampening her mood but cutting into her productivity and her social life, yet she did not want to be accused of acting unlovingly.

In learning to set time limits with her mother, Madeline followed the same basic set of steps as are used to set space limits. *Being realistic*, she recognized that her mother was not going to solve her own problems overnight, evolving suddenly from an emotionally distant, dependent person to an emotionally accessible, autonomous woman. Thus, she also knew that her mother was not about to limit her requests for her daughter's company. She recognized that her success would come not from changing her mother or from "cutting the cord" once and for all but from verbalizing her need to limit time spent with her mother and coming away from those interactions feeling proud and positive about not making her mother's problems her own.

As she turned her attention to *prioritizing*, Madeline decided she could probably manage to have a rather pleasant get-together about once a week. More than that, she believed, and she would start to feel resentful again. Now her task was to *be generous* with her mother and communicate her newfound limits as pleasantly as possible.

Whatever Maternal Style—or Styles—your mother manifests, you, like Madeline, may feel the need to limit the frequency of your meetings, whether to spare yourself emotional turmoil or simply to have more time for other things. How can you convey this to her in a pleasant way? With the three basic steps as ground rules, add to them. Consider something new.

Try praise. Tell your mother how flattered you are that she wants to do thus and such with you. Add warmly that she just can't seem to get enough of you and that she seems to have so much love to lavish she ought to have two daughters. (If she already has two, tell her she ought to have four.) Such comments will not go unnoticed by her. On a conscious level she will hear the flattery. On an unconscious level she will register that you are aware she is the more dependent of the two of you and that she may no longer project that sense of neediness on to you.

Try describing competing demands for your time. Tell her that you would like to spend time with her but that you will have to make an alternative date because work, the kids, or other obligations are pressing. Be sure to cite a real obligation—surely you have dozens—rather than a contrived excuse. Lying about something like this may well imbue you with unease and remorse. The truth will, quite literally, set you free. And once you are ready to make a plan for your next encounter, be sure to arrange an activity in which you genuinely want to partake at a time when you will not feel harried or put upon. Suggest a show you want to see or a store where you want to shop. That way you will be assured in advance of getting something *you* want.

Once again, of course, our old friend Resistance may rear its head. You may well expect to feel guily about setting a limit and getting what you want. You may feel forlorn, too, for who's to say you won't on some level miss the constant demands on your time—especially if that was the primary way in which you felt attended to by your mother. If you let your resistant feelings take charge, you may find yourself making comments to your mother that reel you both back into old, treadworn paths of the Mother Maze, such as, "I just saw a great movie, Mom. You would have loved it. I kept thinking of you while I watched it." But if you take charge of your feelings, you will control the emotional tenor of your interaction without having either to rush to meet your mother's mandates or to argue over why she wants to see you again so soon (an unproductive discourse if ever there was one).

Ending the Broken Record Syndrome

Now for a situation in which a daughter finds the need to stop her mother from "pushing buttons." Here is a scenario where a daughter needed to set a time limit with a mother whom she described as having "Broken Record Syndrome."

Francine, fifty-two, has a seventy-nine-year-old mother-in-law with chronic arthritis. Lately, she and her husband spend a good deal of time at her apartment, shopping, straightening up, paying bills, and generally trying to make things easier for her. At first Francine's mother, who has a Competitive Maternal Style, tended to rail on and on about the situation in ways that caused Francine, in her words, to "bite my lip until I left permanent marks or launch into a high-decibel rebuttal."

"Mom would call up to ask how we were," says Francine, "but soon she would inquire for news of my mother-in-law. If I mentioned anything about our assisting her in any way, my mother would be off and running. Sometimes she would go on and on about *her* aches and pains. She would accuse my mother-in-law of being a hypochondriac and insist that she herself was suffering much more serious arthritis—though she truly wasn't. And of course she would complain that we don't give her the care and attention we 'lavish' on my husband's mother."

Other times Francine's mother would launch into a different but equally grating diatribe. She'd give a detailed account of the many selfless ways in which *she* was helping her infirm, elderly neighbor. "You think *you* do a lot," she would chastise her daughter. "I cook for this woman. I clean. I read to her, write letters for her, and even help with the laundry." Needless to say, Francine's altruism seemed minuscule in comparison. "But that's understandable," her mother would say. "I know how to take care of people. After all, I've been a mother a very long time."

After these talks Francine was left feeling guilty or that her mother had treated her with condescension. The thing that bothered her most, however, was that her mother used the same verbal gambits over and over. She sounded like a broken record. Francine knew she had to get off this conversational treadmill, but she didn't know how.

Here, too, is a case where a grown daughter had to be realistic before she could resolve her dilemma. She had to recognize that she and her Competitive Mother were running two different races and that it was not necessary for either of them to triumph over the other. She then had to decide what she really wanted from these conversations; it turned out she wanted to nip them in the bud. Taking a generous approach, she realized that one way to bring her mother's tirades to an end was to *agree with her rather than oppose her.*

Suddenly, she no longer felt the need to defend her mother-in-law because she realized that doing so was to no avail. Instead, when her mother contended her own aches were more serious, Francine complimented her mother for being able to tolerate such a high threshold of pain so valiantly. And when her mother waxed rhapsodic about her neighborly acts of charity, Francine complimented her for them, too. When her mother felt soothed, the "broken records" wound down.

Whatever your mother's style, you may well be familiar with the frustrating sensation of being on the receiving end of a seemingly one-way conversation in which your mother repeats herself on a topic about which you have heard enough—whether it concerns your father's snoring, your cousin's plastic surgery ("You ought to have a nose job like that, dear") or your children's tardiness in sending thank-you notes.

What can you do? Like Francine, you can try concurring with your mother instead of battling her. (Our next chapter includes many techniques for affirming and validating your mother's point of view even if you *thought* that was impossible for you.) Or you can choose from among these techniques:

Be silent. Yes. Shh! Silence can be a powerful tool in reshaping the interactions you have with your mother. It is simply amazing how often we feed the fires of conflict by feeling compelled to respond to our mother's every comment. We go to a department store with Mother and see that the latest skirt lengths are well above the knee. The issue of skirt length has been a fertile field for battle between us since we were in the sixth grade. Mother once again begins a lament about the indecency of it all and about our "bony knees."

Unable to stop ourselves, we leap to the defense of Cher, Twiggy, and mini wearers across the globe. Why? If we simply counted to ten without saying anything—not biting our lip till it bleeds but breathing deeply and luxuriating in our newfound capacity for restraint—the moment might pass. (If Mother persists in asking, "Didn't you hear me?" you can cheerfully respond, "Yes"—and count to ten again.)

When a person has no willing opponent, the urge to engage in a fracas can dissipate pretty quickly. At the unconscious level, the futility of provocation begins to sink in. Moreover, behavorists firmly believe that by not rewarding behavior one can extinguish it. In this case Mother's "reward" would be your rebuttal, a form of engagement with which she is comfortably familiar.

Terminate the conversation. That's right, end it—*pleasantly.* This is an especially useful strategy in a phone conversation because one can always find a valid reason for getting off the phone. While we must stress again that we do not recommend untruthfulness—not only is it unethical, it will exacerbate your guilt resistance—life is full of legitimate distractions. Rather than saying "The doorbell's ringing" when it's not, try saying, "Oops, Mom, I've just got to run. There's something here that needs my attention." We are certain there is always something that requires your attention, be it paperwork, a boiling pot on the stove, or your eight-year-old hunting for a snack.

Use those non sequiturs. By shifting discourse from the personal to the impersonal, you can very effectively set a limit on the time you are willing to devote to a dissatisfying interaction. "Oh, look, Mom, do you see that cardinal outside by the bird feeder" can be a useful non sequitur as your mother sits at your kitchen table sipping coffee and complaining about your father . . . again. While waiting with your elderly mother in a doctor's reception room listening to her wonder aloud for the hundredth time whether she can trust this doctor you found for her, try, "Mom, do you think that cute receptionist would look better with her hair cut short?" After all, the receptionist's hairstyle is not especially significant to either one of you. What the non sequitur does is steer the two of you away from an impending conflict and put your exchange on a new footing.

Remember, don't move from one potentially heated exchange to another. Use the physical things around you to generate ideas. Practice looking at the places you frequent with your mother and see if you can name five sources of non sequiturs in the room you can use at a moment's notice.

You may resist some of these strategies at first. In fact, at this very moment some of you may be thinking of reasons why you *can't* undertake them. That's understandable. If the currency of your relationship with your mother is near-continual conflict, then you may well ask what exchanges with your mother will be like from now on.

At first they may feel awkward. Conversations may end abruptly once Mother registers that you are not responding predictably to her comments. Take heart. It takes time to adjust to new ground rules, and eventually matters will stabilize. The void you initially experience may in fact be filled with very constructive things, for in setting a time limit, you have made time for progress.

SETTING INFORMATION LIMITS

In general, we have found that women with Competitive, Controlling, and Pseudoperfect Mothers—or any combination of those—experience a need to set time limits on mother-daughter conversations when the focus of those conversations shifts away from anything having to do with them and *their* needs and instead begins to center solely on their mothers' agendas. Women whose mothers exhibit aspects of Merged,

Chronically Worried, or Hypercritical Styles, however, often have a different problem. The conversations they have with their mothers all too frequently focus entirely on *them*. Yet these daughters may be active participants in setting up a lop-sided dynamic. They need to learn to set a different kind of limit—a limit on the amount of *information* they provide about the details of their lives.

Loose Lips Sink Ships

Elizabeth, a thirty-three-year-old special education teacher whose mother's style is a blend of Merged, Chronically Worried, and Hypercritical, is one such woman: As Elizabeth related,

Last year I was flying home from an education conference, and a very attractive, exciting man sat next to me on the plane. We talked and flirted the whole way and discovered we lived near each other. He talked a lot about opera, and when I admitted to knowing nothing about it, he insisted he would introduce me to it—and said I would come to love it as he did. That sounded promising. When we landed he took my number. Then he actually kissed my hand! Well, as you can imagine, I was convinced he would call soon. I was on a pink cloud. So, of course, I went home and called my mother and told her every detail. She sounded thrilled for me.

Well, the man didn't call, but as each day passed my mother would check in with me to see if he had. As the week went by she got more and more anxious and then more and more depressed. This didn't make me feel any better because, of course, I was feeling those feelings, too—plus feeling guilty for inflicting them on my mother *and* embarrassed because she knew her daughter had apparently "failed" to win this fellow's heart.

When something like this happens, you can't help getting down. You start to worry that maybe the right man never will come along. But I wasn't nearly as worried as my mother. Suddenly, she started wondering aloud about my retirement fund, saying that if I never married, I might have to live on it in my old age! I snapped, "Gee, Mom. Thanks a lot." We argued and then she started criticizing me. She actually asked me if I had perhaps done something to discourage the man. She made me recount every sentence of our conversation and then insisted I should have taken *his* number instead of giving him mine.

Learn to hold your tongue.

If, like Elizabeth, you are in the habit of providing your mother with all the artillery she needs for a border invasion, you need a strategy that will help you to be silent. Know that although lying to your mother is not a constructive strategy for improving your relationship, neither is sharing every specific of your existence. Whenever you have the urge to tell your mother something you suspect will come back to haunt you, stop!

Call a friend first.

Think of the people in your life with whom you are comfortable discussing your hopes and fears—calm people, non-judgmental people. Think of them as stand-ins and have their numbers readily available. It's important to have more than one such confidant in the event that you are unable to reach the first friend you try, and it is important to omit from the list anyone who will be tempted to spill the beans to your mother, such as your loose-lipped Cousin Phoebe or siblings who feel it is their duty to divulge all family tidings.

This does not mean, of course, that you should omit telling your mother anything significant, but rather that your stress level—not to mention hers—will inevitably be lessened by sharing information when it is ripe rather than when it is in its budding stage. If, for example, your doctor has just removed a small mole from your back and is running a biopsy, your Chronically Worried Mother will doubtless be thrown into paroxysms of anxiety if you tell her the test is in progress. Call her with the news that the mole turned out to be nothing, and she'll doubtless complain, "Why didn't you tell me?" Be honest. Tell her you wanted to spare her any apprehension. And be generous. Don't mention your observation that panic, rather than reassurance, is her strong suit. If you say instead, "I figured if something were really wrong, I would need you at your best," her unconscious will register your message that you would rather shoulder some problems on your own than risk feeling doubly overwhelmed by wondering how she will respond to them.

Likewise, if your mother is Hypercritical, why call her over the weekend to ruminate about whether or not you should ask for a transfer to your company's new office? If you delay, you will protect yourself from the disturbing and frustrating urge to change your decision once you hear the tone in her voice that connotes disappointment or disapproval.

Elizabeth used an interesting phrase when she described her interactions with her mother. She said her mother *made* her recount her conversation with the airborne Don Juan. But this is Elizabeth's "resistance to change" talking. Feeling habitually anxious and guilty in the face of Mother's probing, she reacts as she did in childhood. But Elizabeth, like you, is a grown woman. Her mother can't really make her do anything, any more than yours can. You have every right to experience the joy of sharing the important events in your life with your mother, but you are also entitled to do so when and how you choose.

SETTING ADVICE LIMITS

Once you have set a limit on what you are willing to give to your mother in terms of space, time, and information, your next task is to look at what limits you are willing to set on what you take *from* her. One thing many mothers like to give freely is advice, and those mothers with Controlling Styles give it especially freely.

Using the Word *We*

Many daughters of such mothers are zealous in seeking maternal advice. For one thing they have never been taught to rely on their own judgment. For another, the routine solicitation of Mother's ideas may be the primary currency of their relationship. It's what they know how to do with their mothers. Nevertheless, they may reach a point where they finally feel as though nothing in their lives is truly their own. As thirty-eight-year-old Valerie related,

> When my husband and I bought our house, my mother had a recommendation about absolutely everything. I mean, *elaborate* recommendations. Other people had always told me I had a knack for interior decorating, but my mother made me feel completely unskilled. Before I knew it my walls were papered in the patterns she wanted, and even my daughter's room was painted in a color my mother chose. But the last thing I had to do was window treatments, and I finally decided to do that one thing my way. I hung country curtains in the living room, knowing full well my mother believed only full-length draperies would suffice— blue silk moire draperies with matching drawstrings, to be precise. The first time she came over after I had hung my curtains, she looked at them and said, "Oh." It was a barely audible syllable, but it clearly meant "thumbs down." Her disapproval was palpable. Part of me felt like cowering in the bathroom for the rest of the night.

Happily for Valerie, part of her decided not to give in to the urge to cringe behind the shower curtain (the shower curtain hand picked by her mother, that is). That part of her which had resolved to take a step toward her own autonomy, no matter how incremental that step, set a limit. Suddenly, Valerie heard herself saying to her mother, "We [meaning she and her husband] talked it over and decided that even though the draperies you suggested were lovely, we'd enjoy a less formal atmosphere in here."

The use of the word *we*—meaning you and someone else other than your mother (your spouse, your children, your best friend)—is an efficient shorthand way of conveying a limit on advice-acceptance. It implies that you are part of other teams as well as a mother-daughter team and that you are open to input from additional sources. It also serves to bolster your resolve to make decisions independently of her on a regular basis. Simply hearing your own words will remind you that you and your mother are not umbilically attached after all.

Certainly, your mother may disparage anyone you name as a "coconspirator" in your drive for liberty, countering with, "What do *they* know?" And that is the point at which you can supplement your limit-setting with an additional strategy. Look around for a handy non sequitur to interject or proffer a compliment, for example, "Mother, I was thinking. You have so many great decorating ideas, it's a shame to give them all away for free. Have you ever thought of starting a little business of your own?" If the compliment is merited, there is no reason to withhold it, for indeed your mother may have many ingenious ideas and abundant good taste. It is none-theless your prerogative not to avail yourself of her talents all the time.

If you are uncomfortable with that approach, you may try offering this compliment instead: "You know, Mother, you've taught me everything I know. Over the years you've helped me so much in figuring out the pros and cons of a situation. It just wasn't hard to come to the right decision this time using the skills you've shown me." Most mothers would be hard-pressed to debate with you on that score.

SETTING GIFT LIMITS

Now we come to the subject of gift limits, an area in which some daughters may at first be unwilling to draw a line. There's no arguing that receiving a new sweater, a used car, or a set of silverware from one's mother can be very pleasant. But how many of your gifts come with emotional strings attached? Perhaps more than you imagined.

Even when they are not consciously aware of doing so, mothers with many different kinds of Maternal Styles sometimes give gifts that are likely to lead to their own satisfaction rather than that of their daughters. Your Chronically Worried Mother may be in the habit of paying for your vacations, but what if the "safe" chaperoned tours she deems appropriate for you are preventing you from embarking on less predictable jaunts? Your Merged Mother may generously offer to buy you a fur coat just like hers, but what if you don't condone wearing fur, yet don't want to hurt her feelings? Your Pseudoperfect Mother may lavish you with countless presents, perhaps even with bountiful sums of cash to do with as you wish, but what if what you really want is less superficial evidence of her devotion? Your Controlling Mother may supplement her advice-giving with material largesse, but what do you do when she actually presents you with blue silk moire draperies rather than simply recommending them? In fact, what do you do if she has contributed a substantial amount to the down payment for your house? Does that mean you will feel even guiltier for refusing to decorate it her way?

Declining Diplomatically

Gifts can be confusing. The truth is that it's hard to feel frustration with someone who is giving you a brand-new shiny this-or-that. Yet your mother's gifts may on some level engender anger in you. The truth is, too, that examining a gift exchange for hidden consequences may make you feel somewhat like an ingrate. Yet unless you come to terms with whatever emotional/material quid pro quo is actually occuring, you may let periodic "gift fixes" forestall your progress in improving your mother-daughter relationship.

What can you do, then, if you come to recognize that setting a gift limit would benefit you and your mother in the long run? Once again the three basic steps to limit-setting will serve you well. *Be realistic.* Gift-giving is routine, to some extent, in nearly all families. Even if your mother does not proffer impromptu presents, birthdays, Christmas or Chanukah, and other occasions offer regular opportunities to give gifts. If your mother is used to doing so, she is not going to halt and desist, nor would you necessarily want her to. It's just for inappropriate giving or overgiving that you need to set limits. Next, *prioritize.* If the effect of your mother's gift choices is to make you feel manipulated or misunderstood, you can begin to manage the situation by suggesting very specific items that you actually want. If your mother simply gives too much and that makes you feel either guilty (because you now owe your undivided allegiance to your benefactor) or empty (because she lavishes presents but withholds herself), you can begin to extinguish her overgiving by gently limiting the extent of her benevolence. You may allow that while you appreciate her offer of a new coat, you simply don't have room in your closet for another thing. Why doesn't she keep the coat since it looks so good on her? Or you may point out that it is she and your father who really deserve a vacation and that they would most enjoy the package tour to the Poconos so graciously offered to you.

Lastly, *be generous.* Diplomacy is imperative when turning down anything your mother offers. Remember, giving gifts may be one of the ways in which your mother infringes on your boundaries, but it is also one of the ways she shows affection. Recognizing her and thanking her for that impulse will make your refusal of a check or an article of clothing easier to bear. And complimenting her for the thought behind her deed will buoy her up when she needs it most.

NEW BEGINNINGS: PUTTING NEW SKILLS INTO PRACTICE

Before we end this chapter on limit-setting, let's reflect on what it's all about and what it's not about. It's not about cunning formulas or quick fixes. It's about diminishing conflict and enhancing mutual respect. It's not about ending but about beginning to mold an enduring new shape for your relationship. Best of all, in redefining the dynamics between you and your mother, you are in truth defining yourself—perhaps for the first time genuinely forming an understanding of who you are and what you really want.

There is an added bonus to all this as well, as later chapters will show. As you learn to set limits with your External Mother, you are actually laying the foundations for limit-setting with your Internal Mother. (Remember our second basic tenet: You can't just "tune her out.") Many of the skills you have become acquainted with here will ultimately enable you to reign in the inner voice that holds the proxy for your mother's point of view.

Though much of this book is yet before you, there is no reason not to begin implementing some basic strategies for setting limits right now. Set tenable goals for yourself, and don't expect to change all interactions right away. Trying out one technique per week is more than enough. This may not seem like much when you think you have plenty to do to change things between you and your mother, but don't be overambitious. It has taken a lifetime for your joint patterns and habits to develop. Patience and perseverance are mandatory.

Finally, don't be discouraged if you find yourself backsliding. Depending on the precise nature of your relationship and on your individual temperament, some resistances will be harder to resolve than others. And some long-standing family patterns and traditions will prove harder to dislodge. (Remember our third tenet: Daughters and mothers do not stand alone.)

You may even find that after initial success, life crises of one sort or another cast you back onto paths of the Mother Maze you thought you had left behind. Don't panic. All of us tend to regress under stress. You need not abandon all your hard work any more than you need to halt a successful diet after a single hot fudge binge.

Besides, even as you practice limit-setting, you can begin to master the next set of skills that chapter 4 will address. In this upcoming chapter you will learn to truly listen to your mother, to help her feel understood, and to discover and share the humor in your exchanges.

CHAPTER 4

❧

LISTENING JOINING, AND JESTING

True listening is love in action.

M. Scott Peck, *The Road Less Traveled*

It is said that in order to comprehend another person we must be able to imitate in our own experience what is going on in the other's mind.

Theodor Reik, *Listening with the Third Ear*

Forty-three-year-old Debra has a recurrent problem. Whenever she leaves her mother's house to drive home—a journey of about fifty miles—her mother, a Chronic Worrier with Controlling tendencies, frets that an accident will occur. If it's snowing, she worries about ice patches. If it's raining, she worries about road flooding. If the weather's fine, she worries about inebriated drivers or bad brakes or simple bad luck. Typically, her litany of worries irritated Debra, and she let her mother know it. For years whenever she and her mother parted company, their conversation went something like this:

MOTHER: Call me when you get home. It's wet out there tonight.

DAUGHTER: Oh, Mother. We've been through this a thousand times. Why should I call you? It will be late. I'll wake you.

MOTHER: What do you mean *why call?* You know I can't
              sleep until I hear from you. Is it such a big thing?
DAUGHTER: I've been driving for twenty-five years, and I've
              never had an accident. I've never even had a
              ticket.
MOTHER: All right, fine. Don't call. I'll stay up all night
              and listen to the radio to see if there are any
              terrible car crashes. No problem. Go!
DAUGHTER: Oh, great. It's clear you just don't trust me, Mom.
              That's the problem. You've never trusted me!

Debra and her mother were off and running again. Whatever
pleasantness may have occured during Debra's visits was
dwarfed by this redundant battle. Moreover, although ultimately Debra usually complied with her mother's request for
an "all's well" phone call, she did so resentfully, feeling manipulated and infantilized.

These days, however, Debra deals with this situation differently. The last time she and her mother said good night,
their conversation went something like this:

MOTHER: Call me when you get home, no matter what
              time it is. It's *foggy* out there.
DAUGHTER: The mist is making you nervous for my safety.
MOTHER: I'll say. Why, I'll bet you can't see two feet in
              front of you.
DAUGHTER: You'll want me to be extra-careful.
MOTHER: That's right.
DAUGHTER: Even if the drive takes longer than usual and I
              get in late, I know you'll want me to call you.
MOTHER: You bet.
DAUGHTER: You can't sleep unless I'm safe. What a mom!
MOTHER: You know how much I love you. Good night,
              honey.

After this conversation, Debra did—as before—call her
mother upon her safe return home. But she did not do so

feeling that her mother had scored a victory or that she had been "bested." She felt better than she ever had before in this circumstance, and her mother felt better, too. She experienced her daughter's telephoning as an act of concern and cooperation—not as an obligation grudgingly fulfilled.

IF YOU CAN'T BEAT 'EM, JOIN 'EM

What changed here? On the surface, not much. Beneath the surface, a great deal. Suddenly, Debra, during an interaction with her mother, allowed herself to experience her mother's positive *int*ent rather than reacting to the frustrating *cont*ent of her demand. By using new language she was able to hear herself stating what her mother actually meant to say. She allowed for the fact that the issue here was not her mother's distrust of her but a well-meant (if annoyingly expressed) preoccupation with her daughter's well-being. Debra then conveyed to her mother a message which acknowledged that Mother's view—though Debra herself might not have wholly subscribed to it—felt emotionally important and, even more significantly, evolved out of good intentions.

You're probably familiar with the phrase, "If you can't beat 'em, join 'em." In effect, Debra reliquished the desire to "beat" her mother by outarguing or outreasoning her. Instead she "joined" her—with happy emotional consequences for them both. Once Debra's mother received what she really wanted from their parting conversations on a *feeling* level— which turned out to be her daughter's affirmation and valjidation—she no longer felt the need to pursue her point ad-infinitum.

This chapter will address the art of validating and affirming, that is, of "joining," one's mother. It will show you how to do this without losing sight of your own needs or being untrue to yourself. Later, we will also address another crucial skill that may be appropriated for bettering one's maternal relations—the creative use of humor. But before we discuss the specifics of these skills, a much more fundamental skill must be addressed. That skill is listening, and it is the key to both successful joining and effective humor.

LISTENING FROM THE HEART

The need to have the genuine meanings of one's communications correctly *per*ceived and acceptingly *re*ceived is a profound need in all of us. How many of us count among our closest friends people who are truly able to tune into us with open minds and open hearts, and who are able not only to comprehend our thoughts and feelings but also help clarify them for us? Conversely, how many of us become irritated with people who just can't seem to get through their heads what we really mean to say or what we really feel? The answer, of course, is virtually all of us—mothers included!

We already know that many mothers adopt frustrating Maternal Styles in order to carry out their unconscious emotional agendas. Merged and Chronically Worried Mothers may indeed cling too tightly to their daughters for fear of their own abandonment. Controlling and Hypercritical Mothers may attempt to impose their will upon their daughters for fear that harm and dissatisfaction will befall those who fail to follow their rigid rules. Competitive Mothers may frustrate their daughters with behaviors derived from their fear of being supplanted by their offspring. And Pseudoperfect Mothers may sadden their daughters with seemingly hollow expressions of affection that evolve from their own neediness and deprivation. But regardless of any such motives on the part of your mother, you can bet she has another, even deeper desire as well: She wishes to be understood. And if you're going to understand your mother, you need to truly listen to her, perhaps in a way you never have listened before.

But we can practically sense some of you objecting. "Now hold on a minute. Why, I've done nothing but listen to my mother my entire life! In fact, you just spent a whole chapter telling me how to set limits on her complaints, her criticisms, her competitiveness, and her controlling."

Well, the truth is that although you have been *hearing* your mother your entire life, you may not have been *listening* to her in ways that enhance your relationship, so we are moving on to a set of more advanced skills in your quest for healthy individuation and relationship harmony. Once you've learned to limit hurtful exchanges between you and your mother, you need to know how to substitute healthful exchanges for them.

To begin this process, we recommend listening in the best and broadest sense of the word.

True listeners give us their attention—no small feat when one thinks of all that can compete for one's mental focus in our frenetic world. True listeners give us their objectivity, for they listen with an aim to discovering, not of reconfirming what they may think they already know. And finally, true listeners give us their trust, assuming the best in us rather than suspecting the worst.

When we listen to our mothers—even as they make comments we have repeatedly construed as inflammatory—it can be exceptionally enriching to our relationships to listen from the heart. But how does one begin to do so?

Distinguishing Intent from Content

The psychiatrist M. Scott Peck has written about the skill of listening with the respect that it deserves. In his book, *The Road Less Traveled*, he says, "An essential part of true listening is the discipline of bracketing, the temporary giving up or setting aside of one's own prejudices, frames of reference, and desires so as to experience as far as possible the speaker's world." In short, the "bracketing" he recommends is the ability to walk a proverbial mile in someone else's shoes, to enter momentarily another's psyche as if from the inside out, rather than from the outside in.

Stepping for a moment into your mother's shoes may net you quite a surprise because they may not be nearly as ill-

fitting as you supposed. Indeed, you may share more of her
emotional perspective than you realized. After all, her *emotional intent* in demanding that you telephone her when you
arrive home may not be very far from the intent you have
when you offer your own teenage daughter elaborate advice
for, say, remaining safe during a camping trip she is planning
with friends. Your intent is not to give the message "You are
incompetent." It is to say: "I am concerned for you always."
Even if you are not a mother yourself, it is likely you will be
able to recall a time in your life when your fears for a loved
one's safety caused your anxiety level to heighten, when you
imagined illusionary disasters, and when the content of your
cautionary messages to that loved person became, shall we say,
a bit overzealous.

Drawing on such recollections from your personal archives
will diminish your anger and lower your frustration level. It
will help you hear your mother's positive intention, couched
though it may be in terms that have long made you bristle.
Perhaps what your mother is saying is not that she doesn't find
you trustworthy but that the very thought that she might somehow, someday lose you frightens her in advance. For along
with the intensity of maternal love can come an equally intense
fear of losing the loved one. Knowing that, isn't it easier to
respond to her in a nonprovocative way—indeed, in a way
that allows you to state clearly what she herself covers up with
elaborate admonitions and demands?

Discerning *intent* from *content* where a mother's communications are concerned is not always going to be easy. For
reasons already discussed, you may have a long-standing habit
of playing out the cause-and-effect scenarios that routinely
unfold in your exchanges. Nevertheless, it is well worth per-
sisting in "keeping an ear out" for the emotion that so frequently fuels a mother's discourse and that forms the core of
her messages: Love and concern. If you *listen for the love*,
chances are you will find it, though it may lurk beneath layers
and layers of superimposed emotional agendas and historically
nonproductive forms of expression.

JOINING: FINDING COMMON GROUND

Once you have enabled yourself to tune in to what is noblest and most nurturing in your mother's communications to you, you are now ready to employ the skill of joining. To clarify that term again, "joining" does not mean linking arms with your mother and walking off into the sunset together. Joining is one alternative to reflexively opposing your mother's point of view. It enables you to make her feel understood, and therefore she behaves less combatively.

Joining is not meant to be manipulative or patronizing. The glorious thing about joining is that it evolves out of a genuine understanding of and empathy for the other person's underlying impulse and emotion. By employing joining skills you will be able to have interactions that are not only less stressful for both you and your mother but that are ego-strengthening for you both. In understanding each other better you will understand yourselves better, and you will both ultimately come to recognize, tolerate, and perhaps even rejoice in the similarities *and* the differences between you.

Joining techniques can be broken down into three subcategories: *echoing, mirroring,* and *silent validation.*

Echoing: Showing Mother You Understand

Echoing involves listening for your mother's underlying intent, gently giving it verbal shape, and giving it back to her so that she is aware you understand it and accept it—*even if you don't agree with it.*

Here is an example that illustrates how echoing can be especially useful in converting diatribe to dialogue. The following exchange is, alas, typical of one that has occurred innumerable times between many a mother and daughter:

MOTHER: There's that smell again. It must be gas.

DAUGHTER: (In an irritated tone) Mother, that is not gas. You *always* smell gas. Ever since I was a child you've been smelling gas.

MOTHER: Why are you yelling at me? Suppose I'm right, then what? Then we're dead, that's what.

DAUGHTER: (Shouting) Oh, come on. I can't *stand* this anymore. We're not going to die. What is it with all this "dying" all the time? Why are you so morbid? Why can't you look on the bright side for a change?

MOTHER: (In a huff or in tears) Well, I'm sorry I mentioned it. I'm just an old know-nothing. (Pause) But it still smells funny in here to me.

When the art of joining is successfully employed, this quintessential "gas conversation" may conceivably go like this instead:

MOTHER: There's that smell again. It must be gas.

DAUGHTER: (In a light, even tone) Yes, you've mentioned a gas smell before, I think.

MOTHER: Well, you don't seem to be doing anything about it! Are you going to wait until we blow up?

DAUGHTER: It does seem to be making you anxious. I guess you think it should be investigated . . . just in case.

MOTHER: What harm could it do to find out?

DAUGHTER: Maybe it's time to consult the gas company. Even if it's nothing, I'm sure they'll understand that my mother doesn't want my house to explode.

MOTHER: (Surprised, pleased) That's my girl . . . but, you know, it probably *is* nothing.

Which conversation would you rather have? The one that ends in tears and recriminations and instigates yet more circular travels in familiar loops of the Mother Maze? Or the one that achieves calm, civility, and perhaps even some closure? Notice that in the second conversation the emotional pitfalls of the first conversation are avoided.

In the first conversation the daughter is immediately on the defensive ("Mother, that is not gas. You *always* smell gas"). She brings up ancient history ("Ever since I was a child you've been smelling gas"). She places a negative label on her mother and illogically demands an instant metamorphosis into a "fantasy mother" ("Why are you so morbid? Why can't you look on the bright side for a change?"). Naturally enough, all of this serves to egg her mother on.

In the second exchange the daughter makes her mother feel credible rather than crazy, appreciated rather than attacked. She does not, it should be noted, promise to take any action. She merely gives verbal shape to her mother's unspoken fears and desires. ("It does seem to be making you anxious. I guess you think it should be investigated—just in case"). And once she states that *perhaps* the gas company should be consulted, her mother is free to back off from her stance rather than hammering her point.

Certainly, not all mothers will necessarily abandon what you may perceive as their annoying or irrational viewpoints once they are responded to in this new, empathic manner. Some, in fact, may resist your new tack by accusing you of condescending to them. "Sure, sure, humor your foolish old mother," they might intone. "I *know* you're not going to call the gas company!"

Should this happen, do not allow your mother's resistance to change to ignite your own resistance and spark your defensiveness. *Keep doing what you're doing.* Once again, hear her underlying wish (she doesn't want to be taken for a fool) and clarify it. "Mother," you may say with complete honesty, "clearly, you are nobody's fool. And you're right. I didn't *swear* to call the gas company, but I do understand your concerns."

After having been consistently acknowledged and echoed, many mothers will feel free to be at least somewhat more flexible. Echoing your mother's suggestions and presenting them back to her in a positive light will be disarming to a mother who is used to fighting with you over every suggestion she makes because you have always heard her grievance rather than her positive intent. A verbal boxing match with Mom is no longer a certain outcome. Your mother and you no longer have to enter each interaction from opposite corners of the ring. Indeed, once you have recognized your mother's positive intent and disarmed her by affirming it, she will be left shadowboxing if she retains her rigid stance. Once you have removed *your* gloves, there will be no one in the ring willing to spar with Mother, save her own shadow. And such a match is, by definition, unsatisfying.

Echoing can be employed universally with mothers who favor all sorts of Maternal Styles. Obviously enough, the hypothetical mother in our "gas conversation" example is a Worrier, as was Debra's mother, who fretted about her daughter's driving. But if your Hypercritical Mother asks you for the umpteenth time, "Why don't you cut those bangs, you have such pretty eyes?" her best intent, too, can be echoed. Try a response such as, "You've always wanted me to look my best. Maybe this is something I should discuss with my hairdresser." Now you have acknowledged her maternal instinct (something virtually every mother appreciates) and at the same time indicated that you will consider her opinion—though not necessarily take her advice.

And if your Competitive Mother begins to elaborate on how wonderful *her* parties are when guests at *your* party are praising your capabilities as a hostess, *listen.* Make an effort to hear Mother's underlying message. "I had something to do with this girl's success. Acknowledge me, too." Then, instead of withdrawing from the conversation so as not to compete or challenging her comments in an attempt to one-up her, preserve Mother's dignity with an echoing response. If you turn to all guests within earshot and inform them, "I learned everything I know from a master," you will be verbalizing the sentiments your mother cannot quite bring herself to articulate and preserving her dignity at the same time. Best of all, you have given yourself freedom to excel without feeling that you have to play down your talents to protect your mother's self-image. You have generously offered her a share of your success. Now you can enjoy your moment in the sun, and Mother can enjoy it as well. All she really needs is not to be left out in the cold.

Often, then, echoing can bring both you and your mother a sense of relief. Simply by clarifying and rephrasing what she says (or what she means to but cannot quite say) you are alleviating a great deal of pressure on you both. Even though you are not necessarily agreeing with your mother, you are not blatantly disagreeing with her. Even though you are not gratifying her by taking action, you are emphatically acknowledging how important her needs feel to her.

But here is a caveat when it comes to giving echoing responses: In order to employ this skill successfully, you must be willing to give up the idea of *convincing* your mother that you are right and that she is wrong. You must be able to tolerate the mature notion that there is room for more than one valid point of view in just about all situations. Your satisfaction in learning to "echo" must come from the fact that you have mastered a new skill and advanced your own maturity—not from getting your mother to agree with *you.*

Mirroring: Acknowledging Similarities

"Mirroring" is the second of our three joining techniques. Just as echoing does not require a trip to the nearest mountaintop to intone your mother's homilies, mirroring does not require re-creating her image. Indeed, mirroring, like echoing, is a kind of emotional communication, yet it is subtly different.

When you echo, that is, when you clarify and resonate your mother's intent, the basic overall message you are communicating to your mother is "I hear what you mean to say." When you mirror, you will be going one step farther. You will basically be communicating a message that says, "I understand how you feel and am capable of similar feelings my-self. I am not unlike you—*though I am still a separate being.*" By using yourself as an example of someone who might share a particular emotion or constellation of emotions, you will open new vistas for your mother and for your relationship with her.

Let's see how this can work by looking at the case of Anne, a thirty-six-year-old woman whose Pseudoperfect Mother used to irritate her greatly by harping on how she was deprived of her rightful inheritance. Mother's specific complaint was that her sister Constance had been willed several valuable family heirlooms by Anne's grandmother, including a pair of silver candlesticks and a Wedgewood tea set. Here is a typical con-versation Anne and her mother would have on this topic before Anne employed the skill of mirroring:

MOTHER: I just came back from your aunt Constance's house, and guess what. She had those candles and that tea set right on the coffee table in plain view. And when someone complimented her on them, she boasted how they were our mother's most precious possessions. How can she be so insensitive?

DAUGHTER: Mom, those things are always on Aunt Con-stance's coffee table. Why can't you give this a rest? It's been years since Grandma died.

MOTHER: How can I give it a rest? I was Mother's eldest child. Those should have been mine. She always gave my sister more. She always loved her best. Now your aunt is torturing me with that.

DAUGHTER: Please, I don't want to hear about this anymore. Why don't you tell Aunt Constance what you think? Or stop visiting her if it makes you so miserable.

MOTHER: What do you mean stop visiting her? She's my sister. What would people say?

However, once Anne employed the skill of mirroring, the next "candlestick conversation" went something like this:

MOTHER: What an awful time I had at your aunt Constance's today. I can't stand looking at my mother's candlesticks and tea set right out on the coffee table. And she just happened to mention again how much our mother had prized them. What nerve.

DAUGHTER: I know how you must have felt. It's not pleasant to be reminded of past hurts.

MOTHER: How could my mother have left her those things? It's so unfair. I loved her the most.

DAUGHTER: I feel sad and angry, too, when I don't think my feelings are reciprocated.

MOTHER: Well, at least I have you, dear.

DAUGHTER: It sounds as if we both want to do a better job with each other than your mother did with you.

MOTHER: But that Constance still infuriates me.

DAUGHTER: Her timing can be just terrible, can't it? Tactless people upset me, too. I can understand how you feel.

In the first conversation Anne pursues the nonconstructive path of minimizing her mother's feelings ("Why can't you give this a rest? It's been years since Grandma died") and ruling herself out as a source of solace and empathy ("Please, I don't want to hear about this anymore. Why don't you tell Aunt Constance what you think?"). Certainly it is understandable why Anne would be so exasperated at her mother's redundant complaints about being cheated out of material things. In part, at least, she doesn't want to focus on those complaints because they remind her that her mother all too often equates love with superficialities. Feeling slighted and ignored, Anne would rather talk about relevant issues between her and her mother than about the unalterable past.

But, as is so often the case, Anne's discontent contained

seeds of its own reparation. Precisely because she truly did understand what it was like to feel rejected by one's mother, she could tap into her own empathy and craft it into a response that mirrored her mother's sense of hurt. By indicating that her own emotional responses to rejection yielded feelings similar to her mother's ("I feel sad and angry, too, when I don't think my feelings are reciprocated"), Anne began to bridge a gulf that had long loomed between them. And by acknowledging that she reacted analogously to her mother when confronted with corresponding frustrations ("Tactless people upset me, too. I can understand how you feel"), she let her mother know that although she was her own person with her own standards, her mother's standards were in no way alien to hers.

Like joining, mirroring can be employed with mothers who favor all variations of Maternal Styles. But because of its usefulness in connoting separateness without stressing opposition, it is an especially constructive emotional communication with Merged Mothers.

Let us imagine, for example, that you have the sort of mother who reacts to your disappointments more dramatically than you do and typically worsens a situation with her histrionics. Such a mother would perhaps become excessively despondent if, say, your child was not admitted to the prestigious college of her choice. You could react with impatience and short-temperedness at her inability to stand back and be helpful, rather than giving you yet someone else to worry about and console. Or you could respond to the emotional intent of her despair and mirror her.

If you do the latter, you might say something like: "Mom, I know how much you want Beth to have her first choice. I feel let down, too, and so must she. It's hard to keep a stiff upper lip, isn't it? But for Beth's sake why don't you and I try to buoy her up and say positive things about her second-choice school. Let's both put our disappointment aside for her sake. It's wonderful for her to have a grandmother in her corner. I know what you think means so much to her."

With this communication you are gently coaxing your

mother out of her relentless symbiosis. You have acknowledged your comprehension of her emotions and, while likening her feelings to your own, have suggested a way you may both constructively harness your feelings—which involve not only disappointment but shared love and concern for Beth. At the same time you have generously added a respectful compliment. As always, generosity never hinders and always helps a tense situation.

Furthermore, your suggestion of how your mother can offer support is both edifying and dignifying. On an unconscious level she will surely register that you do not appreciate the way her Merged Style interferes with genuine helpfulness, but she will also register that you consider her a worthy ally. (A caveat: If you mirror a feeling and Mother responds with "Where did you come up with that? I'm not feeling that at all," you can still leave the door open for her by saying, "Well, I guess if I were in your situation, that's what I'd feel.")

The emotional education of one's mother in such a fashion offers a light at the end of a dark tunnel for all of us. Your mother will have the benefit of that light, and you will have the satisfaction of being the torchbearer.

Silent Validation: Biting Your Tongue

The last in our triad of joining techniques, *silent validation*, has to do not with words but with actions. For many it may prove the easiest of all the joining skills to master, though for some it may require the greatest effort and the greatest patience. What it requires is tacit forbearance, a willingness to make no intervention at all, but rather to let your mother mother without comment by you.

Before echoing and mirroring a mother's comments, you'll recall, it is necessary to listen to the positive intent that is so often the genuine subtext in her remarks. Before silently validating, one must observe the positive intent that is so often the genuine subtext in her behavior. Then one must respond to it accordingly, which in this context means not to respond to it in a negating fashion. Your mother will experience your silence as validation of what she is doing.

Take, for example, the case of Sandra and her husband Michael, two vegetarians who long battled the intent of Sandra's Controlling Mother who disapproved of their dietary regime. Here is how Sandra explains her successful use of silent validation:

My mother was baffled and bothered when I married a vegetarian and soon became one as well. At family gatherings she looked on disapprovingly as we passed up her Swedish meatballs and other meat delicacies. Then when we were ready to leave, she always handed us the same "care package" as she did all my sisters and brothers, regardless of the fact that it contained food we wouldn't eat. First, we tried polite refusals, but she just got more insistent. Then, we got into squabbles. My mother would say, "Take it, take it, just in case," and I would yell, "Just in case of *what?*" It was really irritating. I interpreted her foisting this food on us as evidence that she didn't take us seriously. She was disregarding our needs and our philosophy.

But after going on miserably like this for over a year, I rethought my position. My mother may be controlling, but she's also giving, in her way, and she equates giving food with giving love. If she can't do that, she feels lost. So we stopped fighting and accepted her packages, saying, "Thanks, Mom. We know many people with whom we can share this."

Then a funny thing happened. After we did this for a while, Mom made a really sweet gesture. She gave us a "care package" of what I guess she thought was vegetarian roadfood—a half-dozen cans of pea soup and a head of lettuce. I guess accommodating her by letting her mother us her way for a while enabled her to accommodate us, at least as best as she could muster.

What happened here is that Sandra became an objective observer of her mother's behavior. Having done this, she was free to reinterpret that behavior. Instead of seeing the "care packages" as instruments of control, she saw them, literally, as bundles of care. Thus, she and her husband were able to accept and briefly but appropriately acknowledge the parcels.

They did so out of a sensitive recognition that this was an instance where a mother's need to give weighed more heavily than their need to adamantly express their preferences or to set gift limits.

As for Sandra's mother, once she was silently validated and no longer felt frustrated in her attempts to express her love, she was free to move off the dime, so to speak, and to explore new options. Ultimately, she grew flexible and considerate enough to attempt to meet her daughter's and son-in-law's needs more adequately. Her version of a vegetarian "care package" may have seemed slightly ridiculous on the face of things, but her deep-seated need to nurture was anything but ridiculous. It was a driving impulse that needed to be greeted with open arms.

Like echoing and mirroring, silent validation can be applied across the board, whatever the behavioral style or styles for which your mother has a penchant. The common denominator to all silent validations on a daughter's part is a conscious decision not to engage in a habitually negative reaction to a mother's action but instead to engage in a benign embrace of it.

Silent validation of another human being's deepest and noblest intent and meaning is an extremely potent tool. It is a tool for healing past hurts, for enhancing the other's sense of self, and for opening the door to further expressions of that person's true intent. Who knows what will happen in the long run? Sandra's mother and other mothers like her may become able to express their loving intent more directly, without Swedish meatballs or canned soup as intermediaries.

JESTING: THE SKILL AND THE THRILL OF LAUGHING TOGETHER

Successful joining of all types shifts a relationship from the negative to the positive. Whether joining is achieved through words or action (or possibly nonaction), the result is a change in mood, which in turn can lead to a change in mother-daughter dynamics. Once tension is supplanted by equanimity, combativeness is more readily replaced by cooperation. Suddenly, healthy connections and easy camaraderie are well within range.

When it comes to mood-changing, another skill that will prove immensely fruitful is the use of laughter and humor.

When was the last time you and your mother shared a good laugh? If you can't recall, you may have a problem. But relax. Like so many other problems, this one affords you opportunities for growth and revision.

We are convinced that wonderful new things can happen between you and your mother once you master the skill of making her laugh, but we don't mean to imply that you should don a clown suit and a bulbous red rubber nose or that you should take her to a Marx brothers retrospective. While the latter would doubtless be fun, it would probably not fundamentally alter the dynamics between you. What will alter them is your learning to gently cajole your mother into recognizing the more humorous aspects of her Maternal Style and the behavior that emanates from that style.

When used judiciously and nonmaliciously, teasing, joking, joshing communications release the steam from the pressure cooker of the psyche. When we hear such communications and incorporate them, we are able to stand back and resist taking our own attitudes so seriously. We lighten up on ourselves and, consequently, on those around us.

Many clinicians have written on the cathartic effects of laughter and on the efficacy of gaining an understanding of oneself through humor. Freud described humor as a kind of benign short cut to the unconscious.

Gestalt therapists Erving and Miriam Polster have pointed out that one may explore playfully what may be too painful to explore in a serious framework. To hear or see an aspect of oneself presented through caricature or exaggeration or simple clowning around, they say, is often to identify and acknowledge that aspect more freely than one might otherwise.

When we use humor with our mothers, we are letting the light of recognition of behavior and intent shine on both of us. We bathe in the warm glow of mutual play. If we employ that humor to help us contend with a frustrating aspect of our relationship, we can effectively eliminate a "frontal attack" and instead come to the situation through the back door.

Let's say you have left for vacation, leaving your Controlling and Competitive Mother with explicit instructions on how to babysit Bingo, your cat. When you came back from two weeks away, Bingo and your mother were in mid love affair. Small wonder because your mother ignored your instructions entirely. She let the cat sleep on the bed and prowl across the tabletops. And—big surprise!—she overfed it.

Well, all right, reinstating Bingo's more spartan regime might prove grueling to both you and your pet, but after all, your mother didn't skin your cat, she just pampered it. She wanted your cat to like her. When you think about it, it is sort of funny, isn't it?

Of course, one option here would be to rail at Mother: "How in the world could you have done that? Didn't you hear what I said before I left? You're impossible. You never listen to me!" But this would not likely result in a correction of your mother's future behavior. Indeed, it would probably only complicate matters by fostering a defensive response. Your mother might complain of your ingratitude or contend that you don't know anything about how to treat animals. You would then feel compelled to defend yourself, and on and on the two of you would go.

Suppose, instead, you said (with a smile on your face that reflected your genuine ability to unearth the amusing aspects of this situation): "Mom, it's true Bingo has stripes, but you don't have to feed him like a tiger. No wonder he loves you so much. You give him everything a cat could want. But he's so pudgy now that he'll probably break the bed next time he jumps on the pillow. Maybe he won't be so friendly when we have to put him on the Nordic Track machine."

By responding in such a way you've simultaneously achieved

a number of laudable goals. First, you've managed to flatter your mother at the same time you've nonthreateningly pointed out the error of her ways. Second, you've preempted tension by keeping the timbre of your response in line with what your mother actually did. (As the Lord High Executioner said in Gilbert and Sullivan's *Mikado*, "Let the punishment fit the crime.") Your tone is nonadversarial, leaving the air free of tension and clear enough for a good laugh. Third, you've resisted the temptation to accusingly tie your mother's current behavior to what you perceive as her "prior criminal record." You're keeping the issue in the moment instead of in the Mother Maze where history is a cause of great friction and disappointment.

The truth is, judicious humor allows you to help the other person make the linkage between her current behavior and her historical tendencies and to laugh the laugh of recognition. Once your mother acknowledges through laughter her over-zealous pampering of your cat in an attempt to win its loyalty, give her some credit that she will at some level also be acknowledging to herself that she uses this modus operandi when it comes to people as well.

Needless to say, many mothers will respond extremely positively to judicious jesting. Are you a young woman with a Merged Mother who gives you the third degree when you come home from a dance for which she made you a lovely dress, wanting to know what eligible men you scouted, what was said, what glances—and phone numbers—were exchanged? Instead of cutting her off short and storming off to bed feeling guilty and "mean," imagine tackling the situation with levity: "Gosh, Mom, if you'd made this dress a little larger, you could have jumped in with me and come along. Wouldn't we have been a sight. You've heard of mother-daughter outfits? We really could have started a trend."

However pointed these remarks may be, they are couched in the comfortable framework of humor. A well-chosen humorous statement will inform as well as delight. Mother will probably get quite a kick out of the image of the two of you twirling about the floor, Siamese twin–style, spying prospective boyfriends. Together you and she can expound on this patently absurd—but to her mind somewhat pleasing and whimsical—scenario. What *would* people say? How *might* suitors approach? Naturally, you're not implying that you would in reality even *consider* taking Mother along on social outings. But you are, in effect, creating space for the two of you to do a dance together—a dance of humor, a dance of understanding.

In spite of humor's many benefits, however, we should point out a potential danger in its use: Beware of the almost imperceptible slip into sarcasm—sudden death to your own positive intent. As defined by *Webster's New Collegiate Dictionary*,[1] sarcasm "applies to expression frequently in the form of irony that is intended to cut or wound." Humor, it says, "implies an ability to perceive the ludicrous, the comical, and the absurd in human life and to express these usually without bitterness." Once you have crossed the line into sarcasm you are demonstrating that you are not yet willing to give up your resentments, not yet able to listen to your mother's positive intent—in short, that you are not willing to join with her. A sarcastic slip doesn't mean you need to abandon the tool of humor for good, but it does mean you need to scan your psyche in search of the resistances that have kept you from using humor wisely in any particular instance.

ADJUSTMENTS AND ADAPTATIONS

Listening, joining, and amicable jesting all require a willingness to "take the high road" when it comes to one's mother. They demand more subtle and discerning approaches than many grown daughters are accustomed to taking. Once you do take them, however, you will feel—and be—further along the road toward a mature relationship with your mother. Regardless of your age or your mother's, *you* will actually be more capable of establishing a more mature relationship.

Face it, daughters: No providential intervention is likely to miraculously transform your mother or get her to abandon her basic style. What this chapter has described are ways of altering your responses to your mother so that she, in the natural course of events, will make adaptations and alter her responses to you.

To elucidate what we mean by adaptations, let us for the moment take the liberty of likening your mother to an amoeba. Yes, those single-celled organisms you studied in junior high biology. Though we do not mean to imply that your mother is of such simple origins, you'll see why the analogy applies.

The amoeba travels contentedly on its way in a drop of water until it meets another object, another cell perhaps or maybe the edge of a leaf. When the encounter occurs, the amoeba immediately responds by sending out a pseudopod (fake foot) and changing its shape to conform to the object's presence. The amoeba does not, however, change its molecular structure in order to make this adaptation.

When you consistently listen, join, and jest instead of persistently debating and defending, your mother will experience your behavior much as the amoeba does the leaf. Like the amoeba, she will find a way to conform to the change in her environment, but her basic personality structure will remain intact.

In short, your goal should not be to make your mother over but to get encounters between the two of you to flow more easily.

Of course there remain additional skills and strategies to be mastered in making the fruitful aspects of your relationship blossom. The skills covered in this chapter all have to do with communicating to one's mother primarily through emotional atmosphere, that is, through an ambient affect and positive and appropriate tone. This is reminiscent of the way you and your mother first communicated because emotional communication is the earliest kind of exchange between parent and child.

But before you were very old, you learned, in response to sundry spoken and unspoken messages, how to relate to your mother in another way: as one of several members of your family. Your interactions with her were altered as a result. Moreover, your interactions with other family members were influenced by your relationship with your mother. You may have learned to communicate with your father and siblings through Mother or around her or because of her or in spite of her. In our next chapter we will take a closer look at how family dynamics and family messages continue to impact on your mother-daughter bond.

CHAPTER 5

THE FAMILY FILIGREE

A naive model of the family assumes that it is harmonious under ideal conditions, since that is allegedly how it was designed. But it was not so designed.... Family members are often at odds with each other's ultimate (not merely temporary) purposes.

Melvin Konner, M.D., Why the Reckless Survive

As lacelike and complex as filigree is the life and balance of a family. In filigree jewelry delicate strands of silver or gold link together, filling in a framework design. So, too, in families do individuals interweave, their inextricable "threads" combining to produce intricate patterns that comprise a whole.

Like bits of a filigree ornament, each family member plays a part in sustaining the family's overall structure, and each claims a particular place in its motif. Up close, however, a family looks less like a staid ornament than a living organism—a dynamic, self-regulating system. Family links involve elaborate communications and myriad interactions and reactions. In family life when connections between certain members shift or grow stronger or more slack, other members must make accommodations so that the filigree remains intact.

In our first chapter we noted how important it was to realize that the relationship you have with your mother does not exist in a vacuum. Rather, it exists in a context—the context of your family filigree. The changing ways in which you connect, disconnect, or reconnect with your mother will therefore go beyond the two of you. They will set off a chain of experience that will affect your father, your sisters, your brothers.

This chapter is designed to help you harness the energy inherent in your particular chain reactions so that improvements in the dynamics between you and your mother do not threaten the cohesiveness of your family filigree but rather will reinforce its strengths and minimize its weak spots. It is also designed to help you prevent your father and siblings from unconsciously sabotaging your emotional achievements where Mother is concerned. Be aware: Families are often very good at resisting change and preserving things exactly as they have been.

MAINTAINING THE STATUS QUO

Even if you and your mother lived alone together on an ice floe in the Arctic, instituting the basic skills and strategies described in chapters three and four would prove a challenge. With other family members around, your challenge will prove even more formidable, for as soon as you begin to alter the ways in which you and your mother interact, they will, at conscious and/or unconscious levels, take notice. Once that happens, you may well find that some behaviors of theirs become catalysts for reinitiating your old patterns, potentially stalling your progress.

Take, for example, the young woman in chapter four—let's call her Sally—who returns home from a dance only to find her Merged Mother awaiting her, armed with dozens of questions. Remember how this daughter used a judicious dose of humor and an image of her and her mother dancing together in a single dress to charm and disarm her mother. Sally succeeded in 'breaking the negative cycle of events in which she habitually responded to her mother's inquiries by clamming up and storming off to bed feeling guilty and resentful. Well, suppose the hearty laugh Sally and her mother shared was loud enough to wake up Sally's sister, Sue?

Sue may have been quite startled by the sounds emanating from downstairs. After all, she has rarely heard such a thing before. She knows the relationship between Sally and Mother is often fraught with tension and punctuated by quarrels as Sally struggles against her mother's desire to merge with her. Sue, a more compliant type, is the one in the family who has the calmer, "good" relationship with Mom.

With small alarms going off in her head, Sue may head downstairs to investigate the situation. While she may tell herself she is off to the kitchen to "join the party," she may unwittingly have another mission in mind. She may appear on the scene with the aim of resurrecting a more familiar— and for her more comfortable—scenario, that is, the one where she is the cooperative daughter and Sally is the troublesome, rebellious one.

Plopping herself in a chair and nonchalantly nibbling on the cookie she claims is her midnight snack, Sue may casually turn to Sally and ask, "So, did you dance with Bad Billy Hogan tonight?" This small, seemingly innocuous injection into the conversation is all that may be needed to create a radical shift in the course of events. The knowledge that said Billy Hogan is universally perceived as the local incarnation of James Dean causes Mother to shift back into her intrusive, overprotective behavior. Suddenly, she is interrogating Sally again. Was Billy Hogan there tonight? Did he show up on that horrible motorcycle? Sally didn't ride on the back of that bike, did she? Sally is back on the defensive, insisting that what she does and who she sees is nobody's business. And just as quickly Sue is back in her role of mediator, urging her sister to calm down and doing a predictably fine job of soothing her frazzled mother. Sally is perplexed as to just how her special "moment with Mom" suddenly vanished and the old order of things was restored.

Though the specifics may vary from family to family and from situation to situation, this type of scenario is extremely commonplace. To those who study family dynamics, the thrust toward predictable sameness is known as *homeostasis*. Originally a word used to describe one of the body's self-regulatory biological processes, Nathan Ackerman, the father of family therapy, appropriated it to describe family functioning. Just as homeostasis "preserves the intactness and continuity of the human organism . . . under constantly changing conditions of life," he posited, so does the family unit attempt to "stay the same" despite varying conditions in the inner and outer environment.[1]

Formerly, families were viewed as assemblages whose interactions were largely improvisational, but it has become clear just how swiftly, efficiently, and collusively family members can operate when their equilibrium is at stake. Family members can be extremely adept at deferring the disruptions and anxiety that accompany change and threaten the homeostasis of the family. Unaccustomed to assimilating the unknown, they will cling fiercely to the very things from which they draw their identities: family labels and family myths.

Family labels start out as an innocent attempt, usually on the part of the parents, to understand and encompass the behavior of a child by earmarking that behavior. Yet appellations carry a great deal of psychological weight. The wording of the label can carry a positive or negative connotation. A high-spirited child may be labeled "difficult" or "adventuresome." A sensitive child may be "insecure" or "empathic." A physically active child may be "uncontrollable" or "energetic." Whatever the label and whatever its connotation, sooner or later the child tends to live up to it. As Sonya Rhodes and Josleen Wilson write in *Surviving Family Life*, "In time the child achieves its reputation in the family."[2]

Indeed, in many families each member plays a part in ensuring that everyone else consistently lives up to his or her label. In Sally and Sue's family, Sally was always branded the wild one and Sue the tame one. When Sally ventures into new behavior—jesting with her mother instead of challenging her—these perceptions are threatened, so Sue nudges her sister back into line, and Sally allows herself to be nudged. Then Mother slides back easily into her predominant Maternal Style where Sally is concerned. The family works its homeostatic magic to return everyone to her well-worn path and place.

Like labels, family myths also present a potent obstacle to change. Some myths represent the pervasive collective reality through which a family describes itself—as an entity—to itself as well as to outsiders. Examples of such group identity myths are: *We are a peaceful clan with no disagreements* or *We are better than everyone else in the neighborhood* or *We can only trust one another. No one else is trustworthy.* Other family myths may reflect a family's consensus regarding specific family members. Examples of this type of myth may be: *Helen can't keep a secret* or *Dad isn't well and shouldn't hear bad news.*

Whether family myths contain much objective truth is of little consequence. Whether true or not, the myths become inextricably intertwined with family rules, communications, behaviors, and patterns. Poor Helen, for example, may never be allowed to hear pieces of family news and so may be locked out of participating in her mother's favorite pastime—gossip— and an opportunity to indulge in "girl talk."

A particular myth may be supported *by* and serve as support *for* a Maternal Style. When a Chronically Worried Mother cautions her daughter not to swap sandwiches at school and the whole family chimes in with tales of moldy snacks they've encountered away from home, the myth that *danger lurks outside the bosom of the family* is reinforced, and Mother is gratified at the same time. When a Controlling Mother succeeds in convincing everyone that discussing financial concerns with Dad will give the poor, frail man a coronary, she obtains control of the purse strings. Meanwhile, Dad—who may on an intellectual level be perfectly capable of contending with pecuniary matters—grows more and more emotionally ineffective. Soon he is out of the loop, unable to offer his opinion or his assistance, isolated by a myth.

Thus we see how family myths contribute mightily to the

chicken-and-egg dynamics of family life. It may seem that the net effect of the forces of homeostasis and of family labels and myths would be too overwhelming to buck. "Why bother to adjust my behavior," you may ask, "when my entire family will conspire to keep me exactly where I've been for the past twenty (or thirty, forty, or fifty) years?" The truth is that making changes in a family requires creativity and persistence, but first and foremost it requires sensitivity and awareness. Just as you have become habituated to certain behavior patterns throughout the course of your life, so, too, have other members of your family. Now you are thrusting toward change in your relationship with your mother. Think of that action as you would of skipping a stone across a pond. Everywhere you look there will be ripples, but when the water stills, new aspects of all your family relationships will likely have emerged. Chances are, greater freedom of behavior for all will have occurred.

First, let's take a look at the relationship that, other than the one you share with your mother, could well undergo the most far-reaching revisions.

THE FATHER FACTOR

Though it is true that our maternal bond is considered the most significant in our lives, especially when we are "lap babies," it is imperative that we appreciate the importance of a father's role. As psychologist Louise J. Kaplan has written, a crucial task of the father in family life is that of "helping his child differentiate self from mother, mother from other, maleness from femaleness."[3] The fulfillment of this task is especially helpful to the child in the latter phases of infancy when differentiation becomes the central business of life. For daughters, however, another especially meaningful time in their relationship with father arrives years later, in adolescence, when they begin to see themselves as women, newly reflected in Dad's eyes.

While you and your mother do not exist in a vacuum,

neither, of course, do you and your father: The ways in which you interact with Mother are influenced by the ways you and your father interact, and vice versa. It's also important to note the often profound effect of your mother and father's marital relationship on your individual bond with each of them. Your parents' relationship predated your arrival and had a life of its own. Indeed, it had its own rules, myths, and labels. With the birth of a child, however, the dynamics of a couple shifts. Before having children, your parents' relationship could have been "sketched" by drawing two points connected by a line. Now, with a relationship to each of their children, they form a kind of emotional triangle.

In our opening chapter we talked a bit about the various subgroups or subsystems within the family. How the marital subsystem (the husband-wife leg of the triangle) operated in your family of origin may have deeply affected the relationship you and your mother came to share (the mother-daughter leg of the triangle). Ideally, the husband-wife subsystem serves as the place where executive decisions for the family are made and where each spouse gets many of his or her needs for love, support, and understanding met. No family is ideal, of course, but the more smoothly the marriage functions, the more parents are energized by it and the more capable they are of facing the challenges of raising children without requiring that their emotional needs be met by those children. Should adults' emotional needs be unmet within the marital relationship, spillover may result. A child may be put in the position of attempting to satisfy them. Thus are many parent-child relationships skewed.

Take, for example, a marital subsystem where the following problem exists: A husband sees himself as totally blameless and altogether good, while attributing all friction in the marriage to his wife's inflexibility. All those around this affable man perceive him as Mr. Nice Guy, yet his wife often feels he is not so nice—especially when he gives others the impression that she is unduly sober or harsh. Now a daughter comes along. Dad unconsciously gets that daughter to buy into his

Mr. Nice Guy label by undermining Mother's attempts to discipline the child with comments like, "Oh, Muriel, go easy on her. She's just a kid."

The daughter will soon grow aware of the tension surrounding issues of child discipline that exists between her parents, and it is not unlikely she will learn how to capitalize on Dad's Mr. Nice Guy status. After all, most children seek to avoid curfews, TV-watching limits, and clean-up-your-room dictums as much as possible. She may learn to appeal to Dad each time Mom asserts her parental prerogative ("Dad, do I have to?"). She may even begin to disobey Mother outright, assuming that Father will step in to soften things up for her. In either case, Mom will likely become irritated with Dad. If she does not successfully resolve her issues with him privately, within the appropriate bounds of their relationship, some of her anger will likely cascade over into her relationship with her daughter.

Now we have what appears to be an angry mother-daughter relationship, its redundant combative scenarios being acted out by both parties. The reality is that Dad set up the mother and daughter's rocky relationship by undercutting the mother's authority from the start and deflecting negative feelings away from himself at all costs. Now we have friction in the husband-wife leg of the triangle and in the mother-daughter leg of the triangle, yet there is delightful conspiracy in the father-daughter leg—all of this to reinforce Dad's position as Mr. Nice Guy.

The scenario we've just sketched is not an uncommon one. Many of you may recognize aspects of your own father echoed in Mr. Nice Guy. Indeed, it is a fairly widespread Paternal Style.

Just as a woman's Maternal Style contributes to the shaping of her relationship with her daughter, so, naturally enough, does a man's Paternal Style help define the dimensions of the father-daughter bond. Yet in the intricate web of the family filigree, the Paternal Style serves a secondary function as well:

It contributes to the evolution of certain kinds of mother-daughter dynamics.

Let's take a look at some additional Paternal Styles to see how they may impact on the relationship you have with your mother, keeping in mind that, as with Maternal Styles, some generalization is necessary and some overlap inevitable. You may recognize facets of your father in more than one style.

The Volatile Dad

He always seems to be yelling about something—the way dinner is prepared, the bikes left in the driveway, the nightly traffic jam he encounters coming home from work. If anyone in the household neglects a chore or makes a mistake, he barks his disapproval. If someone does something right, he is loathe to give credit. This curmudgeon seems determined to be unhappy and even seems slightly proud of his grouchiness. Those around him, however, are unhappy by default. They do a dance of contrition, trying to "do the right thing" in hopes of appeasing him.

How might this Volatile Dad affect your relationship with your mother? You may have become Mother's defender and protector, sacrificing yourself in order to spare her some stress and travail. Indeed, if she had a Merged Style, you may easily have adopted it as your own, thus cementing the boundary-blurring merger between you. Yet having been unable to shield her completely—for you were only a child—you may have assumed a heavy burden of guilt. Hence, you continued to put her first even as your own life unfurled before you.

Conversely, out of a strong sense of self-preservation you may have sensed at a very early age that being Dad's accomplice was safer than championing Mom. You therefore may have attempted to distance yourself psychologically from Mother, refusing to identify with her as a role model.

If Dad's relentless expressions of dissatisfaction induced in you the impulse to find fault with Mother, colluding with Dad to label her persona non grata, she in turn may have cast blame in your direction. A reciprocal Hypercritical Style of relating may have sprung into full bloom between the two of you. And why not? You both existed in a critical milieu, the irritable tone of the household set by Dad's insistent grumbling and griping.

The Not-So-Secret-Admirer Dad

He says things about you to your mother like, "She's just like you were when I met you thirty-five years ago, Marge, only prettier." He openly encourages you to pursue things your mother never did. If she had no college education, he may remind you incessantly how "higher education is the most important thing." If she is a homemaker, he may tell you that you are "too smart and full of life to do that." He confides in you about issues your mother may find embarrassing, entrusting you with confidences like, "Mom's hot flashes are driving me crazy."

Certainly, you may have been flattered by all of Dad's positive attention, but when a father clearly appreciates a daughter more than he does his wife and when his relationship with her violates the privacy of the marital subsystem, there may be a trade-off that is not so positive. If you had a Not-So-Secret-Admirer Dad, you may have had to forfeit a genuinely intimate bond with your mother.

One result of your having been the apple of Dad's eye may have been that your mother "wrote off" her relationship with you and "took up" with your sister or brother. This could have happened especially if she had tended toward a Merged Style and was driven to find someone with whom to connect. Another result is that she may have developed a Competitive Style where you were concerned, always trying to "win back" her husband. Living in such close proximity to the constant challenges of a competitive maternal style may have left you little alternative but to adopt the style yourself. Needless to say, this only served to escalate the strain between you and your mother. Finally, she may have decided that your doting dad was not sufficiently preparing you for life's harsh realities and resolved to dole out the brutal facts of life to you herself, relentlessly (advising you again and again, perhaps, that you'd never get into a good school with *those* SAT scores). A Hypercritical predisposition would make this behavior especially easy for her to choose.

Any of these scenarios or any combination of them would have left you with an adversarial relationship with Mother and, consequently, with an unresolved longing, for rarely can even the heartiest endorsement of a Not-So-Secret-Admirer Dad compensate for the hurts of mother-daughter estrangement or hostility.

The Childlike Dad

He is a wonderful playmate when you are young. In fact, he is the household's chief advocate on behalf of fun—pouting even more persuasively than you when you are told it is past your bedtime. Mother often has to yell at him for the same infractions that cause her to yell at the children: "Stop roughhousing!" "It's ten minutes to dinner; no ice cream now!" "Have you spent all your pocket money again? You don't understand the value of a dollar!" You may hear your Mother label him as a perpetual Peter Pan, a dreamer, and, worst of all, irresponsible. And though you may enjoy his lightheartedness, you also sense there is a conflict between your parents. Which side will you be on? And how will your relationship with your mother be influenced?

If you championed your Childlike Dad and balked at your mother's policies, you, too, were in danger of being labeled irresponsible. Mother may have been censorious of you and attempted to "bring you into line" through a Controlling Style. This may have spurred your resentment and incited you to spiteful rebellion.

On the other hand, once again you may have adopted Mother's point of view. Once you yearned to appear mature and put childish things behind you, you may have come to find your father's caprices irksome. You may have found you had more sympathy for a Hypercritical Mother's Style than you had previously, or you may even have become overly concerned for Dad's welfare and attempted to parent him. If your mother was the worrying kind—and Chronic Worrier women often end up with Childlike men as mates since they need someone to worry about—you may have adopted that style in hopes that your father would change when he noticed your fretfulness.

The Passive Dad

While the Childlike Dad treats life like a bowl of cherries, the Passive Dad treats life as a kind of play or movie in which he is not so much an active character as an audience member. He is anything but an executive decision-maker. Indeed, he can't seem to land solidly on one side of an issue or another. His hallmark body language is the shrug. Though he may believe himself to be noninterfering and easygoing, he may be covertly angry and express that anger through withdrawal. Or he may feel inadequate and be anxious that any choice he makes will be the wrong one. He has problems taking the risks inherent in being resolute.

Seductive as this Paternal Style may be to children, who tend to equate nondecision with amiability and see Passive Dads as allies, it can cause many problems in the marital subsystem. Ergo, it can cause resultant problems in mother-daughter bonds.

If you had a mother with a Controlling or Hypercritical Style, she likely found your Passive Dad a suitable foil for her need to orchestrate everything because he offered precious little opposition. Neither, however, did he offer you any support for resisting her domination. When you asked his opinion, he may have mumbled, "Mother knows best." Thus, you may have all too easily succumbed to a position of subservience to

Mother. Perhaps your own frustration with Dad's ghostlike presence prompted you to share in Mother's style. In this way you both have Dad to commiserate about.

If you had a mother with a Competitive Style, things could have also grown problematical. Receiving few compliments from her ambiguous and noncommittal spouse, she may have flaunted her talents before you in hopes of garnering the accolades she felt she deserved. And you may have gotten caught up in a pattern of applauding her accomplishments even while your own were being neglected.

Finally, if your mother had Merged or Chronically Worried proclivities, she may have become all the more clingy and overprotective of you, and you may have allowed her excessive dependence as a way of filling the void in the family matrix. Because Passive Dads seem to blend into the woodwork, mothers and daughters are often left with the feeling that they have only each other.

RESHAPING THE TRIANGLE

The stylistic matches—or mismatches, as the case may be—of mothers and fathers color many of the messages a child receives from her parents. In subtle and not so subtle ways the parents in a marriage under stress can convey to a child how they want that child to "stick up" for them, to affirm *their* version of reality. Alas, in triangulation, when a child is perceived as siding with one parent, the other parent can feel reproached, dismissed, or even attacked. Few children want to deliberately impart such feelings to either parent, of course. Even despite strong preferences for one parent's style over the other's, they feel love for both. Nevertheless, they are frequently faced with no-win situations.

Fortunately, there are three key skills you can employ in successfully reshaping your Mother-Father-Daughter triangle. Begin by *noticing the impulses you have to take sides* in your parent's exchanges. Do you actively and routinely support one and oppose the other? Then *listen to your own voice of experience* and recognize that all such impulses have gotten you in the past was a trip down a well-trodden path in the Mother Maze. Finally, *remember your goal*, which is to blaze a new trail. Pause and check your compass, and let yourself choose a new direction. And remember, many of the skills and strategies you are already learning can help you to better manage not just your relationship with your mother as an individual but also your father as an individual—and your parents as a duo.

Here are two scenarios that illustrate how well these skills can work:

Scenario Number 1: A Visit to Phoenix

You arrive at Phoenix Airport for a long-planned visit to your parents' new condominium at the Sunlight Retirement Community. Your father's letters from their new locale have been filled with descriptions of the many attractions of Phoenix, all the activities available at their community center, and his many new cronies. Your mother's letters have told you how she is carefully decorating the new apartment, how the food brands are different at the supermarkets, and how she hopes the climate will agree with them. Inevitably, this Chronically Worried Mother adds postscripts that chronicle your Childlike Dad's misdeeds—how he climbed up on a chair to hang balloons on the walls of the recreation room for the Valentine's party though he could have fallen and hurt his already ailing back.

Mom and Dad appear at the gate all smiles and kisses, overjoyed to see you. To outsiders you are the perfect loving clan. You bask in the glow of family harmony, momentarily forgetting that synergy is the exception and not the rule in your relationship with Mom and Dad—and in theirs with each other. By the time you have reached the car, the luster of your greeting has begun to tarnish. You suddenly find yourself engaged in a chafing exchange with your mother. You are on a familiar, worn path of the Mother Maze, and you are not even quite sure how you got there.

Well, here's how:

DAD: (En route to the car) Say, girls, let's take a ride around Phoenix now. It's so lovely with the lights ablaze in the desert night. We can stop for sundaes at Frostine's Ice Cream Emporium and then go over to the rec hall and introduce my Deirdre around.

MOM: Martin, you don't have your glasses with you. Anyway, the drizzle has made the roads slick. You know Deirdre must be tired and in no mood to meet a bunch of old geezers. Don't be foolish. Let's just go back to the apartment.

DAD: You just have no *joie de vivre*, Ellen. Live a little!

You have heard this exchange in one form or another your entire life. Your Childlike Dad wants instant gratification, but to your Chronic Worrier Mother all gratification is suspect and comes with a heavy price. What a combination.

As usual you find yourself agreeing with Dad. After all, it is only 7 P.M., and it would be fun to drive around and get ice cream. So you chime in.

DAUGHTER: Oh, Mom, leave Daddy alone. Why must you worry about everything? Dad obviously got here without wearing those glasses. Seeing some sights will be fun, and I'd love to meet Dad's friends.

MOTHER: You encourage him. You know he hasn't been well lately.

DAUGHTER: Well, maybe if you didn't fight him so much, his health would improve.

On you go until you wish you had never embarked on this lunatic expedition to visit your folks at all. Get the three of you together, and it always ends up like this. You are trian-

gulated in the conflicts between them in which Mother per-
ennially voices pessimism and Father goes for the gusto, even
if a bit irresponsibly at times. They argue through you, each
one appropriating you for his or her emotional ends and attempting, at times, to speak *for* you.

Now you and Dad have won a Pyrrhic victory, one that is
far too costly emotionally. Your "majority rule" has won the
right to take a drive, but Mom is pouting in the backseat, and
you and Dad sit up front trying to act as though you don't
notice the black cloud looming over your adventure.

Learning to neutralize this kind of triangulation requires
grace under pressure. You'll need to keep your wits about you,
for after all, there are two of them and one of you. And despite
the fact that your parents are at odds, their combined force
exerts a powerful pull toward old patterns for everyone in the
family. But things can be made different. With your new
awareness and the use of your new skills, the foregoing exchange might have gone in another direction. Let's take it
again, from the top:

DAD: Let's take a spin around Phoenix, then head to Fros-
         tine's for double fudge ripple. After that we can stop
         off at the rec hall and have my Deirdre meet the guys.
MOM: Oh, Martin, don't be silly. You don't have your glasses,
         and the roads are slick. Besides, Deirdre's too exhausted
         to socialize with your cronies. Let's just go home.
DAD: You just have no *joie de vivre,* Ellen.

Now hold it right here before you say a word. Employ these
three key steps in reshaping this triangle: (1) *Notice the impulse*
welling up in you to defend Dad and his pursuit of fun. Recognize your complementary impulse to stifle your mother. (2)
Listen to the voice of your own experience. You know that if
you give in to these impulses, you will antagonize Mother and
preclude any possibility of having fun with her. (3) *Remember
your goal.* You want to blaze a new trail in the Mother Maze
but without alienating Dad. Now you are ready to speak:

DAUGHTER: Look, folks, the truth is I am a bit tired (you validate a little of what Mom just said), but I would love to see this ice cream parlor. It sounds like fun (you validate Dad's belief that fun is good), and the food on the plane left something to be desired (so a snack would be practical, which appeals to Mom). Besides, we can see a bit of Phoenix along the way (you go for the gusto but in a limited way). But how about saving the visit to the rec hall for tomorrow. Dad, I'd love to meet your friends when I'm rested and can make my best impression. Anyway, I'm just dying to see your new apartment (in a wise compromise, you show interest in things that are important to Dad and to Mom).

So far, so good. Or is it? Your mother will be pleased by the fact that you didn't automatically and totally side with Dad as you have done in the past. She will appreciate your valuing her point of view rather than disparaging it as Dad is wont to do. Dad, however, may feel a bit stunned and lost. He expects you to side with him one hundred percent. He expects to win these skirmishes. He may not be thrilled by the diplomatic tone you've set. Who are you anyway, Henry Kissinger? *Watch for maneuvering on his part to reestablish the familiar dimensions of the triangle,* such as:

DAD: Oh, come on, you will see the apartment for the entire week you're here. There's plenty of time for that. And you're too young to be tired. Don't tell me you're turning into your mother.

Ouch! Your father has said the magic words in an attempt to bring back what has been your all-too-predictable behavior. Don't take the bait. Take three deep breaths and recall your three steps: Watch out for your impulse to comply with his agenda; listen to your voice of experience; and remember your goals. Instead of attempting to prove how unlike your mother you are and alienating her by leaping on Dad's bandwagon, try this:

DAUGHTER: Actually, Dad, you're right. I do have lots of time here, and I want to do it all! So let's start with ice cream and a tour of your new home.

Scenario Number 2: Dressing for a Cousin's Wedding

You and your parents have been invited to the wedding of your younger cousin. You're excited about the prospect since you're bringing as a date a young man to whom you're quite attracted. You and your Competitive Mother shop for dresses together, and you purchase a turquoise outfit you like, though she tries to talk you into a beige ensemble that you feel does little for you but that she says *hides those hips*. The night of the big event you come downstairs and await your date. Your Not-So-Secret-Admirer Dad beams as Mom looks on.

DAD: Well, Pumpkin, don't you look wonderful! What a glorious color for you.

DAUGHTER: Well, thanks, Daddy! But do you think I look a little wide in the hips in this? Mom says so.

DAD: What? Why, you look as slim as a willow. In fact, you look just like your mother did at your age.

MOM: Well, Fred, she certainly has my legs, but I was never very broad in the beam.

DAD: Oh, Miriam, don't be silly. Look at this radiant young flower of mine. Isn't she something?

DAUGHTER: (Glumly) Mom's right. I'm a tub. I wish I looked as good as she does.

DAD: Pumpkin, to me you'll always be the most beautiful girl in the world.

MOM: Well, anyway, dear, here comes your young
man. Be sure not to step on his toes when you
dance with him. Doesn't do a thing for romance.
My, he's attractive. I'll have to be certain to get
a dance with him myself.

There you are again, stuck in the triangle. The more your
Not-So-Secret-Admirer Dad praises you, the more your Competitive Mother picks on you. That makes you mad. You've
become accustomed to fishing for Dad's compliments, even
putting yourself down so he'll rush to your rescue, but, of
course, his accolades begin the whole cycle anew. Now Mother
has no kind words for you. What's more, since Dad will not
pay attention to her, she may be tempted to charm your other
admirers into doing so. All of this is hurtful to you because
in many ways she is your ideal. Her approval would mean so
much.

Now let's take another shot at this scenario, using new skills
and strategies:

DAD: Pumpkin, you look fabulous in that dress.

DAUGHTER: Thank you, Daddy. Mom helped me shop for
it. (You graciously give your mother credit and
remind your father that you and she share a bond
as well.)

MOM: Well, really, I did prefer the beige one. It made
you look a bit less hippy.

DAUGHTER: (Resisting the impulse to retaliate) You have such
good taste. It was hard to choose.

DAD: Pumpkin, you'd look great in anything. You're
the spitting image of your mother when she was
your age. In fact, to me you're the most beautiful
girl in the world.

DAUGHTER: Well, aren't you lucky to be going to this wedding with two such such gorgeous girls (you generously share the spotlight with Mom and let Dad know she should not be ignored). And aren't I lucky to have such a smashing-looking couple for parents (you clarify that you and your parents are in different generations). Oh, my date is here. I hope we cut as good a figure when we dance as you two will (you reinforce clarification of your generational place, affirming that you don't want to end up in your father's arms but in the arms of your date).

MOM: I'm sure you and your beau will do just fine, dear.

In this revised scenario you have successfully recalled the essential truth about you and your Competitive Mother, that is, that you and she are running two different races. Your part in this conversation has reinforced this. You have established that your dad is your mother's "prize," and yours is your own escort. Once this is clarified, your mother can relax and be supportive of you. In a very real sense your interventions here have served to reshape the family triangle.

In chapter two we alluded to the quintessential Oedipal battle in which young children become enamored of the parent of the opposite sex. This is a natural developmental stage. Typically, a young girl (between the ages of three and five) will develop an innocent crush on her father and attendant rivalrous feelings toward her mother. In most cases this dynamic tends to "go underground" after age five, only to reassert itself strongly for a time in adolescence, before diminishing again as the daughter transfers her affections to boys her own age. Yet it never disappears entirely. Most women want their father to approve of them as females and appreciate their charms. Where the marital subsystem is healthy and strong, it can absorb this emotional reality without trauma. Where it is not, things go askew. As a small child you had no way of diffusing the ways in which your father may have "skipped over" your mother and, much to her dismay, doted on you. But as an adult you can exert some influence.

In this scenario, as in the "visit to Phoenix," the daughter's success revolved around the three crucial skills initially outlined. There was an awareness of the impulse to revert to old habits, but as a result of the awareness, the impulse was resisted. There was a willingness to listen to the voice of experience. And there was a focus on remembering the goal of blazing new trails in the Mother Maze.

We have now seen, however, that in families where patterns of cross-generational misalliances repeatedly impede harmony, a fourth skill can often come in handy. Where Father ignores Mother to dote on Daughter, as happened in "dressing for a Cousin's wedding," the daughter must hold fast to her generational identity.

Remembering one's generational place can also be helpful in other situations. If, for example, your mother is joined at the hip to *her* mother and "abandons" your father, your impulse may be to dote on him. Identifying yourself with your generation can serve to nudge your parents back into an identification with theirs. This, too, is part of improving your relationship with your mother.

SIBLING SCENARIOS

In addition to bringing a new awareness to how your father affects your bond with your mother, many of you will also need to develop awareness of sibling involvement in your maternal relationship. As you'll recall, we began this chapter with the example of Sally and Sue, illustrating how profoundly the role one sibling plays with regard to Mom may influence another's. Any number of variables affect the role-determined behavior of each and every sibling with one another as well as with their parents. Birth order and temperamental matches between mother and child, as well as father and child, are potent determining factors in role assignment. Other factors are the number of children in the family, how far apart in age the siblings are, how many are girls, how many are boys, and so on. Moreover, if any one child becomes especially "fused" with the parents—that is, singled out for excessive positive or negative attention and deeply bound up in triangular parental dynamics—the intensity of the other's roles will shift accordingly.

For example, imagine that you are four years old and overjoyed at the prospective birth of a younger sibling whom you envision as an ever-present playmate. But soon your mother's messages may alert you that new circumstances will afford you less time for fun and games. "When the new baby comes," she informs you, "you are going to be my big girl, my big helper." Gulp. Suddenly a new level of maturity is expected of you, and you may be less indulged by Mother. Moreover, if the new arrival is a better temperamental match with your mother, you may notice your family label diminishing in status. Where you once overheard statements like "Melissa, our one and only, was a feisty baby," you may now hear "Billy is so good, not cranky like Melissa was." Hmm, you think, maybe this new baby stuff isn't so hot after all. Your new sibling may have, albeit innocently, knocked you off your pedestal, and so the seeds of sibling dynamics and rivalry are sown.

Well, like it or not, as the shape of your family changes, so does your role in the family. Myriad messages will filter down to you, setting rules for the revised role you are to play. Which filament of the family filigree will be yours to realize in thought and deed? Here are some of the many possibilities:

The Parentified Child

This role often, although not always, falls to the oldest sibling who is expected to conduct herself as an adult rather than identify with the children's generation. Often she is given "jobs" to do with relation to her sisters and brothers, such as looking out for them in the schoolyard or helping them with their homework before Mom and Dad get home from the office. Sometimes these sisters and brothers are anything but appreciative of the Parentified Child's duties as overseer. They may keep secrets from her or band against her. On the other hand, the Parentified Child may have a grateful mother with whom she shares a strong bond and whose Maternal Style she especially wants to mimic.

The Keeper of the Flame

This role often, though not always, falls to the youngest child. Both Mother and Dad may convey to her messages that communicate she is their "last, best hope"—their final chance at doing this parenting thing successfully and the one who will be around to take care of them in their old age. Since, statistically speaking, a mother is likely to outlive a father of approximately the same age, Mom may particularly stress this latter aspect of the Flamekeeper's role. "It wasn't easy bearing a child so late in life," she may remind her, "but I know you'll always be here for me." Since all the Flamekeeper's siblings will be as aware of her designation as she is, they may feel they are "off the hook" and abnegate responsibility as both parents age. Consequently, the Keeper of the Flame may resent them while feeling guilty toward Mother and fearful of letting her down.

The Confidante

An especially empathic child is predisposed to accept this role. If her parents' relationship is strained, she may form an alliance with one or the other, listening to grievances, offering solace and companionship. The parent who is attended to in this manner is usually thankful. The other parent may feel relieved, but along with that relief can come a growing distance from the Confidante. Thus, Mother's Confidante may move ever closer to Mom and farther from Dad as the years go by. Dad's Confidante will do just the reverse. Distance may also occur among siblings who experience jealousy toward the Confidante.

The Scapegoat

The misdeeds and problems of all other siblings pale in comparison to this child. She is the one labeled as "bad." She is by nature a defier rather than a complier with rules inside and outside the family. She may have eccentric interests and unorthodox friends, and even though she may be highly creative and bright, she may not fare as well in school as her brothers and sisters. Or maybe she is not so radically different from the others after all, just different enough to be earmarked as such. Often families unwittingly collude to label one child "bad" even when the term doesn't really fit. All their distress can then be "expressed" through one member. Consequently, as Rhodes and Wilson write in *Surviving Family Life*, "Everyone else in the family may appear normal and healthy because they permanently detour all family conflict to one person."[4] The Scapegoat's siblings may be eternally grateful to her for being who she is, though she may always be treated as though she is on the outside of their relationships. Needless to say, when a daughter is a Scapegoat, her relationship to her mother is bound to be rocky.

The Peacemaker

This role sometimes falls on the middle child, but it can fall on any child who is compliant and who has an inherent dislike of conflict. Once parents recognize her need for tranquility, they may overtly recruit her to mediate her siblings' conflicts with one another or with parents. They may also covertly communicate to the Peacemaker that she is never to assert herself, never to add fuel to the fire. The Peacemaker role often brings with it a certain status. Everyone may respect her equanimity or admire her ability to cajole other family members out of bad moods. However, the personal needs of the

Peacemaker may be given short shrift by everyone else, not least of all Mother.

The Golden Child

Favored by Mother and often by Father, too, this child can seem to do no wrong. Though the maternal and paternal relations of a Golden Child may be extremely harmonious, she may feel somewhat overwhelmed by parental attention and expectation. She may also evoke profound envy among siblings.

The Second-Class Citizen

In contrast to the Golden Child, the plight of this sibling is hardly enviable. Here is an anecdote that Sigmund Freud's sister, Anna Bernays—who played the second-class citizen in her family—recounted after her brother's death.

> In spite of his youth the regulations and desires of Sigmund were respected by each member of the family. Before I was eight, my mother, who had been very musical, permitted me to study the piano, and I began my hourly exercises. Since the piano was not far from Sigmund's room, it disturbed him. He told my mother that the piano would have to be moved or he certainly would leave the house. The piano disappeared and with it any chance for his sisters to become musicians.[5]

Being a Second-Class Citizen in the family can engender one with a sense of futility. For neither Mother nor any other family member tends to consider this child's needs and preferences of paramount importance.

THE SIBLING AXIS

Within any one family many varied sibling personae can co-exist, and the possible permutations of combinations can be mind-boggling. Indeed, it may sound as if the more siblings one has, the more difficult it is to carve out a constructive, peaceful relationship with one's mother. But this is not necessarily so.

If any of the labels mentioned so far seem to apply to you and if your relationship with your mother seems to suffer as a result of it, take heart. Together with your siblings you have the potential to build a power base from which to improve your relationship with your mother. Even if you are the maternally fused child in your family, designated for overinvolvement with Mother—whether it be in the form of excessive affection or antipathy—the key to achieving separation and individuation may lie, at least in part, with investing more of your energy in your sisters and brothers.

In family therapy lingo there is a term called the *sibling axis*, reminiscent of the Allied Axis powers in World War II. It refers to a coalition of children within one family who have a cooperative relationship among them and use that relationship to gain ground for their generation of the family.

Sonya Rhodes and Josleen Wilson write, "The most positive aspect of having more than one child is that the children have a chance to form an impressive coalition of their own. . . . Acting as a team, they can negotiate for bigger allowances, later curfews, more privileges."[6] But there is something else that can be negotiated by joining a coalition with one's siblings, and that is a more balanced relationship with Mother.

Needless to say, as with any attempt to change you will experience your own resistance. Giving up your designated role can be a mixed blessing especially if it affords you some much-coveted approval from your mother. To overcome the resistance you must acknowledge to yourself the "downside" of your role and anticipate the "upside" of joining with one or more of your siblings in creating an effective axis.

When your new skills and strategies impact the whole family, resistances will emanate not only from you but from your father, your siblings, and, of course, from your mother. And their resistances to change may magnify your own hesitation. Remember, as a whole the family—on a level below conscious awareness—aims to reinstate the status quo. You, however, have awareness, and that is a powerful tool.

The following scenarios illustrate how the sibling axis can work:

Scenario Number 1: The Keeper of the Flame and the Scapegoat

As the youngest child in your family, born a "menopause baby," you have been designated by your mother as Keeper of the Flame—the child who will handle her affairs and her emotional needs when she is old and gray. Your sister, eight years your senior, has always been the family black sheep, the Scapegoat who got blamed when anything went wrong or when fighting broke out between any of the siblings. The Scapegoat, understandably unhappy at home, married early to get out of the house. She divorced two years later, "proving" how correct her label was in the first place.

Now, years later, although she is a very successful pension and health insurance manager for a large firm in a nearby city, she is still deemed unsuccessful by your mother because she has never conformed to the rest of the family's expectations (that is, she does not have a husband or children of her own).

A few years ago, your father passed away, and right now your mother is in need of advice regarding his estate, specifically some pension and insurance matters. You have always considered such matters akin to rocket science in complexity, and the thought of consulting your sister passes fleetingly through your mind. You dismiss it and instead plunge into the Mother Maze, landing in the midst of this typical chafing and frustrating exchange:

MOTHER: I need you to handle these financial matters, darling. I get these documents in the mail, and I don't understand a word. You will manage it somehow, I'm sure. I rely on you for this sort of thing.

DAUGHTER: *I* don't know anything about this stuff, Mom. I'll have to call a professional.

MOTHER: No! I don't want a stranger knowing my business. You have to do it. You can figure it out. Otherwise I'll have to try. That print is so tiny, don't be surprised if I go blind.

DAUGHTER: What do you want from me? I would have to take a course in money management to be able to advise you, and I'm up to my ears in my own work.

MOTHER: Fine. I'll just lose my eyesight trying to read it. Fine, fine. You're busy.

DAUGHTER: Okay, I'll try, Mom. I'll try to figure it out.

Watch out here. At about this point you're giving in to your impulse to agree to do something you don't want to do and don't feel capable of doing. The *voice of experience* should tell you that if you give in to the impulse you will end up resentful. Remember your goal of blazing a trail in the Mother Maze.

Now blaze that new trail. Remember that fleeting thought you had about calling your sister, the one you banished from your mind because of her Scapegoat label? Take a chance and utilize the sibling axis. Recognize that your sister's label no longer has any merit, if it ever did in the first place. By aligning yourself with her you can in fact improve your relationship with your mother—not to mention that between you and your sister. Call her and approach her not as a Scapegoat but as the expert she is. Invite her assistance and express your respect for her abilities. Communicate to her that you and she have in common a less-than-ideal relationship with Mother ("You know how Mom is, Sis. It's not easy to reason with her when she has an idea fixed in her mind").

Initially, Big Sister may resist. She may begrudge assistance to a mother who has chastised and often rejected her for years. She may take a kind of defiant pride in her outcast role and find it hard to relinquish. She may even resent the role you played in perpetuating her Scapegoat status over the years and resist helping you resolve your conflict with Mother. Indeed, secretly she may enjoy watching you struggle for a change. Your own resistance may kick in here as well, for part of you may relish enacting singlehanded, herculean rescues of Mom. Be cognizant of these resistances. Allow yourself to experience the feelings they evoke, then try again.

In your discourse with Big Sister, traffic on the positive results that are likely to occur if you and your sister tacitly agree to disregard the labels each of you has been given and explore new options. Consider acknowledging how misguided you were in accepting your parents' view of her. You could end up less burdened and your sister less isolated. Mother wins, too, for her needs can be more efficiently met by the child best suited to meet them.

Assuming your sister ultimately does offer her aid, you of course, will have to "fess up" to Mother. Courage. Tell her that you would never go against her wishes and consult a stranger, so you went to your sibling instead. Your own blood. Wax eloquent on how helpful your sister was. Your mother may be irritated—and, remember, she is entitled to her feelings—but she will begin to get the message that her children are no longer willing to accept her stereotyping of them. They have expressed the fact that they have outgrown this. The seeds for new beginnings are now sown.

Scenario Number 2: The Second-Class Citizen and the Golden Child

You come home from college for spring break hoping, as always, that things at home will be different for you. You haven't seen your mother for months and hope she will now pay a good deal of attention to you. But soon you realize nothing has changed. Your little brother Tom, now a high school junior, is still the Golden Child, garnering most of your mother's accolades, and you are a Second-Class Citizen.

Things have been this way for a long time. It seems your mother embraces a Pseudoperfect Style of parenting, and your brother was a good temperamental match for her from the start, an independent child who did not require intensely emotional parenting. Also, Tom is a musical prodigy, and Mother, who would have liked to have a musical career herself, likes to bask in his reflected glory. You, on the other hand, were a more maternally attached child whose requests for more open affection felt overwhelming to Mother. Moreover, your talents and accomplishments lie in areas with which she cannot identify. Much as you have always wanted Mother's approval, you have often felt as if you received the short end of the stick. Little brother, on the other hand, seems to have his every wish catered to.

On your first night back you and your mother have a conversation that goes something like this:

MOTHER: Hmm. What should we have for dinner tonight?

DAUGHTER: Can we have Mexican? I've really missed good tacos up at school.

MOTHER: You know your brother hates tacos. Besides, he likes a light meal before school orchestra performances. We'll have tuna salad tonight.

DAUGHTER: Why do we always have to eat what Tom likes? Why can't I ever choose what I like?

MOTHER: That's a very ungenerous attitude to take, dear. Your brother often eats what you like.

DAUGHTER: Yeah, if he happens to like it, too. And he's the pickiest eater I know!

MOTHER: Your brother does so much for you. I don't see why you can't do this for him.

DAUGHTER: What about what I do for him? What about all
these Saturday nights I give up to go to his stupid
concerts. Well, I'm not going tonight. I'm going
out for Mexican food!

Now no one likes to be a Second-Class Citizen, and envious
resentment of your brother and mother's relationship is an
understandable response. Let's be honest here and acknowledge the often bitter and enraged feelings one can have toward a sibling who effortlessly garners Mother's favor and
attention.

But once again you are doing little for your cause if you
give in to the impulse to act out on resentments. Here, you've
put Mother on the defensive and, to her eyes, sharpened the
distinctions between you and your brother. Once again she
perceives you as being difficult. You've forced her to take
sides, knowing full well which side she is predisposed to
take.

Historical evidence should teach you that if you pursue this
stance, you will spend your entire vacation giving the cold
shoulder not only to your mother but to your brother as well.
This is sad because you really do love and admire Tom, who,
by the way, does love you and, as Mother says, does a lot for
you—from fixing your car to trying to cheer you up when
you're blue.

To achieve your goal of a different sort of homecoming,
avail yourself of the sibling axis. Remember that your mother's
affinity for your brother is more a product of her temperamental
"fit" with him than of anything he has deliberately done.
Rather than dwelling on how unfair life is in your family or
pointing out your brother's flaws, try something like this:

MOTHER: Hmm. What should we have for dinner tonight?
DAUGHTER: How about Mexican? I really miss the local tacos.
MOTHER: You know Tom likes to eat light before perfor-
mances. We'll have tuna salad.

DAUGHTER: Oh, that's true. I guess a heavy meal would make it hard to hit the high notes on that clarinet as well as he does.

MOTHER: Yes, and he's doing a new solo tonight. He makes me so proud.

DAUGHTER: Me, too. I can't wait to see him. But, how about it, Mom? When can we have some tacos?

MOTHER: Oh, must we decide now?

DAUGHTER: Come on, Mom. When?

MOTHER: All right, how's tomorrow? We can stop at that Mexican restaurant at the mall and look at new spring fashions, too.

In this exchange you have echoed your mother's admiration of your brother (and since you do admire him, you are not sounding a false note). You have resisted the temptation to undermine him. Then you have asked for something for yourself in such a way that it does not interfere with your brother having his needs met. At the same time you have been persistent in making certain your needs will be met as well. As a result, your mother is able to act more generously toward you.

What you are left with is certainly not a perfect situation. Chances are your mother will always get along more smoothly with your brother than she does with you, but you can be satisfied that you have taken a new path in the Mother Maze. You and she may not be bosom buddies, but you have expanded your repertoire beyond trading accusations. Meanwhile, you and your brother are not set up as adversaries. You are free to enjoy his company and he yours. Though he may register some confusion as he notes the increased calm between you and your mother, he also registers that you no longer feel the need to subvert him. He *may* start championing your needs and desires—at least now and again. Both of you are now free to explore with each other the possibility of a closer relationship, perhaps sharing the sort of easy, genuine camaraderie with which Mother is not comfortable.

BYPASSING ROADBLOCKS: ESTABLISHING
DIRECT LINES TO FAMILY MEMBERS

As useful as the sibling axis is, we must append a caveat concerning its use. In some families mothers seem to work hard at obstructing meaningful communication between their children—and, in fact, even between their children and their husband. Such mothers perceive themselves as the family nerve center and tend to act as Communication Central. All messages between family members seem to be processed through them. Those messages sometimes emerge from the maternal switchboard censored or skewed, and they often emerge infused with her feelings and interpretations.

Perhaps something like this has happened to you: You are trying to arrange a family gathering—such as a picnic in a nearby state park—so your children can spend time with their grandparents, aunts, uncles, and cousins. The first person with whom you raise the subject is your mother. Indeed, broaching the subject to anyone else without her go-ahead seems unthinkable.

She immediately launches into a litany of reasons why such an outing is impractical: "Oh your dad wouldn't want to spend hours in a park. He hates bugs. Billy has final exams sometime around then, and your sister Emily and her husband are already planning a vacation to the Grand Tetons. Besides, don't you remember that time Uncle Alfred got sunstroke?" Before you know it, planning this affair seems as daunting as scaling the Grand Tetons themselves. Nice try, but you give up.

Isn't your mother amazing in her magical and omniscient power? She seems to know what everyone thinks, what everyone wants. But wait just a minute. What really happened here? If you think about it, you might realize it's your mother, not your father, who is squeamish about bugs. She has projected her own feeling and attributed it to someone else. Far be it for her to take responsibility for putting a damper on your plans.

And what about your brother and sister? Would final exams or an upcoming vacation really preclude an afternoon's picnic? Couldn't you work around their schedules? And, by the way, what about Uncle Alfred? As a matter of fact, you don't remember the infamous time he got sunstroke. Even if he did, hasn't he heard about sunscreen by now? The truth is, you don't know the answer to these questions because all information is being selectively channeled through your mother.

Of course, your mother may not even be aware of the effects of what she is doing. To her conscious mind she may simply be relieving you of the burden of contacting other family members, but her unconscious agenda may be to erect roadblocks to intimacy. If each person in the family must communicate through her, she gets all the attention and makes all the decisions.

If such emotional maneuvers are typical of the way your mother operates, some creative strategies are needed. If you feel blocked from other members of your family, you may have to try an end run around Mother. A tactic so successful in football may result in a communications touchdown.

Consider a new approach to Mother's secondhand objections to your plan. First, try to get your mother to speak for herself.

MOTHER: Billy couldn't possibly come. He'll be busy study-
            ing for finals.
DAUGHTER: Mother, I was really wondering what *you* thought
            of the idea.
MOTHER: Oh, I love the idea. But your father will just hate
            being outdoors with all those bugs.
DAUGHTER: Maybe so. I'll have to investigate further. Perhaps
            there's a screened area. But at least I know *you*
            like the idea.

At this point it falls to your mother to make her preferences known, to take responsibility for her point of view. If she is projecting her concerns onto your father, she may own up to them overtly or decide to come to the picnic and make a temporary truce with beetles and ants. On the other hand, she may press on:

MOTHER: Yes, I like it fine. But your sister Emily is getting
                   ready for her vacation. You can't expect her to
                   come. And your uncle Alfred can't be in the
                   sun. You remember what happened last time.

Gently join your mother:

DAUGHTER: Certainly everyone's schedule and needs should
                   be taken into consideration.
MOTHER: Yes, so you see it's impossible.

Now use skills you've already honed. Bring the conversation to an appropriate, friendly conclusion or employ a Creative Non Sequitur to change the subject. You have established that everyone's needs must be considered, so go ahead and communicate with everyone to determine what those needs actually are.

Rather than rely on your mother's weekly conversation with your sister Emily in Des Moines to hear about her vacation plans, call Emily yourself. Consider employing the lost art of letter writing. Drop your brother Billy a cheerful, newsy note at college—he may well be delighted to receive an unexpected missive. Brighten Uncle Alfred's day with a fax from his favorite niece.

Your resistance may assert itself when you inadvertently let slip to your mother that you are individually polling members of the family. If she knows this, she may shift into high gear to reestablish her role as Chief Channeler. Faster than you can say "matriarch," she will be on the phone projecting her own thoughts and feelings across state lines and informing everyone why everyone else can't attend your festivity. Try to restrain yourself from alerting Mother of your new strategy before you've had a chance to implement it. If you can manage to get a quorum together for your picnic, your mother will very likely attend. Remember, she doesn't like anything to take place without her! She may complain a bit, and that's her right, but nevertheless you will have made a constructive change in your family filigree. Furthermore, you will have made great strides in the Mother Maze, for you will have learned how to gently and strategically circumvent Mother's roadblocks without directly challenging her authority. You will have learned to speak for yourself while subtly getting your mother to speak for herself and not the rest of the family.

And so we have the family filigree, with its intricate weave casting an indelible mark on your life. No matter how far away your family members are, they influence your perceptions and your behaviors. But your awareness of family myths and labels and roles will serve you well as you follow the steps of *combatting your impulses, heeding the voice of experience,* and *remembering your goals.* Do not be too hard on yourself when you lose some ground in the Mother Maze. Remember the steps you learned earlier: *Be realistic.* You can't change everything, and certainly you can't change anything instantly. *Prioritize.* Concentrate on the aspects of your maternal relationship that frustrate you most. And *be as generous as possible* wherever possible—to your mother, to your other family members and, last but not least, to yourself.

In our next chapter, The Mother Within, which begins Part III of this book, we'll say some more about being generous to yourself. This is the chapter that addresses the maternal voice women internalize, the one that can be more difficult to contend with than even the most vexing conflict with one's "real life" mother.

PART III

ADVANCED
SKILLS
AND
STRATEGIES

CHAPTER 6

MANAGING THE MOTHER WITHIN

The fundamental difficulty in undoing introjection is its
honorable history as a generic learning process.
Erving and Miriam Polster, *Gestalt Therapy Integrated*

Imagine, if you will, your mother in miniature taking up residence inside your head. She behaves within you much as she behaves in her own home. If she has a fretful, Chronically Worried Style, she paces back and forth across your synapses, musing about your latest impending disaster. If she has a Controlling Style, she taps on your neurons as though pressing the keys of a personal computer—deftly pushing the buttons that make you behave in maternally programmed ways. If she has a Competitive Style, she snuggles up against your gray matter, looking as elegant and cool as she does on her own living room sofa, pointing out how much better she does things than you do.

Now imagine this Miniature Mom also has a shuttle car that ferries her from your head to your heart at a moment's notice. She will whisper her thoughts into your psychic inner ear and then shuttle down to your heart where she will stir up old, familiar feelings that only an exchange with your mother can engender. Oddly enough, however, this split-second thought-feeling reaction is happening while you are entirely alone. Your real-life mother could be on a remote hilltop in Nepal, in your sister's living room in Des Moines, or on a beach in Florida minding her own business. Nevertheless, to you it feels as if she is *everywhere*. No matter what you do or where you roam, the spirit of your mother seems to tag along.

Does it sound as though you've entered the realm of science fiction? Well, you haven't. What you're experiencing is a ubiquitous psychological phenomenon. Your Miniature Mom—so-called because we believe this can help you easily conceptualize the *maternal introject*, or Mother Within—does reside in your head and heart, and she is there to stay.

How did she get there in the first place? How can you recognize when she is operative? How can you learn to distinguish her voice from your own? How can you untangle your moods from her attitudes and your priorities from her values? How can you let your true voice ring forth without having to silence all of her counsel forever? These are the issues this chapter will address.

THE MOTHER ELECTRICIAN: GETTING WIRED BY MOTHER'S MESSAGES

In our first chapter we said the process of acquiring an internal representation of one's mother could be likened to "swallowing" her value system. The metaphorical imagery of ingesting the outlook and beliefs of our childhood caretakers and role models is widespread in the literature of psychology. Yet it's a bit misleading in that we don't simply gulp up our mother's essential character features—that is, her outlook on life and way of relating to others—in one sitting, the way we might gulp a soft drink on a hot day. Acquiring a Mother Within is a subtle process that occurs over many years.

Let's return to our visualizations once more. This time, imagine a wire running from your mother to you. Through this wire runs the current of love, concern, and care that lights your way through life. Coursing through it as well are the thoughts and feelings Mother has about what's good and bad, right and wrong, reasonable and irrational, appropriate and impolite, safe and dangerous. Gradually, imperceptibly but unremittingly, you are being infused with your mother's world-view.

Though on a conscious level neither of you is aware of it, it is as if you are being wired with Mother Current by the Mother Electrician. It's through the exquisitely delicate trans-mission of this current that a facsimile of Mother is incor-porated into your psyche. This "double" will always dwell somewhere inside you.

Some aspects of this "wiring" process can be enabling. When positive signals from the mother are internalized, they help to build a strong foundation for the developing ego. By transmitting messages such as "You are wonderful! You can do anything!" the Mother wires the daughter to be confident and resilient, and the daughter's sense of self blossoms.

But some aspects of this process can be debilitating. Though it is part of a mother's job to help shape a child's conscience or superego by conveying and demonstrating appropriate rules of conduct, her corrective messages, when proffered too em-phatically or harshly for her child to comfortably assimilate, may be experienced as punitive. Later, when Mother is not around, the child may punish and frustrate herself by replaying in her mind stern reprimands she absorbed long ago.

Hence, a child who learns from her mother that it is not mannerly to monopolize conversation obtains a useful social skill. On the other hand, a child who learns from her mother that opinionated people are unattractive to others may be se-verely sanctioned by her own superego—the part of her psyche to which her mother's wagging finger of disapproval has been relegated—each time she returns from a dinner party at which she dared venture a comment about anything more contro-versial than the weather. "I was too loud," this daughter may chastise herself. "What I said was too strong. Now everyone thinks I'm a loudmouth. They'll never invite me back." Of

course the "entity" who is speaking here is not really the re-
morseful dinner guest at all but an embodiment of her mother.

We do not mean to say that the diner's mother consciously
set up her daughter to suffer in the wake of every social engagement. Chances are when she originally instructed her
child she did so out of a genuine effort to impart to her a
useful ground rule of life as she experienced it. Furthermore,
had this daughter's mother actually been on the scene of the
"crime," her assessment of the wrongdoing might have been
somewhat more merciful. The truth is that while human
beings have the potential to occasionally surprise you, their
"carbon copy" introjects invariably sing the same old song.

Like so many grown women, this daughter was doomed to
play that tiresome tune over and over. She was wired to dis-
approve of qualities within herself that she believed would be
displeasing to her mother.

BLOWING A MATERNAL FUSE

For some women the introject wired in by the Mother Electrician is a more or less continual source of misery, especially
when they are temperamentally mismatched with a mother
whose Maternal Style imposes excessive demands. Thirty-two-
year-old Meredith describes her experience of this phenomenon:

My whole life I have been a relatively slow-moving person, at
least in comparison to my mother. She will make decisions and
take action quickly. I mull things over and take my time. It's the
way I am, yet I can't help feeling it's somehow wrong to be this
way. I'm not lazy, but my mother made me feel I was. Ever since
I was little she would ask me, "Can't you do that any faster?
What's taking you so long? The earth won't stop turning while I
wait for you!" Today, I still deliberate over decisions. I guess it's
my nature. But the whole time I'm deciding I'm in agony. Somewhere I hear a voice whispering, warning me that life is passing

me by. And when things go wrong for me, I tend to blame myself for not having acted more swiftly—even if the logical part of my mind tells me that haste wouldn't have made any difference.

Meredith was temperamentally mismatched with her Hypercritical Mother. Nevertheless, while quite young, she dutifully and necessarily took on her mother's value system, labeling herself lazy rather than methodical, thorough, unhurried, or relaxed. *Necessarily* is the operative word here since we really have little choice as small children: We absorb what Mother says. For quite some time we may know no other truth but hers.

As adults we like to think we are free to discover our own realities and make individual choices. We are. Yet it's not a simple matter to exercise that freedom. Though we forget how abjectly we may have surrendered to Mother's truth way back when, it often comes back to haunt and daunt us.

The Mother Within is as elusive as she is persistent, and coping with her presents a formidable, ongoing challenge for most of us. It is impossible to simply dismantle or exorcise our wired-in maternal introject. After all, without current from the Mother Electrician, Daughter Current would never have flourished at all. Remember, we started out life in symbiosis with our mothers, and it is often through identification with her that we experience the greatest sense of closeness to her. Thus, even when our Mother Within criticizes us, we may get some satisfaction from agreeing with her, a kind of "fellow feeling," a sense that everything is humming along as it was meant to. When we depart from her viewpoint and betray her value system, we can receive a shock. Sometimes, as fifty-year-old Dolores tells it, we may even blow a fuse:

I spent nearly two decades taking care of the house and the kids. Even when all my friends got jobs or went back to school, I continued to be the ultimate homemaker, and I enjoyed it, I really did. But when the last of my children left for college, I realized I had some interests I wanted to pursue. I decided to take some art and photography courses at a nearby college. At first I was a little scared, but mostly I was excited. School was fun! But all of a sudden I started to feel panic. What was I doing here with kids less than half my age? What if one of my own three kids needed me, and I wasn't there to answer the phone? What if I got so bogged down with assignments that I couldn't have my husband's dinner ready when he came home?

My children and my husband told me that was silly. They were one hundred percent behind me, really encouraging, but in my mind I kept hearing, "Dolores, you're an old fool." And when I imagined myself needed elsewhere, I started skipping class. I justified this by saying the classes were "only" for my own enjoyment, which turned out not to be enough of an incentive. I soon dropped out altogether. Part of me felt good about that; I guess it was the part that was loyal to my mother's way of thinking. You see, she always told me: "The most important thing in life is family. Get a good husband and he will take care of you. It's okay that you don't do well in school. Girls don't need to. I left high school to marry your father, and see how happy I am."

I know most mothers push their kids to get good grades, but with my mother, educated people, especially other women, made her nervous. But here's the ridiculous part: My mother passed away years before any of this happened, and I still didn't want to make her uncomfortable.

Here we have a woman who lived most of her life hooked up to the Mother Electrician with nary a power interruption. When she decided to flip a switch and connect to her own desires, she promptly got zapped. In spite of Dolores's interests, in spite of a supportive family of her own, and in spite of the fact that there were no reality-based reasons to keep her from furthering her education, she was unable to do so. She heeded her mother's voice even though her mother was deceased. Of course, the person Dolores was making uncomfortable by going back to school was not her actual mother but her Mother Within, that is, the part of her psyche where her Miniature Mom was perched. But since it is Dolores's psyche we are talking about here, it was, ipso facto, Dolores who experienced the discomfort. When she was out of sync with Mother's value system, she short-circuited, so she returned to it again though it meant sacrificing so much else.

COMPLIERS AND DEFIERS RESPOND TO MOTHER WITHIN

We do not mean to imply, of course, that all women defer to their Mothers Within as consistently and completely as Dolores, nor that they will rush to reestablish a smooth rapport with their Mother Within after even a mild defection. Far from it. We wrote earlier about compliant and defiant daughters. Dolores is, overall, a compliant type, highly invested in confirming and perpetuating Mother's opinions. Thus, her Mother Within had the final say just as her real-life mother invariably did. But, as we know, many grown daughters act in ways that seem to indicate reckless disregard for Mother's edicts. They have a Mother Within, too, but they defy her on a regular basis.

There are no hard-and-fast rules about who will become a complier and who a defier of Mother. It's partly nature and partly nurture. Obviously, some people are more content than others with the path of least resistance. And family roles and mythology also play a part. We have also noticed that certain Maternal Styles tend to engender more of one type of daughter than another.

Though there are numerous exceptions, in general the Maternal Styles that most effectively instill self-doubt and low self-esteem in a daughter—Controlling, Competitive, and Hypercritical—tend to produce compliers. After all, the more insecure one is about one's own judgment and perceptions, the more likely one is to seek the counsel of others. Often those "others" are psychic internalizations of authority figures, especially Mom. Another way of saying this is that where the ego is weak, the superego tends to be excessively powerful and especially punitive.

Mothers with Pseudoperfect Styles, as we know, generally engender compliant daughters as well. These emotionally fragile mothers, though unable and unwilling to experience let alone reveal their deep-seated emotions and perceptions, are often flawlessly socially appropriate. Their daughters, infused as children with their Mother Electrician's exquisite sense of etiquette and belief that appearances are what matter most, may rely on the Mother Within for ongoing instruction in "doing the right thing"—or at least the appearance of doing so. In the bargain, by continuing to preserve a "perfect" image of Mother in their psyche, they get the satisfying feeling that they are still protecting and insulating her.

Mothers with Merged or Chronically Worried Styles, on the other hand, seem to produce a higher ratio of defiant daughters. This may seem surprising. After all, these mothers work so hard to preserve symbiotic ties with their female children. Indeed, such mothers tend to convey to daughters the message that pulling away from them or challenging them may result in damage to Mother's life and daughter's limb, and some daughters cannot bear to take that chance.

But the overwhelmingly stifling effects of these intrusive Maternal Styles compel a fair number of daughters to try to wrestle free. For them, challenging their real-life mother as well as their Mother Within is tantamount to survival. They recognize that if they don't wage some sort of freedom fight, they will have to live their lives within extremely narrow confines.

Some daughters evidence defiance early on. They struggle against the rules and requests of their mother since the first day they are able to utter the word *no*. More daughters shift into a defiant mode in adolescence when the drive for independence and self-assertion blossoms and when the desire to conform to peer pressure outweighs the drive to conform to Mother's value system. Some of these recalcitrant toddlers and teenage rebels become defiant as a way of life. So frustrated are they by the kinds of messages they receive from Mother that they unilaterally decide if Mother says yes, the only smart thing to do is say no, and vice versa. When their real mother is not around, they use their Internal Mother as a measuring stick. The louder the introject's voice shouts *stop*, the more likely they are to proceed. They become totally reactive and reflexive. They are in the grips of a behavior that psychologists term a *reaction formation*.

Is defiance a helpful or a detrimental thing? Well, let's say it's a mixed bag. Defiance can liberate a daughter in some ways, but it can enslave her in others. Whoever reflexively engages in a blatant negation of Mother's value system will have to contend with the consequences. Specifically, two rather troublesome consequences may result:

The first of these is the defiant daughter's chronically anxious sense that she is somehow an imposter. Let us say, for example, you are the naturally feisty daughter of a Competitive Mother. Despite the childhood conditioning messages that told you "Mother does it better," you set out to gain a top executive position in the corporate world. Your powerful drive to react in opposition to the voice of your Mother Within may spur you on as you work long hours, forfeit vacations, exceed your job description, and lift yourself by your bootstraps through your company hierarchy. Finally, the key promotion you always dreamed of is within reach. Still, even as you are poised to leap ahead, you cannot help looking back over your shoulder and wonder: What will happen if it's discovered that I don't really deserve to be here, that someone else could do it better?

The fact is that, like so many defiers, even as you've openly behaved in ways that contradict the edicts of your Mother Within, you have not gained peace of mind. Though your outer self appears strong and competent, your inner self is still torn by wearisome second-guessing. In a sense you feel uncomfortable in your own skin. Your accomplishments, no matter how numerous, cannot assuage the feeling that you are an imposter.

The second unhappy consequence of reflexive, habitual defiance or reaction formation to the Mother Within is that daughters risk throwing the proverbial baby out with the bath water. Let us say you are the defiant daughter of a Chronically Worried Mother who harangued you with innumerable warnings about the dangers of sandwich-sharing, mascara-wearing ("You'll blind yourself!") and roller-skating ("You'll break your neck!"). In spite of her admonitions, you went ahead and determined for yourself that none of these activities was actually life-threatening. Since not participating in them would separate you from your friends, you undertook them anyhow. Now let us say in your teenage years you also took up cigarette smoking, another activity in which your friends engaged and which would have sent Mother into a tailspin had she ever chanced upon the crumpled packs you secreted away. Now, years later, part of you would like to give up smoking. You've been convinced, at least on an intellectual level, that it actually can be life-threatening. Still, you may be emotionally unwilling to relinquish your habit. Your Mother Within is telling you to quit right now, and therein lies your problem. You don't want to believe that she could possibly be right about anything. Your pride is at stake!

Clearly, unilateral reactive defiance of the Mother Within is not the way to manage her, any more than is automatic capitulation to her commands. What is needed are some strategies to help you lower the voltage you receive from your Mother Electrician without forfeiting the empowering aspects of her energy. We call these strategies Circuit Breakers. Like the circuit breaker devices in your house, they are designed to interrupt the flow of an electric current—in this case the Mother Current—when it becomes excessive.

We are aware that you will experience resistance to giving up your introjected value system. It is old, familiar, and as comfortable as a well-worn sweater when the breeze is chilly. Do not set a goal of undoing overnight what has taken decades to become established.

Managing the Mother Within is a task to be approached gently and judiciously. Before we can even break old circuits, we must become aware of the signals that indicate Daughter Current is being overloaded with Mother Current.

SUBTLE SIGNALS: KNOWING WHOSE VOICE IS SPEAKING WHEN

Is it me or maternal Memorex? That is the question we must ask ourselves when we feel compelled to obey or defy a voice we hear inside our heads. It is no small achievement to figure out whose voice is speaking when. What follows are some clues to help alert you to the fact that the voice of the Mother Within is about to drown out your own:

Abrupt Changes in Feeling

Earlier we saw a college-bound mother of three shift precipitously from enthusiasm and self-confidence to apprehension and self-doubt. For a while Dolores's own value system was operative. Her genuine voice rang loud and clear in her head: "My kids are grown. My husband thinks it's great I'm back in school. I know I'll do fine. I was always good at helping my kids with their homework, especially art projects. This is a new chapter in my life." Suddenly, her mood changed. She was no longer happy about the prospect of a "new chapter." Her self-appraisal changed as well. Just as suddenly, Dolores no longer believed in her abilities. What had seemed like an interesting challenge was now anticipated with dread.

Whenever you experience meteoric shifts in mood or in your evaluation of your competence level, do some reality testing. Ask, "who's talking now?" Chances are your Miniature Mom has been piping up.

If you tend to be a compliant daughter, ask, "Does this mood make me feel compelled to stop doing something I want to do?" If your answer is affirmative, you are in danger of veering off a new, adventurous course and back onto old, worn paths of the Mother Maze. If you are a defiant type, ask, "Does this mood make me feel as if I have to respond to a 'dare' to proceed?" If your answer is affirmative, you know you are in danger of behaving in a completely reflexive manner rather than honestly evaluating your genuine priorities. You, too, are stuck in the ruts of the Mother Maze.

Heightened Emotions and Excessive Concerns

You'll recall that along with her enthusiasm Dolores experienced normal fears when contemplating signing up for college courses. These were her own natural emotions. It's commonplace to be somewhat nervous in the face of a new situation. Humans are made that way, and a good thing, too, for it's part of our survival instinct. But Dolores's mild case of nerves blossomed into a case of acute anxiety, and her appropriate concerns erupted into obsessive ruminations. This exacerbation was a homage to her Mother Within.

Should you experience mild nervousness that becomes panic or a low mood that ignites a bonfire of depression or a wee bit of annoyance that threatens to set off a temper tantrum, or if you suddenly find yourself frequently prognosticating worst-case scenarios, you should heed these shifts as warning signals.

Be aware that such psychic signals are often accompanied by actual physical sensations. Many women, both habitual compliers and defiers, have expressed to us that they experience symptoms such as a tightening in their chest or a tension headache just as their introject is about to "take over" and hold forth on yet another doomsday scenario. If this happens to you, know that these, too, can be telltale signs that you are getting a voltage jolt from the Mother Electrician.

The next three signals should clue you in to the fact that you are now responding to your Mother Within by outwardly behaving like her:

"You Sound Just Like Your Mother"

Sometimes we get a helping hand from others when it comes to recognizing warning signals that the Mother Within is acting up. Have you ever been told by your spouse or children or even your best friend that you seem to be mouthing verbatim your mother's words, as though you were possessed? If you have, you've probably felt a chill down your spine. Perhaps you've gotten extremely defensive, effusively denying that any such thing is taking place. We suggest that before you start defending, you take a minute to consider. Is your Mother Within playing ventriloquist again? Chances are the more you feel like protesting this possibility, the greater the likelihood that she is.

Let us say you and your family are finishing a pleasant meal when your daughter asks to be excused from the table. Well, that's fine, you think, except she hasn't eaten all her vegetables. Now you're off and running: "You can't leave the table until you finish that broccoli. Why do I slave to make nutritious dinners if you're not going to eat them? Besides, it's cold season, and you can't afford to miss any school. What about the science fair?" Now your daughter is sulking, and you are fuming. Your husband is perplexed. Is there really some mystical connection between broccoli-eating and the science fair? "Honey," he says, "calm down. You sound just like your mother."

In the frame of mind you are in, part of you considers this an ideal moment to fling whatever is left of the broccoli directly into your husband's lap. Instead, ask yourself, Doesn't your daughter get a multivitamin daily? Isn't it true she's at an age where Spaghetti-O's are considered the height of gourmet fare? Mightn't it be your Chronically Worried mother who believes every meal must include a vegetable, or dire consequences will ensue? Hear this communication from your husband as helpful, not hurtful, and you will do everyone at your table a favor.

"She's Just Like I Was as a Child"

Another indication that it may be time to take stock is if you observe your own daughter behaving in a manner that causes her—and/or you—distress. You may see that she is responding to you in much the way you responded to your mother. Let us say your Pseudoperfect Mother gave you the message that crying was unacceptable because it upset her and gave others the impression that yours was not a perfectly happy home. Now you notice your own little girl bites her lip and runs from the room every time she thinks she might shed a tear in front of you. You wonder, Why does she feel she must be so stoic? Think about it. Do you sometimes say, as your mother did, "Don't cry. Crying is for babies. You are a big girl." Is this the value you really wish to convey? Or is it solely your mother's? Ask yourself, Is it "me" or "she?"

"Whose Husband Is It, Anyway?"

Perhaps your mother sacrificed herself to meet your father's needs—because, as she said, Daddy is so helpless—and then resented it. She maintained, with a sigh, that her husband was impossible at times. In fact, it always seemed as if your parents struggled along in their relationship. You grew up telling yourself that things would be different for you. You would find a different kind of man than she did. And so you do. Nevertheless, the more intimacy that develops in your relationship with him, the more compelled you are to think of him and treat him the way your mother did your father.

Let's say you marry a very independent man, a man who throughout many years of bachelorhood managed to get his shirts washed and his pants pressed without any help from you. Now, although you work full time and are as busy as he is, you become obsessed with his laundry. "I can't ever get to my chores," you complain to your mate one Saturday afternoon, "because I'm always doing your wash." Why are you doing it, anyway? He hasn't asked you to. Why? Because he's "helpless."

Or let's say you become involved with an easygoing man. Unlike your "impossible" father he is not rigid but very flexible. He's happy to do most of the things you want to do except maybe one or two. For instance, he'd really rather you went to the ballet without him. So okay, you'll just go to the ballet with a girlfriend as you've done for so long anyhow, right? Wrong. You nag your spouse relentlessly until he agrees to accompany you, and then, fuming that he sits there sound asleep, you think, He's impossible.

If such scenarios sound familiar to you, take note. A tendency to see men the way your mother did or to repeat vivid patterns found in her marriage may lead you to lose sight of who the man in your life really is. It's yet another signal that your maternal introject is overpowering your own perceptions.

Certainly, it is not true that every time a woman has a quick shift in her emotional state, excessive concerns, a profound allegiance to a particular green vegetable, or a misunderstanding with her daughter or her man that she is conforming to the values and desires of the Mother Within. But should any of the foregoing signals manifest themselves, it couldn't hurt to perform what we call a Believe-It-or-Not Checkup.

First, examine the premise that underlies your feelings, thoughts, words, and actions. My husband cannot find the dry cleaners on his own. A meal without broccoli is not worth eating. Or perhaps: I can't balance a checkbook. Or: I'm too fat. Now ask yourself, do you (yes you, not your mother) believe it or not? If you believe the premise is true, fine. Do what you need to do about it. Draw your husband a map, sneak broccoli bits into the Spaghetti-O's, consult with your banker, go on a diet. If you recognize, however, that you don't believe it but your mother does, it is time to employ a circuit-breaking strategy.

CIRCUIT BREAKERS: INTERRUPTING MOTHER CURRENT

There are a few encouraging things to say as we embark on this practical section on circuit-breaking skills. First, the introjected voice, though wired in by the Mother Electrician, is a part of you. Thus, working on managing it is personal, intrapsychic work. You won't have to deal with impulses on the part of your real-life mother, let alone your father and siblings, to bring things back to status quo. You'll have resistances to doing this work, but at least you can claim them all as your own. Second, though you likely cannot change the things that your Mother Within says to you, you can alter the way in which you allow the maternal voice to converse with the rest of your psyche.

Here are some strategies you can bring to bear on modifying the effects of the Mother Within.

Good Old Echoing and Mirroring

In chapter 4 we discovered the beneficial effects of "joining" one's mother through echoing and mirroring communications. Remember, echoing is used to help clarify Mother's intent and to assure her that her position, as well as the loving impulse which often fuels that position, is heard and duly noted. Mirroring is used to communicate that you sometimes experience feelings similar, though not necessarily identical, to hers. What we're going to suggest now is that you employ those joining skills to ameliorate messages from your Mother Within which routinely block you from achieving *your* goals and remaining faithful to *your* priorities.

We'll see in the following case how an Internal Mother can be joined and mirrored in much the same way as a real-life mother:

Claudia works for a home furnishings design firm in Chicago. She is asked by her boss to attend a major trade show convention and present a new product line to key customers. She is thrilled to have the opportunity and excitedly tells her husband and nine-year-old twin sons that she will be spending a week in Los Angeles.

The boys think that's neat, and Claudia's husband is happy to contribute some extra effort on the domestic front while she's gone. The housekeeper agrees to work extra hours, too, so the coast is clear for a smooth departure.

Enter the Mother Within: "What are you thinking of? Leaving your small children with your helpless husband and housekeeper? They'll miss you so. They'll be lost without you. They'll have fast food for dinner every night! And I shudder to think what the house will look like when you get back. All this for some dumb convention. What's the point? You'll feel lonely for your family and worry about them, and do a lousy presentation anyway. You'd better tell your boss the trip's out of the question."

Claudia feels frozen with fear and indecision. Dare she comply with the maternal voice and back out of her obligation now? Dare she defy it and carry out her plan to go away?

Claudia's psyche is inhabited by a Merged and Chronically Worried introject wired in by a Merged and Worried mother who dreads separations and fantasizes all manner of disasters. She can comply with her introject, disappoint her superiors, and let a career opportunity go by the wayside. Or she can grit her teeth and defy her Mother Within, but that would practically guarantee a week of major-league guilt pangs. Indeed, it feels as though her Mother Within is even more adept at inflicting guilt than her actual mother.

But Claudia has a third option. She can take note of the warning signals that indicate her Mother Within is operative (her *abrupt changes in feeling state* and *excessive concerns*). Then she can do a Believe-It-or-Not Checkup. Will her trip inflict terrible suffering? Hmmm. She, Claudia, doesn't think so. She can choose to use a Circuit Breaker by echoing and mirroring her mother in an internal dialogue:

MOTHER WITHIN: You can't go away. Your family will miss you, and you'll miss them horribly.

DAUGHTER: It is always difficult being separated from the ones you love. (She clarifies the feeling that drives her Mother Within, that is, the part of her psyche dedicated to her mother, to seek a merger.)

MOTHER WITHIN: The kids will be lost without you.

DAUGHTER: I know concern for the kids is a testament to love. (She reflects the loving intent behind the worry.)

MOTHER WITHIN: You'll do a rotten job presenting. You'll be too preoccupied with what trouble everyone might be getting into back home.

DAUGHTER: It's true, I often do fret too much about things that needn't bother me or that are beyond my control. (She acknowledges that she has feelings similar to her mother's.) But I'll just have to persevere. I am willing to tolerate a little anxiety if it means making the most of a wonderful opportunity. (She then differentiates her true self from her Mother Within: Though I share some of your emotions and traits, I am my own person.)

Now the maternal voice is soothed, which means, of course, that Claudia herself is soothed since she is really having this dialogue with a part of herself, a part that is not usually subjected to scrutiny but instead obeys blindly or opposes reflexively. When this grown daughter echoes and mirrors her introject, she is affirming she is aware that she sometimes has conflicting impulses, that she accepts *all* her thoughts and feelings. This very acceptance liberates her to make the wisest and most logically considered choice on behalf of her own well-being.

If you're someone who thinks that talking to oneself is crazy, think again. Isn't the greater madness to ignore yourself? Of course, we're not suggesting you have this internal dialogue aloud at the A&P. Simply sit calmly for a time—perhaps in the tub where no one will disturb you—and let your mind's eye summon up your Miniature Mom for a chat.

A Laugh Couldn't Hurt

Also in chapter four we explored the immeasurable benefits of cultivating a sense of humor when it comes to mother matters. Why stop at jesting and joshing with your actual mother? Just as pointing out the lighter side of a situation may help you to get your mother to recognize her patterns, it can help you develop an awareness of when your own patterns are "under the influence" of her introject.

Do the ideas in your head or the words coming out of your mother sound a little, well, silly sometimes? Do you ever, for example, find yourself asking your daughter or son, "If all the other kids were going to jump off a bridge, would you do it too?" Or as part of the ongoing broccoli refrain, "How can you leave that on your dish when people are starving in Asia?" Do you say, as your Competitive Mother did, "Well, something just like that happened to me—only worse"? Or, as your Merged Mother did over and over again, "Like mother, like daughter"? That would be a good time to allow yourself a little grin at your own expense. It might also be a time to give your husband a wink and a friendly nudge, even before he can say, "You sound just like your mother." And don't be afraid to share a smile and a shrug with your kids as well.

Miniature Moms can be a source of frustration, but with luck they can sometimes be a source of amusement as well. There's no rule that says you can't have fun learning to manage your responses to Mother, whether she's the actual one or the one in your mind.

Mothering Yourself: Installing an Alternative Introject

Earlier we noted that our psychic representation of Mother might well judge our behavior more harshly than our actual mother would. Alas, it is the more frustrating, punitive messages that tend to end up stored in our superego. There, unexposed to the light of conscious awareness, they grow more tenacious. Through their endless repetition it's as if they're flexing the same muscles again and again, and overworked muscles can become hard as rock.

Thus, while your Controlling Mother might have expressed doubt about, say, your financial capabilities (complaining, for example, when you ask for an advance on your allowance, "Why don't you put some money aside every week like Mommy does? You don't want to end up poor as a church mouse, do you?"), the doubt your Mother Within instills in you might be even more severe. In the face of even the most minor pecuniary setback you might berate yourself ceaselessly, tuning into a punitive inner voice that virtually shouts, "You should have listened to your mother. Now you'll *never* have a dime to your name. You'll spend your old age sleeping in the park!"

And while your Hypercritical Mother might have found fault with your taste in clothing ("Must you wear those empire waists? They don't exactly help that flat chest of yours"), your inner maternal voice may take things even further. Selecting a dress to wear to your own fiftieth wedding anniversary celebration, you may still see yourself through the *Hyper*-Hypercritical eyes of the Mother Within. Each garment you try will appear to accentuate some heinous figure flaw until you systematically rule out high necks, low necks, short sleeves, above-the-calf hemlines, polka dots, stripes, sequins, and so forth, and arrive at your own party sporting a floor-length dark-brown muumuu that, though ideal for smuggling out floral table centerpieces, does nothing to enhance your appearance.

Remember, though wired by the Mother Electrician, it is your psyche that has accentuated your mother's most frustrating proclivities. Now we are suggesting that you deliberately manifest a counterbalancing maternal voice that incorporates the most affirmative messages your mother imparted to you, accentuates those, and spices them up with your own compassionate and loving instincts.

Draw on your most positive childhood memories, the times when you actually felt soothed, protected, and encouraged by your mother. Then use these feelings to create a second Miniature Mom—the Benevolent Mother Within—who embodies the quintessence of all that is noble about mother love. Mentally install her in your psyche alongside your negative Mother Within, and the next time you find yourself struggling with your old, familiar negative maternal introject, allow your new Benevolent Mother Within a chance to voice her opinion as well.

In creating this alternative introject, draw, too, on your natural impulses to comfort and nurture your own child or, if you have no children of your own, a niece or nephew or a neighbor's child who comes to you with some sort of physical or emotion pain. If you have within you the ability to reassure a weepy little girl that her freckles are not blemishes but beauty marks, you have the power to remind yourself that you, too, are beautiful. If you have within you the capacity to instill a sense of optimism in a child who has endured a disappointment at school, reminding her that one failed test is not a stepping-stone to a lifetime of disgrace, then you can apply a similar optimistic attitude to your own life.

We have said over and over again that it is completely unrealistic and self-defeating to pine for an actual mother who is perfect and ideal in every way, but when it comes to your deliberately created Benevolent Mother Within, the ideal becomes attainable. Stir into this mother's pot all the care and approval you can muster. When you feel worn down by the complaints and rebukes of your nay-saying, guilt-invoking maternal introject, turn to your Benevolent Mother Within for some extra-supportive mothering.

In short, mother yourself in the kindest, most generous way you know how. A helpful first step in this process is taking a breather from your routine and getting cozy if you can. Ease yourself into your favorite chair, or turn on your favorite piece of music, light some candles, and soak in a hot bath. The important thing is that you soothe yourself and cherish yourself. You may be surrounded by the trappings of your adult life, but the feelings you are accessing and responding to with your own positive current of mother love are as old as you.

As you pamper yourself, remember that mothering through support and encouragement is essential for growth. If you didn't get any of that, you wouldn't be here! Offer yourself some warmhearted words. You have always deserved to hear them, though they might not have come your way with optimal frequency. Give yourself permission to have your feelings, to have your failures, to have your moments of hesitation and confusion without negative self-judgments butting in on you. And if negative thoughts do intervene during this time of tranquility, remember there are now two sides to the story. If your frustrating introject starts to tell you how bad you are, allow your supportive one ample time for rebuttal. Soon the turmoil in your psyche will mellow. You will not feel compelled to reflexively comply or defy, and you will have blazed yet another new path in the Mother Maze without involving your real-life mother at all.

Choosing a Champion

There is no question that some women find it easier than others to mother themselves via a supportive and encouraging Benevolent Mother Within. The women who find it easiest are those who, despite some inevitable frustrations and conflicts with their mothers, generally have mothers who are willing and able to make room for their daughter's emotional point of view.

For example, a daughter might have had a Controlling Mother who she recalls questioned her accounting abilities or housecleaning talents but who also held her in her arms after a monster-filled nightmare and assured her that she knows how scary bad dreams can be and that Mommy is there to make certain she's safe. Likewise, a daughter might have a Merged Mother who, although inordinately possessive of her child, might also have been her daughter's greatest cheerleader, bubbling over with pride and joy when her daughter came home to announce that she had won the lead in the school play. "I know how hard we practiced those lines, honey," she might say, "and how nervous you must have been. What an accomplishment!"

Women who received insufficient emotional validation as children, however, might find it more difficult to conjure up a validating introject. Often, in fact, such women go through life in a kind of psychic seclusion with few people, if any, really knowing their feelings. They are unsure if anyone else in the world shares the kinds of thoughts and emotions they do, and they often shelter from scrutiny their most private hopes, dreams, fears, and shames because they perceive them as somehow insupportable or unacceptable.

One of the things we hope this book has shown is that many women share common experiences and common feelings. That pool of community emotion can be a magnificent resource. If your Benevolent Mother Within needs bolstering in order to ameliorate your negative introject, we suggest you start searching for a champion, someone you believe understands you and is an advocate for your point of view. Such a person's messages of advocacy can also be internalized.

Who should be your champion? It may be another family member—an aunt, a sibling, a grandparent. It may be a good friend. It may even be a therapist. Whoever it is, the main criterion any suitable champion must meet is that she dignify your feelings through the simple act of endorsing their legitimacy, allowing you to feel happy or sad or just plain mad without giving you the message that such feelings are unwarranted.

When the going gets tough, turn to your champion. Either speak to her directly or have an *internal* dialogue with her. Her input can stem the flow of harmful current from a punitive introject.

For example, if you are struggling to set limits with your mother, and your Mother Within is berating you for not sharing with Mom the intimate details of your latest romance, your champion will gladly remind you that it is not appropriate at age forty-three to share with Mother your memories of each endearment and caress, or even your rising hopes that this man may be the one. "Hold on," your champion will counsel you. "You'll have plenty of time to clue Mother in about your happiness in the future. In the meantime, tell me about it!" What's more, your champion will understand and accept the anxiety you feel in breaking the habit of immediately confiding all to Mother. She will reassure you that that feeling, that resistance, is natural and understandable. She will remind you, too, that you are strong enough to tolerate it while adhering to your plan of limit-setting. She will support your struggle and your decision, and she will help you break the circuit that engenders your compulsive confiding.

One last word about your champion and about your newly created Benevolent Mother Within. Don't be surprised if every now and again you notice them agreeing with your old, familiar Miniature Mom. Once again we must remind you that it is most likely many of the lessons your mother taught you about values and priorities were quite worthwhile. You probably realize, as you mature, that some of her teachings were wiser than you first thought. Some of them may be well worth passing on to the next generation. Your champion and your Benevolent Mother Within can help you separate the wheat from the chaff.

MOPPING UP INTROJECT SPILLS

Naturally enough, it takes considerable concentration, courage, and practice to learn to differentiate "me" from "she" and to activate Circuit Breakers with regularity. Sometimes the familiar, frustrating introject seems to take over your psychic reins with awesome speed. Before you know it, you are thinking and talking like your mother—or to be precise, like a caricature of your mother in her least admirable moments.

With time and practice on your part, this seemingly automatic process will slow down, but until it does, and even occasionally after, you may be subject to what we call introject spills. There will be times when your Miniature Mom, despite your best efforts to modulate her voice, will leap forth suddenly and become not only a source of intrapsychic frustration but a source of irritation for those with whom you interact.

Like an expanding oil slick that causes more and more damage to your environment, that is, your children, spouse, friends, and coworkers, your introject, once "released" from the corner of your superego where it usually hovers, will be wont to spread out in all directions. But all is not lost.

Take, for example, the story of thirty-seven-year-old Jeannie. Over the course of many years she had applied herself to managing her response to her mother and to monitoring her maternal inner voice. She was successful most of the time, but her Controlling introject nearly wrecked a family vacation. Jeannie recalls:

Last spring my husband suggested we take our ten-year-daughter and eight-year-old son to Disney World and Epcot. At first I thought that was a great idea. The kids would have a good time and learn a lot, too.

As the time drew nearer, I started getting obsessed with the trip's logistics. There would be long lines, I knew, since our vacation coincided with spring school break. If we didn't have a fully thought-out game plan, we could spend our whole trip standing on line. I determined to find out what the most popular attractions were and plan a schedule for each day so we could queue up for them first thing in the morning. Of course, sleeping late was out of the question, and I figured we should plan on early lunches and dinners, too, to avoid the rush.

I started going on and on about these concerns, but when I revealed my master schedule to the family, my children groaned and rolled their eyes. Why couldn't we just have fun at Disney World like everyone else? My husband tried to calm me down.

"Honey," he said, "vacations are supposed to include some down time."

I disagreed, and he grew impatient with my need to put the kibosh on the family fun. After much arguing I agreed to play things somewhat by ear—but only grudgingly. We definitely did spend some time on lines, but somewhere on our journey, a funny thing happened. I started enjoying myself.

Standing on line was a chance to improvise pastimes, play games, and just catch our breath and look around. Then I remembered that when I was little I had pleaded with my mother to take me to certain events where she feared there would be long lines. She would agree only if we did it her way, and that meant planning a siege. I guessed I had been following her lead.

So I got into the spirit of things. I was able to tell my family I was sorry for the fuss I'd made. And one day, waiting on line to get into the Haunted House attraction, the kids asked to hear a scary story, and I told them a tale about an imaginary creature— the behemoth that ate good times. That had been me! They all thought that was very funny. I'm glad they were so understanding.

Clearly Jeannie had an introject spillover. Despite her usual high level of awareness when it came to mother matters, she hadn't heeded the warning signals that abounded as the family holiday approached. Her change in feeling, her excessive concerns, and the feedback she was receiving from her husband and children should have served as an introject alert, but few of us are flawless observers of our own motivations all the time. The signals went unnoticed, and Jeannie persisted in tormenting herself and hindering her entire family. Fortunately, once she successfully assessed the reality of the situation, she was able to initiate damage control. She apologized to everyone and joked about her own bewildering behavior. She "mopped up" after the introject spillover.

As in the aftermath of any environmental disaster, the speedier the cleanup and the containment, the better for all. Your Miniature Mom may simply take over from time to time. It happens. Afterward, you may feel embarrassed, even ashamed, yet you may feel too proud to own up to what happened. Try not to let this false pride stand in your way. First, forgive yourself. Next, apologize to the appropriate parties. Go easy on yourself and see if you can find the humor in the situation, for there often is a lighter side. And, most of all, remember that people love you for you, and that includes all the parts of you—even those that are not entirely under your conscious control at every moment. Keep that in mind and the "behemoth that ate good times" will not seem quite so frightening.

Introject spills are most likely to occur under two conditions. Stressful situations can stir up your Miniature Mom with great intensity, and so can the opening of new vistas in your life. When either of these conditions arises or when they arise in tandem, as is often the case, there is generally an impulse to fall back on old patterns, old rules. Initially, this may provide a feeling of safety, but soon enough this Miniature Mom redux may feel anything but soothing.

In our next chapter we will explore how the Mother Within can manifest her presence during key rites of passage in her daughter's life—at weddings, graduations, and other occasions that pave the way for mother-daughter separations. We'll also look at how mothers get stirred up during these important transitional stages, and we'll discuss how daughters can manage their response to both real-life and internal mothers during these exciting but trying times.

CHAPTER 7

❧

A Daughter's Rites of Passage

We are a generation of women who, with every act of self-assertion as women, with every movement into self-development and fulfillment, call into question the values by which our mothers have tried to live.

Kim Chernin, *The Hungry Self*

In every woman's life, crossroads on the journey from girlhood to adulthood are marked by rites of passage. Sometimes these rites involve elaborate rituals, from sweet sixteen parties and "coming out" balls to wedding ceremonies. On such festive occasions, friends and family gather around to celebrate the transition from one phase of life to the next. Sometimes, transitional phases are less formally acknowledged, but informal rites of passage—which may include everything from buying a first bra to accepting a first date to heading off to college—can be as emotionally momentous as the most decorous public event.

Such turning points are psychically significant not only for maturing women but also for their mothers. This phenomenon is nothing new. For countless centuries women have begun their menses, married, borne children, cared for the elderly, and watched their own children begin the cycle of life all over again. And for countless centuries each step on life's journey has affected the bonds between generations.

But something is different now.

In centuries past the traditions of life that surrounded a mother and her daughter were defined by and large by social custom and usually went unquestioned. Everyone knew pretty much what was called for at each stage of life and what to expect. Moreover, when daughters grew up, they did not tend to grow away from their mothers. They likely remained in the same community and lived the same kind of life as their mothers and grandmothers before them. As a result, a maturing woman and her mother, while slackening certain aspects of their bond at each successive stage of life, would forge new ties—ties secured by years and years of socially sanctioned convention and conduct. Mother would serve as guide and counselor as her daughter confronted each of life's stages.

Nowadays, however, more than in any other time, women are able to avail themselves of innumerable options when it comes to choosing the direction of their lives. For many daughters, growing up may well mean moving away from mother's mode of life, abiding by different "rules," and setting radically different goals. Often it may involve literally moving away, perhaps hundreds or thousands of miles from the place where Mother makes her home.

Doubtless there has been some emotional upheaval involved in a daughter's rites of passage since the dawn of family life itself because change, no matter how happily anticipated, is invariably attended by a degree of anxiety. Now, however, the extreme nature of the change virtually assures that life's crossroads will be laden with mines.

How so?

During the stressful times of rites of passage, your mother's Maternal Style will likely be accentuated. Thus, a Merged Mother may become more oblivious to boundaries, a Hypercritical Mother more judgmental, and a Competitive Mother more resentful at exactly the moments you take a step away from the nest. And as we noted in the last chapter, the voice of your Internal Mother will likely grow louder and more exaggerated. Consequently, all kinds of relationship struggles and intrapsychic struggles will arise.

What's a daughter to do? As she moves forward in life, part of her longs, understandably, for liberation from Mother's purview. But as we noted in the first chapter, total emancipation from Mother, or at least from Mother's influence, is not only impossible to achieve but fundamentally undesirable because daughters, deep down, still want Mother's emotional endorsement.

This chapter is designed to help daughters navigate through life's transitional phases in order to achieve a comfortable balance of emancipation and support. For while one's relationship with Mother during successive rites of passage will never be completely stress-free, a daughter's frustration level can often be reduced if she understands what is happening, why it is happening, and what can be done to ameliorate the level of anxiety involved.

THE ANXIETY AXIOM

In chapter two we learned about the developmental transitions of infancy, the stages of separation and individuation. During those phases, you may recall, a mother should, ideally, be emotionally available to assist in her child's quest for both freedom and protection. She should encourage her daughter to explore the world but help her "refuel" by offering encouragement and reassurance. Practically speaking, striking the optimum balance between these dual maternal duties is difficult: In truth, of course, separation and individuation are never-ending processes, and each successive rite of passage in life drives this fact home—both in your mother and in you. You probably already know what we mean.

Did your mother weep when you boarded a school bus for the very first time? Was she unnerved when you made the change from anklets to stockings, necessitating shaving your legs? Did she perhaps neglect the requisite discussion of menstruation because she could not quite believe you were old enough to have such a thing happen to you? Did the announcement of your first date with a boy prompt her to proclaim that she wouldn't sleep a wink until you returned?

And what about you? Were you keenly aware of Mother's reluctance to part from you? Did her misgivings about your development make you uneasy? Did you tremble with trepidation when you asked for permission to wear pantyhose? Or recoil with embarrassment when you told your mother you needed to borrow a tampon? Did you ever inwardly question your ability to take a new step in life just as your mother questioned it outwardly?

Chances are that at these pivotal moments in your life both you and your mother fell prey to anxiety. That's understandable. There is nothing like the unknown and the untried to marshal anxiety's forces. And there is nothing like anxiety to blur the vision and cloud the judgment of all of us, mothers and daughters alike.

For mothers, anxiety surrounding a daughter's rites of passage may take the form of separation anxiety—a keen sense of loss and abandonment. It may also take the form of anticipatory anxiety—a sense of hyperresponsibility for the way her child's life "turns out." For many mothers it is not easy to come to terms with the fact that the years when she was able to "possess" her daughter, even a little, represented but a brief prerogative—one to be returned to the child at the earliest possible moment.

For daughters, some rite-of-passage-related stress may evolve from a sense of guilt in leaving Mother behind especially if a forward step for the daughter involves surpassing her mother in some actual way. The strain in a young, accomplished woman's voice as she informs her homemaker mother of her latest on-the-job promotion exposes the tension between her satisfaction in her own success and her anguish at calling her mother's life into question in any way. As we have already seen, daughters often manifest a kind of hypervigilance when it comes to their mother's emotional reactions. Consequently, the mere possibility of causing Mother discomfort can make any woman of any age extremely uncomfortable.

Anxiety connected to rites of passage may also be attributable to feelings of self-doubt on the part of both mothers and daughters. A daughter's utterly natural sense of insecurity in the face of new situations may be aggravated if Mother—the original role model with whom she has identified for so long and so strongly—never confronted such a situation herself. ("How can Mother know which law school I should go to?" a daughter may wonder. "She never went to college!") Likewise, Mother may feel inadequate if she believes she is ill-equipped to advise her daughter at some critical juncture or shepherd her through a circumstance she herself has never encountered.

With so many opportunities for anxiety to spring up, it is inevitable that transition will elicit conflict between daughters and mothers. Before we can discover how to diminish or at least weather the conflict, we must discuss another element that enters the rite-of-passage equation: Whenever we have anxiety, we have something else that goes along with it—defenses.

WHAT ARE DEFENSES?

Defenses are the mind's way of attempting to cope with a flood of anxiety. Unconsciously and automatically we find ways of erecting defenses to mediate between our private fears and the demands of social propriety. Defenses may allow us to "save face" in front of others and to comply with our own "observing ego," the part of us that stresses appropriate behavior over irrational impulse. Defenses may allow us to function appropriately in the world when we feel like falling apart.

Somewhat paradoxically, defenses oftentimes enable us to negotiate reality by skewing that reality. For example, we manage to tolerate some anxiety-provoking situations by "not noticing" their more upsetting aspects. When someone gets through the nerve-wracking chore of paying monthly credit card bills by meeting minimum payments while "blocking out" or excluding from consciousness the full balance due on the bottom line, he is illustrating a defense of *selective inattention.*

Defenses, by definition, involve some self-deception, which is not always a negative thing. As Daniel Goleman points out in his book on the subject, *Vital Lies, Simple Truths,* some measure of self-deception is essential to our psychological existence. We certainly don't want to be "defenseless" in the face of anxiety! We all require some psychic armor to keep overwhelming stress at bay.

But just as defenses can sometimes be helpful to individuals, they can sometimes do damage—especially in the area of interpersonal relationships. Sometimes, for example, in the throes of defending against anxiety, a mother may be unable to talk about or face up to what's actually going on in her daughter's life. She may be unable to give her a daughter a boost when she needs it most—for example, when she is going off to school, moving away from home, or getting married.

In the remainder of this chapter we'll show you some of the most common frustrating defenses mothers employ during their daughters' rites of passage. These defenses often baffle and infuriate daughters but, like most things, they may not be so daunting once they are understood. We'll also offer you some mature defenses of your own to help you get through your transitional times and move onward and upward without alienating your mother. Remember, it's *emancipation* with *support* you're after.

Bear in mind: The defenses and rites of passage we will be exploring are linked "randomly" in the sense that any configuration of defenses may manifest itself during a time of great stress. As you interact with your mother, remain open and aware while you observe the repertoire of defenses both of you tend to use.

First, we'll look at a protracted period that includes numerous rites of passage for a daughter. Even if you are far beyond this phase, stay tuned because there is something to be learned from it that can be helpful at successive stages of life.

ADOLESCENCE: MOTHER AND DAUGHTERS FACE OFF

The years between girlhood and womanhood offer a plethora of opportunities for mothers and daughters to frustrate and even infuriate each other. This extended transitional phase encompasses within its parameters countless "firsts"—from the aforementioned first bras and first dates to first cars, first jobs, first trips with friends, and so on—and each creates an excellent forum for a mother-daughter rift.

To a daughter, each new endeavor and accomplishment primarily signifies motion toward adulthood. To a mother, on the other hand, each one may symbolize primarily a tearing asunder of the old order of things. Both perceptions are correct, of course. To some extent "in with the new" means, ipso facto, "out with the old." In such a climate of continual change, anxiety can sprout up with weedlike tenacity and speed.

During these years that are, by definition, difficult ones, daughters may express desires for things they never acknowledged wanting before. They want freedom to make their own decisions and to come and go independently of their parents. Most important, they want their maturity recognized. When these new desires and expectations are thwarted by Mother, as they invariably will be at some points along the way, even the most compliant girl can turn, seemingly overnight, into a defiant teenager. And even the most loyal daughter may switch her allegiance abruptly, heatedly declaring to friends, classmates, teachers, neighbors, and perhaps even to her siblings and/or father that her mother should be outfitted with a broomstick and a pointed hat.

Mothers of adolescent daughters, as confounded and enraged as their metamorphosing offspring, may be heard loudly lamenting the fact that their formerly attentive and cooperative daughters have obviously struck some sort of pact with the devil. "I don't understand what's happened," they bemoan. "She never listens anymore. I can't get any respect in my own house. She only wants to be with her friends. It's as if she's embarrassed by me."

Inevitably, the sideswipes give way to head-on confrontations. But no matter what the ostensible catalyst is for the quarrel—the eyeliner, the short skirt, the boyfriend—mother-daughter arguments coalesce around a nucleus of consistent rite-of-passage anxiety themes, such as:

MOTHER: Where have you been? I lent you the car, and you thank me by coming home late. I was worried sick!

DAUGHTER: I'm only forty-five minutes late. You never let me do anything! You don't trust me.

MOTHER: Don't talk to me in that tone, young lady. I'm still your mother.

DAUGHTER: You want to lock me away so I'll never see my friends!

MOTHER: How can I trust you if you act like this?

Under all the recriminations, of course, the daughter is expressing a desire for more autonomy while the mother is expressing a desire to reinstate the status quo that existed before hormones and high school. But saying "Mother, you must let me go" and "Darling, please come back" would simply be too painful and too threatening. Instead, angry thrusts and parries are used as a defense mechanism.

But is using anger as a defense mechanism healthy or unhealthy?

All in all, anger is a necessary part of adolescent rites of passage for both mothers and daughters. As Sonya Rhodes and Josleen Wilson put it in *Surviving Family Life*, "Adolescents use anger to liberate themselves emotionally from the intense bonds of affection and dependency that bind them to their parents." Mothers of adolescents, it should be added, use anger to divert their attention from the poignant sense of sorrow they experience as their daughters' growing independence becomes a reality.

Defenses help us to cope with reality without feeling overwhelmed, and defensive anger assists mothers and daughters to traverse the adolescent battleground without becoming shell-shocked.

Often, in the post-adolescent years, defenses invoked by mothers and daughters will be more subtle and thus more complex than simple shouting matches. We'll examine some of these more "sophisticated" defenses next. But remember, with every rite of passage you incur throughout life, there will be potential for anger to be invoked as a defense and for fiery arguments to transpire. Those quarrels will not be pleasant, but they may not be so enervating if you remind yourself of the purpose they serve. Anger can have a hidden agenda that actually eases pain and disappointment at parting and lessens the sense of bewilderment which inevitably accompanies the new.

GOING TO COLLEGE: NEGOTIATING FAREWELLS

Let's move a bit forward in time to a rite of passage that commonly occurs as the turmoil of adolescence draws to a close. After years of following the trajectory of their anger side by side, many mothers and daughters are faced with a situation that calls for increased distance between them—in a physical as well as a psychic sense.

In the summer that marks the passage from high school to college, eager young women begin to pack up their blue jeans, their T-shirts, and their expectations about life away from Mom's apron strings, readying themselves to take on the identities of undergraduate women. In many households where such preparations are underway, the din of adolescent battle subsides somewhat. Such shaky truces are often punctuated by skirmishes, each flare-up engendering under-the-breath muttering in which Daughter declares, "I'm glad I'm getting out of here," and Mother implores the Fates to please hurry and grant her some "peace and quiet" at last. Underneath all this defensive intoning, of course, is apprehension, perhaps even alarm.

As autumn looms closer and closer, Mother's vague defensiveness may give rise to behaviors that seriously thwart and frustrate a daughter. To some extent, of course, her Maternal Style will influence what form her defenses take.

In the following recollection, shared by twenty-one-year-old Patricia, now a college senior, we'll witness a rite-of-passage defense frequently—though not exclusively—employed by Competitive Mothers. Here is what Patricia recalls of her relationship with her mother during her pre-freshman summer.

I was more and more thrilled with each passing day, but nervous, too, of course, about what college would bring. I remember a letter arriving with the name of my new roommate. She was from a small midwestern town, and I was a city slicker. Would we get along? I went on and on about it, but my mother didn't seem to want to speculate. In fact, she didn't really want to discuss my departure at all, except when we ran into one of her friends, and then she would always say how proud she was that I was going to an Ivy League school. She made a big deal out of the Ivy League thing, even though she herself had gone to a local community college.

Whenever it came time to talk about specifics, such as going to the bank to arrange for my dorm deposit and spending money, she put it off. Also, she couldn't seem to remember the exact date I was leaving.

Finally, she proved just how forgetful she was about that. She went out and bought opera tickets for her and my father for the very day they were supposed to drive me to freshman orientation. When my father asked her to exchange them, she said she couldn't. The performances were sold out, she insisted. It ended up that she went to the opera with a friend, and my father drove me to school by himself.

I told my father it was fine that it was just the two of us, especially since it was his alma mater I was attending. Part of me *was* glad, but I was upset and disappointed, too. How could Mom forget the most important day of my life?

The defense mechanism that allows Patricia's mother to "forget" is known as *passive-aggressive behavior*. Faced with a situation that she found threatening (her daughter was not only going away but going to the prestigious Ivy League school where Dad had gone and she herself had not), she unconsciously used indirect measures to deflect anxiety and to avoid assuming an overt competitive stance. Her procrastination and denial she attributes to absentmindedness, which is at least socially acceptable. What would not be acceptable, to her way of thinking, would be to admit to herself that she fears her daughter is going somewhere where she can never follow. Even though such fears are commonplace and understandable, her style is such that she defends against them.

In any situation where a rite of passage has the potential to propel a daughter "past" a Competitive Mother who still thinks she and her child are running in the same race, passive-aggressive behavior may materialize. So what is a daughter to do?

If she is unaware of the defense that is operative, she may, as Patricia did, simply reenact an old, familiar emotional scenario. She may flip-flop between feelings of furious indignation and mournful longing toward her mother. She may seek solace in commiserating with her father about the failings of her mother, reinforcing a pattern that in the past has only served to exacerbate mother-daughter rivalry.

If Patricia knew then what we know now, she might have helped precipitate a different outcome by utilizing the three basic skills: *being realistic* (that is, acknowledging that her mother was bound to have some mixed feelings about her foray into academia), *prioritizing* (deciding what form of support she most wanted from Mother and setting her sights on attaining it), and *being generous*. As we've already learned, being generous with a Competitive Mother can take the form of bringing her into the family loop and praising her for the part she has played in her daughter's accomplishments. Remember, a Competitive Mother is uncomfortable unless she feels she had something to do with her child's success. Since she probably did, a daughter can be "generous" simply by acknowledging that fact.

Imagine Patricia and her mother had had a dialogue like this:

DAUGHTER: Mom, I know how much you were looking forward to seeing *Carmen*, but I was hoping you would come along to help me set up my dorm room. No one can whip a place into shape like you!

MOTHER: Oh, you and your dad will do just fine. He knows his way around campus, and he can introduce you to everyone.

DAUGHTER: Yes, but I'm really more concerned with getting settled, and Dad's no match for you when it comes to that. Dad can help carry my cartons, but he doesn't know a thing about organizing shelves. You've always helped me get things together. If it wasn't for you, I'd still be in high school trying to find my lost algebra homework.

Now Patricia's mother has some real incentive to relax her passive-aggressive defense. Her daughter made her feel needed and appreciated, and she pointed out that Dad, for all his helpfulness, couldn't fill Mother's unique role.

Along with all this, Mother has ample psychological room to change her mind about the opera because her daughter did not attack her defense but joined it instead. ("I know how much you were looking forward to seeing *Carmen*.") This is a very important point. Had Patricia said, "Going to the opera is just an *excuse!*", her mother would have felt exposed and vulnerable. She may have felt even more compelled to stay home because changing her plans would have been an "admission of guilt." But by letting her mother's defensive stance go unchallenged, Patricia enabled her mother to soften it.

In the foregoing example are lessons for *anyone* whose Mother seems to be using a passive-aggressive defense during an important rite of passage. Keep in mind that your mother's noncooperation, her procrastination and the forgetfulness are probably masking deep feelings of anxiety at physically losing you and at the loss of a heretofore shared identity. Since she feels her maternal footing is slipping as you glide into the next phase of your life, you must be careful not to knock her off balance any further. Understanding the feelings behind the passive-aggressive behavior is the key to responding compassionately and to enabling you to garner emancipation with support in spite of it.

Before we leave the scenario of departing for college, let's use this particular rite of passage to illustrate how the Internal Mother might behave at such a juncture. No matter how successfully one negotiates farewells with one's mother, the Mother Within will accompany you on your college journey, as she will on subsequent journeys, whether you like it or not.

Here's how Yvette, now twenty, recalls her first weeks as an eighteen-year-old undergraduate:

> I remember feeling completely confused and inept. I couldn't do anything right. I kept getting lost on campus and arriving late for classes. I always seemed to have read the wrong pages in my textbooks. My roommate ignored me and hung out with girls she knew from back home. I felt as if my mother had been right, I should never have gone away to school. I wasn't mature enough. I wasn't ready. There were plenty of good colleges back in Atlanta, and here I was all alone in Virginia. Ridiculous!

Every time I had another mishap or disappointment those first weeks, I heard my mother's voice saying "You can't take care of yourself, and you're so far from home. You'll be back." You see, she didn't seem to think I could get along by myself, and she made this prediction once when we were arguing about my applying to out-of-town schools.

I almost did go back home. Once I even started to pack. But I pulled myself together, sat down, and made a list of all the reasons I could get along. I'd had good grades in high school, even though my mother said I could do better, and I'd had plenty of friends, even though my mother didn't approve of most of them. I was still the same person, and so what if I was feeling a little overwhelmed? That was probably par for the course. I'd get used to the mazelike classroom buildings, and I'd leave extra time until I grew more accustomed to the lay of the land. I would organize my schoolwork. I would go to a few mixers and meet some people. I'm friendly. I told myself that soon I'd be having a great time and more freedom than I'd ever known in my life.

At first I went along on sheer willpower, gritting my teeth when the alarm clock rang each day. But after a while I found my niche and didn't feel like fleeing anymore. I still heard my mother's voice, of course, but I didn't have to obey everything it said. It was as though a spell was broken.

During her period of adjustment to college, Yvette turned up the volume on the voice of her Hypercritical Mother Within. That's understandable. These weeks away from home marked the first significant length of time she ever spent physically separated from her mother. Replaying her mother's opinions in her own mind, no matter how discouraging those opinions might be, was a way of maintaining a connection. Yvette's introject wreaked havoc. She actually began to sabotage herself, as if to prove her mother's point. She'd be back, all right, if she kept this up.

Yet, intuitively, Yvette saved herself from retreat and surrender. She mothered herself in benevolent ways (which leads us to believe, by the way, that her real-life mother must have given her some positive, loving messages along with judgmental ones). She comforted and encouraged herself, and she allowed herself to have feelings. ("So what if I was feeling a little overwhelmed? That was probably par for the course.")

In addition to all this, she instinctively employed what can be a very useful and mature defense in the presence of a nay-saying introject. Yvette called upon the defense *anticipation*. She bolstered her self-confidence by visualizing the successes and pleasures that lay ahead of her, rather than dwelling on the confusion and irritations of the day.

Whenever a Hypercritical introject or any punitive introject threatens to cause you to retreat from a rite of passage, you, too, can resist turning back by using as many of your Circuit Breaker strategies as necessary. Comfort yourself or call your champion for a pep talk to get the support you need. And think ahead. Allow yourself to envision all the positive things that might result from your emergence on the other side of your current transitional phase.

Change brings uneasiness, but it also brings expansion. Indeed, in the Chinese language the same calligraphic character that denotes "crisis" also denotes "opportunity." Reminding yourself of this and allowing yourself to indulge in futuristic scenarios in which you not only survive but also thrive can alleviate some of the pressure in the present. With *positive anticipation* at your service, you can conjure up a good deal of your own support to help you through.

MOVING AWAY: A NEST OF ONE'S OWN

In most cases, of course, going to college does not constitute a full-fledged flight from the maternal nest. Undergraduates still tend to spend holiday periods and perhaps even summers at home. They are often financially dependent on their parents as well, a fact that tends to reinforce emotional dependence. But in our society it is not uncommon for a recent college graduate to decide she wants to live permanently in a faraway place.

Perhaps she wants to do this for career reasons. After all,

it's hard to commute to Wall Street or Capitol Hill from Duluth. Or perhaps she wants to do this for romantic reasons. If the man she loves relishes wide-open spaces, Chicago may seem less compelling than it once did. Or perhaps she wants to move away just because she feels like it, because she wants to reinvent her possibilities, satisfy her curiosity, sample the joys and challenges of new places and new people.

The first two scenarios are often difficult for a mother to accept with equanimity, the third nearly impossible. A mother whose daughter opts to move away for no apparent reason may not only experience a sense of loss but also feel some sense of disgrace. With no legitimate reason to validate this inexplicable rite of passage, how will she justify it to herself and to others?

If your mother has a Controlling Style, your opting to move away permanently may feel like an especially acute disaster. It can imbue in her a sense of powerlessness that she is not accustomed to and most certainly does not appreciate. In this situation one often sees another maternal defense swing into action. Twenty-three-year-old Gina did.

A year after receiving a nursing degree, Gina chose to leave her hometown of Eugene, Oregon, and relocate to Minneapolis. She knew Minneapolis offered abundant opportunities for anyone in the medical profession, and, besides, she wanted a city that offered more in the way of cultural events than Eugene. But neither of these was her driving impetus. In truth, Gina would have moved to any number of cities because she wanted to emerge from under the wing of her Controlling Mother and felt that, even though it would not solve all of her mother-related frustrations, one way to begin was to put some distance between them. It was time, she felt, to start claiming more responsibility for her own choices.

For months Gina withstood her mother's tirades as she finalized her plans. Though her mother attempted to be more controlling than ever, Gina set *limits* on the amount of information she gave her and on the advice she sought from her. She utilized *silence* while her mother espoused all the reasons she simply couldn't go. ("You don't know anyone." "You'll be so lonely." "It's freezing in Minneapolis, and you know how easily you catch cold.") She even came up with some funny and fabulous jests and *creative non sequiturs* to deflect the energy of some maternal histrionics. Nevertheless, moving day found her mother in a rapidly accelerating state of desperation. Gina recalls:

It was 8 A.M. and the phone rang. I thought it was the movers, but it was Mom. She sounded totally distraught. She told me that her back was out and that she could hardly move. She said she needed me to go over and put her to bed, that she couldn't possibly manage by herself. What about Dad? He was already at the office, an hour and a half's commute away, and, besides, she said I was the only one who knew how to set up the traction and rub her back properly.

Well, this was not the first time her back had gone into spasms. I knew she wasn't in terminal danger, and I was tempted to enlist someone else to assist her, but then she sobbed that she had probably thrown out her back when she helped me pack my dishes. Actually, she'd insisted on *repacking* my dishes "the right way" after I'd already done it. I felt horribly guilty anyhow, so I called the movers and told them to hold off for a few hours. Then a few hours turned into a few days. After this episode I reorganized the entire move and—guess what—my mother's back went out again, and again.

As the correlation between Mother's aches and pains and her own departure grew indisputably evident, Gina came to suspect that something other than Mother's back was awry. Like many Controlling Mothers, hers had opted for the defense of *hypochondriasis* to up the emotional ante surrounding her daughter's rite of passage. Hypochondriasis enables such mothers to translate their anxiety and bereavement at their daughters' "desertion," as well as their reproachfulness toward their daughters, into physical complaints.

In such cases a mother's physical symptoms may give her a resurgence of the power she fears relinquishing. Indeed, part of that power lies in the ambiguous and enigmatic nature of her symptoms.

Is Mother's ailment, so incredibly timed to coincide with a daughter's departure, real or not? With complaints such as back pain, headaches, and other sundry "spells," it can be hard to know. Indeed, what constitutes real? Symptoms may well feel real to the ailing mother and look real to the observing daughter, even if there seems to be no purely physiological basis for them. (How heavy were those dishes anyhow?)

The symptoms that result from hypochondriasis may be psychosomatic but, contrary to what many people think, this term does not imply that such aches and pains are imaginary but rather that the psyche has played a primary role in generating a bodily affliction. Someone engaged in manifesting psychosomatic symptoms may be doing so at a completely unconscious level. At a conscious level, on the other hand, someone like Gina's mother may have thoroughly convinced herself that rearranging her daughter's dishes did cause her back to go out.

Again, what's a daughter to do? Obviously, if Mother's complaints seem even remotely plausible, one must respond by arranging for immediate medical consultation. But what if the doctor maintains it is nothing serious, a nonevent? Should a daughter continue to alter her plans for as long as Mother's alleged infirmities exist? Suppose the symptoms are ongoing or recurrent? Surely she cannot be expected to stay and minister to Mother forever. Or can she? If Gina's mother had had her way, one suspects that would have been the outcome.

If you find yourself in a situation similar to Gina's, that is, with a Controlling Mother—or, for that matter, any type of mother—whose physical complaints repeatedly coincide with your attempts to separate from her, be *realistic*. Recognize that in many cases a mother simply cannot let her daughter move away without attempting to forestall the impending loss. *Prioritize*. You want to leave, but you also want to go without feeling like a heel. *Be generous*. Pause to help and do what you're able. (You really must if you want to feel comfortable about your rite of passage.) But then carry on with your own life.

Above all, in coping with hypochondriasis, we especially suggest that you remember and call upon your *joining* and *mirroring* capabilities. Validate your mother in whatever way you can. For example:

MOTHER: You can't leave today. My back is out again.

DAUGHTER: I know it's very painful even though the doctor say it's not serious. I'll call Mrs. Weston (Mother's next-door neighbor). She can come in and help fix you lunch so you can rest until you feel better.

MOTHER: I don't want Mrs. Weston. She's half senile. How will she find her way around the kitchen? You're the only one who knows where everything is! Can't you just delay this move of yours a few more days?

DAUGHTER: I would love to continue to help, Mom. I know this will be especially hard because I'm moving away, and you'll miss my help and I'll miss helping. But I can't change my plans at this late date. You are so strong, though, I know you'll be on your feet in no time.

MOTHER: How can you go? You know I rely on you at times like this. What's another day or two when I need you?

DAUGHTER: It's going to be hard on me, too, when I have problems and you're not right there to help me as you've always been. I guess we'll both have some adjusting to do. We'll have to commiserate on the phone about how we're doing.

Earlier, we stressed that it's important never to directly challenge Mother's defense. In instances of hypochondriasis, this translates as: *Never contradict your mother's perception of her symptoms.* Recognize that your mother probably is experiencing the sense of physical pain she claims. And even if she is dramatizing that aspect of her suffering, you know she is in psychical pain. Her symptoms are not a manipulative trick. They are her defense, her armor. And you don't need to feel guilty about going on with your life once you've paused to be generous.

Give your mother the support she needs so that, down the road, she can muster up some support for your emancipation. It may be late in arriving, but you will have sown the seeds that make it possible for maternal support to grow. Remember, too, that your budding personal emancipation reveals itself in the fact that you have followed through with your plans.

Needless to say, moving away, like going to college, also means taking along one's Internal Mother. As you settle in to new surroundings, your Miniature Mom will doubtless be your unseen, albeit frequently heard, companion. Your internal representation of her and the way you manage it will affect the ease or uneasiness with which you adjust to new surroundings and to this new phase of your life.

Consider the daughter of a Chronically Worried Mother who despite her real-life mother's continual calls to caution— or, more precisely, *because* of them—has mustered the goodly amount of defiance necessary to relocate to a distant city. Even after negotiating land mine–laden parting scenes and arriving at her new home, she will have to contend with misgivings that approximate and perhaps even exaggerate her mother's uneasiness.

"How can I trust the superintendent in my apartment building? Suppose he uses the set of keys I give him to come in and burglarize the place."

"Why did I invite that guy at work over for coffee? I don't really know him well. What if he's dangerous? I'd better call off the whole thing."

"I must have been crazy to move to Los Angeles where you have to drive on freeways. I don't know how all these exit ramps work. This is hopeless. I'd better take buses."

In a state of panic she may question her judgment at making this major move and consider changing her mind. In such an event, a daughter must remember to check for warning signals that indicate her Mother Within is calling the shots. Here, *heightened emotions* and *excessive concerns* are tip-offs, as is *rapidly plummeting self-confidence.*

At these moments it's wise to initiate a Believe-It-Or-Not Checkup and consider each concern individually. Does this young woman really believe that her superintendent is a thief? Probably not. Nevertheless, it may be wise to think twice before giving out keys to her apartment. She can confer with the other tenants about his reputation. Does she really think her date is dangerous? Probably not. Still, she can amend their plans and meet him for coffee in a public place. Finally, is getting around Los Angeles by bus a practical plan? Alas, it is not, but she could drive very carefully while she acclimates to freeways. Soon she'll get the hang of it.

In calmly examining her concerns in this fashion, this grown daughter does not give short shrift to the part of herself that has been wired for prudence for many years by the Mother Electrician. She does not engage in *reaction formation* that might cause her to "throw the baby out with the bath water." But she does draw a line at excessive worry accompanied by paralysis. She's not going to cut herself off from the rest of the world because Mother encouraged her to play it safe.

Still, she'll need to deal with those nagging worries that resonate in her head even though she's decided not to act on them. She should have a little "chat" with her Miniature Mom and acknowledge the loving *intent* behind the *content* of her cautions. She should consider calling her champion for a pep talk that will help her gain perspective and restore her fortitude.

In addition to all this, she could implement a mature defense mechanism known as *suppression*. Suppression involves a conscious decision to postpone focusing on a particular impulse or conflict. You probably have used it instinctively many times already.

We like to call this the Scarlett O'Hara defense. As *Gone with the Wind* fans will recall, the determined and spirited southern belle managed to survive the burning of Atlanta, the devastation of her beloved Tara, and even the loss of Rhett Butler by telling herself she would think about it tomorrow. What she meant was that she would tackle her problems when she was calm enough to deal with them effectively.

Suppression allows one to take things one day at a time by putting redundant anxieties on hold. It is a very effective way to defend against the excessive concerns of a Chronically Worried Mother Within or, for that matter, with messages from *any* inhibiting maternal introject, long enough to allow oneself to settle into a new mode of living.

The daughter who moved to Los Angeles could, for example, postpone any decision about freeway driving versus buses. In the meanwhile, she can drive alternate local routes and think about those daunting exit ramps tomorrow. There are many adjustments she will have to make as a result of her move, and many choices. She certainly does not have to overwhelm herself by making them all at once.

One caveat: To ensure you are using your "think about it tomorrow" defense to your best advantage, be certain to deal with the issue you've deferred once your acute anxiety has subsided. You will continue to receive signals from your psyche that let you know you have placed an important issue on hold. As you wait for the hundredth traffic light to turn green en route to your office, you will have fleeting thoughts about negotiating the freeways after all and saving time. Those thoughts will be your ongoing reminder that you and your Mother Within have some unfinished business. One day you will attend to it. One day you will want to try your hand at those exit ramps.

GETTING MARRIED: A NEW ALLIANCE, A NEW ALLEGIANCE

Of all the rights of passage in a daughter's life, none since the cumulative trials of adolescence offers as many opportunities for Sturm und Drang as a wedding. Certainly, some mothers slide gracefully into new ways of relating to a daughter when she takes on a new role as someone's wife and life mate. But a great many do not. Indeed, from the moment impending nuptials are announced until the last forkful of wedding cake is consumed, a degree of intergenerational discord is more often the rule than the exception.

Weddings bring to the fore any dissimilarities in attitude and priorities that may already exist between a daughter and her mother. Endless skirmishes involving everything from appropriate table settings to whether or not Aunt Winifred gets to sing "I Love You Truly" become more than irksome differences of opinion, they become symbolic expressions of a major contest of will.

Most important, weddings underscore the fact that mothers and daughters are moving inexorably from unity toward separateness. It is not surprising, therefore, that in the months preceding their weddings, brides-to-be and their mothers may heatedly reenact old familiar run-ins reminiscent of their most tempestuous battles of yore.

With all the anxiety that usually attends wedding planning anyhow, it is easy to see how a daughter might let frustration overwhelm her and readily slip back into the traps of the Mother Maze. Make no mistake, this is a very common occurrence, but a daughter will enjoy her wedding a great deal more if she can manage to use her skills and strategies to obtain emancipation with support.

One of the Maternal Styles that makes this hardest for a daughter to achieve is the Merged Style. Naturally enough, no one is likely to experience the diminishment of mother-daughter unity as profoundly as Merged Mothers, and it is likely no one will employ frustrating defenses as persistently as they will in the face of a daughter's "defection."

Instinctively, their daughters seem to know this. Countless women have confided to us the enveloping sense of dread with which they broke the news of their engagement to their Merged Mothers. One of the most common reactions seems to be the one described by thirty-one-year-old Lila:

> I wanted to tell my mother the news that my boyfriend and I had decided to marry before I told anyone else. I figured I should do it in private so she could get a grip on herself before we shared the news with Dad and my brother and sister. I dropped by when I knew she would be home alone and sat down at the kitchen table. "Mom," I said, "I have something to tell you. I'm engaged to be married."
>
> The first thing she said was, "Who are you marrying?" I told her it was Steven, of course. I'd been seeing Steven for years. But again she said, "*Who?*" as if she'd never heard of him.
>
> After I reminded her that this was the man who had had holiday dinners with us for the past two years, she seemed to recall him vaguely. But then she said, "Well, he's still in medical school. You can't afford it. Where will you live? Don't be ridiculous!" and on and on. She suggested a nice, long engagement, like another two years, and was appalled when I said we wanted to be married by Christmas, which was four months away. She said we'd never be able to make arrangements in time. Even later, when I told the rest of my family the plans, Mom sniffed and said, "Well, they'll see. If you want a nice wedding in that period, it simply can't be done."

If you have been girding your loins for a similar discussion, know that your mother may also employ the chosen defense of Lila's mother—the defense of *denial*—in order to cope with the anxieties your potential loss has elicited in her. Denial means exactly what it sounds like: One way we self-deceptive humans have of dealing with a stress-inducing situation is simply to pretend to ourselves and insist to others that it is not happening. Denial is different from the more mature defense of suppression in that it does not involve a conscious choice to defer dealing with a perceived problem or conflict. Rather, it incites a fantasy that there is no problem or conflict.

If your mother shifts into denial mode, you may feel very disheartened. Chances are that if you and your mother have shared a great closeness, you really want her to share in the joy of your wedding. It can feel very hurtful if she is loathe to acknowledge the source of your happiness. How can you enlist some support?

We suggest *setting limits* from the very first wedding-related conversation. You don't have to play along with Mother's script. You can set the agenda for the conversation by enforcing various kinds of boundaries. For example:

MOTHER: Who are you marrying?
DAUGHTER: Oh, Mom, how funny you are! Anyway, Steven and I have thought a lot about it, and we'd like to have the wedding before Christmas.

Here you are setting an *information limit*. You are fighting the temptation to describe the man you are about to marry, with whom she is already well acquainted. Obviously, she does not require such information. You are also invoking the word *we* at the earliest opportune moment, which signals to Mother's unconscious level of receptivity that there will, in fact, be a dissipation of her sense of her merger with you. Still, Mother continues:

MOTHER: You can't get married so soon. You need a long engagement to plan a big wedding. I've always dreamed of what your wedding would be like. The bridesmaids would wear lavender—I love lavender! And I would wear a deeper shade of purple that would match the flowers in your bouquet. Also . . .

DAUGHTER: What a lovely image, Mom, but Steven and I
thought we'd have a simple ceremony without
bridesmaids or ushers. I'm not sure what I'll wear
yet or if I'll carry a traditional bouquet, but I do
think you'll look wonderful in purple if that's
what you'd like to wear. By the way, do you think
Uncle Phil will be able to fly in from Denver?
We haven't seen Uncle Phil in ages.

Here you are setting an *advice limit*, being gracious about
Mother's opinions but not deferring to them. You are also gently
replacing Mother's merged image of you and she as the "stars"
of the wedding with an image of you and your fiancé. Finally,
you're invoking a *creative non sequitur* to redirect the flow of
conversation. Nevertheless, Mother has an ace up her sleeve:

MOTHER: Don't be silly! You're probably just saying you
don't want a big wedding because you can't afford
it. I'll pay for the reception if you'll just wait
until we can do it right!

DAUGHTER: That's awfully generous of you, Mom. I am
really very grateful. But a simple wedding is more
our style.

Here, of course, you are setting *gift limits* because it's clear
your mother's largesse comes with emotional strings attached.
However, you are not forgetting to express your gratitude, and
you are using diplomacy while you decline her offer.

If you gently but consistently set limits, chances are the reality
of your marriage will gradually permeate the consciousness of
your Merged Mother. But now there's something else you may
need to be aware of. If you have siblings, your Merged Mother
may utilize a defense called *displacement* and shift the focus
of her attention, heretofore reserved mainly for you, onto one
of them.

You'll recall from our discussion of family dynamics that families seek homeostasis. Where one member's actions or attitudes tilt the balance of the family unit, a corresponding tilt in another direction may take place. As you prepare to take your wedding vows, therefore, your mother may begin doting on your kid sister in a way she never has before. This realignment may be disconcerting to you, to say the least. After all, you have been the one who has received the bulk of Mother's attention, and even though it's been somewhat stifling, it's been somewhat satisfying, too. Your resistances to increased autonomy may spring to the fore. You hate being displaced, which is completely understandable, and you may get inklings of yearning for your former maternal connection.

You may find yourself slipping a little bit, reverting to old, familiar behavior in an attempt to reinstate the status quo. You may solicit and take advice you don't really want, and accept gifts that leave you beholden. If you can, try another tack. Be *realistic*. Recognize that what you really need at this stressful juncture is support in the form of camaraderie and comfort. *Prioritize.* Know that to get this from Mother in the short run requires reinstating your symbiosis with her and potentially putting stress on your relationship with your fiancé. In the long run, however, you will feel more supported by a mother who has learned to respect you as a separate being. Consider whether your immediate needs can be met by someone else. Do you perhaps have an older sister who has successfully negotiated her own separation from Mother? If so, avail yourself of the sibling axis and give her a call. If this is not your situation, employ the tried-and-true strategy of calling a friend first whenever you feel the urge to merge with Mother. Lastly, *be generous.* Allow room for Mother's suggestions and wishes where you can without compromising what's important to you.

While the subject of marriage is still at hand, there is one more aspect to examine. Of course, you will not be surprised to learn that a daughter's Miniature Mom has much to say about her choice of mate as the ceremony draws near. Whatever Maternal Style your Mother Within is inclined toward, rest assured she will let her opinion be known. But perhaps one of the most difficult introjects to contend with when one is on the verge of marriage is that of the Pseudoperfect Mother.

The Pseudoperfect Mother, you'll recall, is extremely concerned with public opinion. Thus, her representative "voice" inside her daughter's psyche will likely enumerate a compendium of wedding etiquette "do's" and "don'ts" that would put Emily Post to shame. More deleterious to the bride's enthusiasm, however, will be the introject's probable listing of her fiancé's many shortcomings.

The status-oriented Pseudoperfect Mother will likely feel disappointed if her daughter does not marry "well," and to her this may have more to do with the groom's outer trappings than his inner qualities. If on the brink of wedlock you begin to have second thoughts based on doubts about your partner's financial prospects, social background, or even his physical appearance, do yourself a favor and employ your Circuit Breakers immediately to sort things out. A voice in your head may be saying "He's not good enough for you," but do you believe it or not? If it's your Mother Within talking, beware; she may well think this about any man with whom you become involved. And Pseudoperfect Mothers, with their need for things always to appear flawless and exemplary, are known for their unrealistic expectations. What man can measure up?

Last-minute jitters of this nature pose an especially tricky quandary for the daughter of a Pseudoperfect Mother because beneath the doubts about her mate may lurk deep doubts about her own ability to be intimate, to trust, to love, and to feel lovable. Indeed, if you have been raised by a Pseudoperfect Mother, a deeply intimate bond with your spouse may prove elusive unless you mindfully work at it, but you *can* work at it successfully.

Your very awareness of the realistic limits of your mother's emotional support may help you get what you need from your spouse—and give him what he needs in return. Remember, Mother's emotional limitations were likely a result of her unmet needs. You can overturn this legacy.

Marriage is your opportunity to start a new family. You now have a chance to redirect the future by consciously steering clear of quicksand on the path of the past. With your mature defenses such as *anticipation* and *suppression*, with empathy and humor at your service, with your compassion for your mother intact, and with your husband by your side, you can find emancipation in the truest sense.

All in all, the most important thing that can be said about any rite of passage is that daughters have *rights* during their passages. They have the right to change and grow, for that is what life is about. They have a right to feel excited, even elated, about new freedoms and about breaking away. But along with rights come obligations and responsibilities. Just as daughters are entitled to have all their feelings, so are their mothers entitled to have emotions, including anxiety, anger, and sadness. If they don't always handle these feelings to their daughters' liking, that's frustrating, to be sure, but it's also manageable.

Having said all that, we are still not entirely through with our rites-of-passage discussion. There is one occasion so momentous, so joyful, and yet so potentially stressful that we have reserved a separate chapter for it. Next, we will look at what may happen between a daughter and her mother when the daughter becomes a mother herself.

CHAPTER 8

❦

BECOMING A MOTHER

I am every woman who has ever honored her mother by becoming a mother.

Phyllis Chesler, *With Child*

Perhaps you are a twenty-two-year-old, recently married to your high school sweetheart, and for you family planning means letting nature take its course. Perhaps you are a high-powered executive who has deferred marriage until age forty, interested now in conceiving a child as soon as possible. Perhaps you have been wed for years, living a frenetic dual-career existence, and have now opted to make time for a baby in your busy life. Perhaps you are even a single woman who courageously chooses to raise a child alone.

The decision to embark on the path of motherhood is, in some ways, different for every woman, yet whatever your individual circumstances, the realization of this choice is a dramatic, life-transforming event. Many of its ramifications are impossible to grasp fully until this new life has actually arrived to share your life day by day. But from the moment the reality of pregnancy sets in, one's impending responsibility seems awesome. You who have always defined yourself as a daughter are now going to nurture and care for a child of your own.

And that small being will be as reliant on you, as bound to you, as influenced by you, as admiring of you, and perhaps—dare you think it?—even at times as frustrated by you as you are by your own mother. There's a concept to get your mind whirring!

Inevitably, in pondering what lies ahead, connections are made between what the future holds and how one's own mother has coped with motherhood until now. Did your mother convey joy and pride in her own maternal status, or did she seem burdened and harried much of the time? Was she able to find a comfortable balance of fulfillments in her own life, or did she live "for you" and thus through you? Did she encourage you to be yourself or to be only like her? What did she say about pregnancy itself? Did she thrive or simply endure? Did she say her delivery of you was relatively easy, or difficult but "nothing compared to the happy end," or "the most painful experience of my entire life"? Many of Mother's actions as well as many of her words will probably flash before you as you prepare to have your baby.

Also vying for a front-and-center spot in your psyche will be broader messages from your past, those hand-me-down generational mandates concerning the "rules" of motherhood. They may be: "A *mother should sacrifice everything*" or "A *child is a complete reflection of its mother*" or "A *mother must guard her child from the harms of the world at all costs*" or perhaps, more reasonably, "A *mother should guide her child safely through childhood but allow her freedom to make her own way in the world.*"

Regardless of what kind of impact her mother's attitude and her family's mandates has had on her own life, an expectant mother may consciously or unconsciously adopt both. For some women this appropriation of style and mandates comes out of a genuine, conscious desire to re-create a mother-child bond they found largely satisfying; for others it comes directly from their maternal wiring. Either way, the result is an approach to motherhood that is more or less synchronized with Mother's.

Some expectant mothers, on the other hand, may emphatically reject the guidelines they've been handed, proclaiming, "I'll never do this. I'll never be like that." These women may recall their mothers' words—"Just wait until you're a mother, then you'll see"—as more of a threat or a challenge than a promise that she had something to teach and share. Looking back on years spent locked in conflict with their own mothers, highly frustrated grown daughters may head straight into full defiant reaction mode. That mode can impact each maternal decision they make regarding their child, for they have resolved to be different from their mothers in every way.

In the middle ground are mothers who consciously choose to adapt a priori guidelines rather than simply adopt them or reflexively defy them. They may recollect their own mother's messages, while at the same time separating the wheat from the chaff. While acknowledging, for example, that a child is likely to identify with its mother, they may determine it's wiser to be a good role model than to insist their child act like them and think like them. While acknowledging that a mother must make some sacrifices in order to raise her children, they may eschew staying at home full-time as something that would not be beneficial to their state of mind—and thus not serve their child either.

Regardless of how much of their mothers' type of mothering they hope to re-create or terminate, it would be nice indeed if all expectant and new moms could feel as though they are getting something of value from their own mothers as they themselves encounter the formidable tasks of childbearing and child-rearing. What's to be gotten at this juncture? Some support, some nurturing, and some empathy, naturally, but some "emancipation," too, in the sense that feeling truly comfortable in assuming the role of Mother requires that a woman know in her bones she herself is no longer a child.

In truth, nearly all women on the threshold of motherhood can experience some sense of enhanced mother-daughter bonding, even without full compliance to Mother's maternal mode. But becoming a mother can simultaneously offer abundant opportunities for accentuated conflicts. The latter need not obliterate the former if you keep your wits about you. Care must be taken from the very first, however, to keep one's goal of blazing new trails in mind and to maintain an awareness of the complex emotional dynamics that surround a woman's indoctrination into motherhood.

You *can* move closer to your mother (in the sense that you can enjoy increased mutual appreciation and reciprocal respect) while still differentiating yourself from her in positive, mature ways. You can continue to use your skills to manage responses to Mom while becoming a mother yourself.

SHARING THE NEWS

Let's take first things first. Upon discovering she's pregnant, the natural inclination of a mother-to-be is to let a few special people in on her little secret. The baby's father usually tops this list, of course. But, not uncommonly, her mother follows.

No matter how different from her mother a woman is or perceives herself to be, by becoming a mother she is validating her mother's experience in some manner. It's not surprising, therefore, that many women view the advent of their own pregnancy as not only a bona fide admission ticket into the sisterhood of adult women but as a shortcut to mother-daughter unity, or perhaps a "tonic" that can magically obliterate manifest differences between them. In many cases this vision of unity and harmony means that the anticipation of sharing with one's mother the news of a prospective grandchild is imbued with dreams of ideal mothers offering ideal responses. Indeed, this occasion may feel to an expectant mother as if it is the last time her mother can mother her *perfectly* before her baby comes along and requires her to shift from the role of nurture-seeker to primary nurturer.

The good news: For some women, expectation indeed coincides happily with actuality. The imparting of the momentous news of pregnancy has been known to elicit warm hugs and tears of joy even from mothers who have not always responded to their daughters with such spontaneous and unconditional affection. The not-so-good news: Other women may find their mother's Maternal Style so deeply informs her every action and reaction that even news such as this is not enough to serve as a "temporary restraining order" on her frustrating behavior. If you have such a mother, you may receive a less-than-ideal response to your announcement.

"Oh how wonderful," your Merged Mother may exclaim. "We're having a little baby." True to form, she seems to take the same kind of proprietary interest in your child that she has in you. She may even be upset that she was not the very first to know.

"That's terrific. But you just spent all that money getting a Ph.D. I just hope you really know what you want this time. You're always going off in two directions at once! Having a baby is a real commitment." Your Hypercritical Mother follows up her expression of enthusiasm with a judgmental tweak.

"How charming! I can't wait to tell Mrs. Miller," your Pseudoperfect Mother says delightedly. "She's always asking me when I'm going to be a grandmother. She already has three, you know." Once again, her concern about how the world views her puts a damper on intimacy.

"Marvelous. Now you'll want to watch your weight," says your Competitive Mother. "I gained only fifteen pounds when I was pregnant." Once again she seems to be initiating some sort of contest between the two of you. Help! You've already gained five pounds in the first eight weeks.

"Oh, my goodness! But aren't you a little old? I've heard women your age have high-risk pregnancies. What if something happens? You might get sick." Your Chronically Worried Mother manages once again to anticipate worst-case scenarios.

"Of course you'll use Dr. Garfinkle. And you'll have the baby at Manley Memorial. I'll arrange for a private room. Isn't this a thrill? Soon I'll have to help you pick out your layette. I assume you'll use our family surname as a middle name, but what about a first name? And there's a college fund to begin." Still in character, your Controlling Mother seems to have not only your pregnancy but your child's entire life mapped out to her specifications.

If your announcement is met with any such rejoinders, you may feel grievously disappointed. *I can't believe she's still doing it to me,* you may lament. But remember, your pregnancy is a rite of passage and, as such, likely to provoke anxieties. For all the satisfaction your mother may glean in seeing you join the ranks of childbearers and for all her pleasant anticipation of a grandchild, she may also experience a deep-seated dread that your new role will propel you further from her orbit. Certainly, some aspects of your life and her place in that life will alter significantly. And, as we already know, the threat of change—even the most positive, expansive sort of change— can lead some mothers to maneuver defensively and exaggerate the most disconcerting aspects of their style.

If your mother has traditionally reacted to your rites of passage with evident emotional discomfort, you will do yourself a disservice by assuming your pregnancy will occasion anything different. It may, but then again it may not. The most helpful thing you can do is anticipate a less-than-perfect response on her part while still listening for the love so often couched in its somewhat irritating framework.

A Merged Mother's boundary-blurring, a Worried Mother's hand-wringing, and a Controlling Mother's excessive bent for participation do not negate their genuine pleasure and pride at your life-changing, life-affirming condition, nor, in most cases, do the self-referential reactions of Competitive and Pseudoperfect Mothers or even the judgmental missives of Hypercritical Mothers. So remember to look past Mother's Maternal Style to the underlying bond between you. Your pleasure and pride in your condition need not be diminished if you *remain realistic.*

Once again, follow up your reality testing with *prioritization.* What do you want from your mother now? You may find at your disposal a potential wealth of information, gleaned both from folk wisdom and from real-life experience, if you open yourself up to hearing it. You may find a wellspring of comfort and commiseration upon which to draw when you need it most.

Be generous. Why not? In a way your pregnancy already makes a generous nod in your mother's direction. In choosing to have a child of your own you are according your mother the honor of knowing that you see what may well have been her most difficult and most magnificent challenge—the challenge of mothering—as important enough to repeat.

But the question still remains: How much conflict will arise if you choose to repeat her experience in your own fashion?

IN A FAMILY WAY: BALANCING AND LIMITING YOUR MOTHER'S ROLE

Once a pregnancy is confirmed and announced, a contemporary woman is apt to spend much of her time engaged in certain prenatal activities. We mean other than coping with morning sickness. One such activity is reading. Today a plethora of information exists about the maternity months, advising expectant mothers on everything from how to talk to their in utero baby to what exercises will help them keep in shape to what sort of stimulating mobiles should be hung above the baby's crib.

Another consuming prenatal activity is networking with friends who have recently undergone childbirth. Not surprisingly, nearly everyone who has recently borne a child has sage counsel to offer in abundance. Just try to stop them.

In a way this profusion of information is a boon. So much knowledge, both physiological and psychological, is available today that was not available before. Yet in a way so many expert opinions can be confounding. Furthermore, the resultant anxiety and confusion can intensify when the "newfangled" knowledge received by an expectant mother runs smack dab into her mother's long-cherished beliefs.

What if, after digesting countless tomes on bottle versus breastfeeding, an expectant mother decides to prepare for the latter, but a casual mention to her mother that she is off to buy a nursing bra elicits a barrage of nay-saying: "You'll ruin your figure, and you'll get sore. Besides, not all babies adjust to that very well. Why, your baby could starve to death."

What if, after polling dozens of friends, a grown daughter opts to sign up for Lamaze classes rather than plan to give birth as her own mother did, from the vantage point of "twilight sleep" during which one feels relatively little pain but misses out on the very parts of the event now deemed so essential. A word to her mother that she and her husband are practicing their breathing can incite a lecture on the unendurable agonies her choice will doubtless entail: "You say this is modern. It's back to the stone age. Why suffer when you don't have to? You'll never be able to stand it!"

What's a daughter to do now?

First, we suggest you *remember the context*. When she was an expectant mother, your mother felt pressure, too. As much as you feel duty-bound to do the right thing for your baby, so did she. And just as surely as you think breast-feeding is the right thing, she may have felt pressured to bottle-feed because that was considered the right thing. Who knows what will be in vogue when your own daughter has her children? Remembering the context of your mother's communication enables you to hear her positive *intent*, to focus on the concern that fuels her decrees rather than the decrees themselves.

But what about the decrees themselves? Though they may not be your focus, should you ignore them entirely? Should a point of view that seems out of fashion always be discarded out of hand? We suggest taking what mother says and adding to the grist in your mill.

The last several decades have surely done much to broaden our understanding of pregnancy, birth, and child development. But just as surely generation after generation has been cradled in the arms of the "psychologically unaware" and emerged healthy, upstanding human beings. (Psychology, after all, is often just a "scientific" extension of common sense.)

You think breast-feeding helps a baby bond? Fine. Your mother says the baby might have difficulty feeding. True enough, as your expert sources will certainly confirm. Doubtless you will take the appropriate precautious so that your baby isn't malnourished, and doubtless you will persist with your plan as long as it seems viable, in the belief that long-term benefits will outweight initial difficulties. All fine. But it would be as misguided to unilaterally screen out anything and everything your mother tells you as it would be to heed no voice other than hers. In this case—histrionics aside—your mother's communications do contain some worthwhile information. Try to balance her advice, which may be intrinsically valid, with newer, more popular approaches.

Of course, some mothers-to-be may find themselves in circumstances where mother's counsel seems unduly persistent, to the point of being overwhelming. If this is your situation, it is clearly time to set limits.

Humor Me!

As an expectant mother you'll be pleased to discover that you have a kind of built-in limit-setting prerogative where your mother is concerned. We call it the "Humor Me" strategy. Now a word to the wise: This strategy involves playing into the politically incorrect notion that a pregnant woman is a bit fragile and should not be unduly upset. We do not recommend its use as an across-the-board policy, but when it comes to maternal limit-setting, you may find it rather handy. Let's say you find yourself in the following situations:

After having read numerous articles on life in the womb, you have become enamored, in your sixth month of pregnancy, with the idea of singing lullabies and reading Dr. Seuss aloud in the direction of your bulging tummy. Your Hypercritical Mother thinks all of this is, to put it mildly, ridiculous, and she loses no time in telling you so.

Fine. "Humor me, Mom. I'm pregnant!"

You are determined to have a Le Boyer–style birth, complete with Mozart in the delivery room. You've gotten your obstetrician to agree, but your Chronically Worried Mother is aghast: "What kind of birth? Is it safe? Music? You want music? Is this a delivery or a square dance?" Again and again, she questions your approach to childbearing.

"Okay. But you'll just have to humor me, Mom. I'm very pregnant. You remember how it is!"

If you gently, lovingly, but firmly persist with this approach, your mother may well get the idea that her objections are futile. But if there's just no reasoning with you about some things she can chalk it up to "hormones" instead of personalizing it.

Limit-setting of this sort and of all the sorts mentioned in chapter three—including information limits and gift limits—are crucial and often very effective strategies to use during the pregnancy rite of passage. Nevertheless, the issue of balancing how actively Mother participates must be addressed.

A Place for Mother

What do we mean by balance? Simply this: Most expectant mothers would serve their own interests well by remembering not to overly restrict their mother's role in this happy event. After all, they do want their mother's support for themselves, and they want to pave the way for a healthy grandchild-grandmother bond. So care must be taken not to undermine Mother's genuine sense of connection.

Let's say your baby is due any day and your Merged Mother, more relentlessly symbiotic than ever, has been calling every few hours to make sure "we haven't gone into labor yet." Though, in response to your Humor Me strategy she stopped nagging you about your choice of natural childbirth, she seems to have mentally blocked out your husband's role as labor coach. She is determined to be at the hospital with you and, in her mind, has assigned your baby's father no task more significant than parking the car. How can she? To acknowledge his pivotal participation in this event would be to acknowledge the strength of your alliance with him.

For the fourth time today your phone rings. Rather than giving in and inviting your mother over for a second-by-second countdown or fueling a quarrel with your feelings of frustration, you might try something like this:

MOTHER: How are we doing?

DAUGHTER: Great, Mom. Just great.

MOTHER: No pain, no contractions?

DAUGHTER: Not a thing, Mom.

MOTHER: Well, you make sure to call me the second you feel anything so I can be waiting for you at the hospital.

DAUGHTER: You know, Mom, my doctor says there's a chance things could happen so fast we might not get a chance to alert you right away.

MOTHER: But I have to be there. Only your mother can really help you through this.

DAUGHTER: Mom, Jeff and I have been to every Lamaze class together. He knows what to do. Anyway, we'll need you to help in another way. Someone has to come back to our house and finish getting the baby's room ready. Can I count on you to do that? You have such a knack with that sort of thing.

Notice that in this conversation a number of limit-setting strategies have been used. The invocation of the doctor's advice communicates to Mother that an "authority" other than herself is on the case. The use of the word *we* (as in "we might not get a chance to alert you") is, as always, an efficient shorthand way of erecting a healthy boundary. And it is important to remind Mother that the rightful place for baby's father is the delivery room, not the parking lot. Just as important, however, this sagacious daughter has figured out a way to include her mother in a suitable way even as she prevents her from acting inappropriately. She has managed to give her mother reassurance, a necessary ability since every choice that differs from mother's can be misconstrued by Mom as rejection.

Granted, there are many other issues on an expectant mother's mind, but it's best not to lose sight of one's mother even as a new life comes into this world. For indeed, once your baby has arrived, you may feel more needful of your mother than you have for quite some time.

THE BABY AND THE BATH WATER: RECOGNIZING SOUND ADVICE

What will be wrought from this needfulness? Once again it depends on individual temperaments and circumstances. But regardless of whether a daughter is compliant or defiant, in postpartum months, just as in prenatal ones, she must learn to take her mother's input as grist for her mill. Some realistic thinking would serve to remind a daughter that her mother, for instance, bathed *her* and apparently never drowned her in the attempt. Mother never threw the baby out with the bath water in a literal sense. Why should she persist in doing so in a metaphorical sense? Oftentimes, a daughter may find that even suggestions which sound like superstitions or old wives' tales or folk remedies are, in fact, sound bits of wisdom. Mother's hands-on experience is a valuable resource that must not be discounted.

We know a new mother who, quite understandably, grew increasingly distressed because her baby would not go to sleep unless rocked by her. The child was almost eighteen months old, and not only were this mother's arms aching, but the process seemed to take longer and longer every night. She told her mother of her increasing frustration and concern. Her mother replied, "Oh yes, dear, you were the same way as a baby. Finally I just laid you down in your crib, said good night, and left the door slightly ajar. After a week or so of crying yourself to sleep, you began to fall asleep peacefully. Try it. I'm surprised you haven't already."

But this grown daughter was not so sure. Her impulse to draw on her mother's counsel was undermined by a habitual stance of opposition. *Mom doesn't know what she's talking about,* she thought. *She's suggesting something so hard-hearted.* She consulted her pediatrician, expecting a different opinion. Surprisingly, however, the doctor told her that in the past thirty years the entire medical community had not figured out anything more efficient and effective than her mother's plan of action. He felt helping one's child adapt to falling asleep alone was a fine practice. He advocated the same method as her mother had, adding that it would be good to go into the child's room at intervals to offer reassurance. "Rub his back for a few minutes," he advised, "and take your leave again." He described how her baby would at first resist breaking the habit of falling asleep in his mother's arms and assured her that although this habit-breaking would be hard on the parents at the outset, the child would readjust quickly.

The technique worked, but the aftermath of the incident left this grown daughter feeling, as she told us, "awfully silly," not because she consulted her pediatrician, which, of course, was the proper thing to do, but because she was flabbergasted when the doctor said her mother had been right.

Just like the pregnancy months, the first months of caring for a child yield many questions. A new mother must find answers that work for her. Why not stay open to the possibility that Mother may have at least some of these answers? If you allow for the possibility that tried-and-true experience can be happily melded with modern mothering, you can allow for the possibility of stronger feelings of camaraderie with your mother.

But what if, in your particular situation, Mother's helpful advice rapidly exceeds the bounds of the "suggestion" category? A daughter's initial impulse to include her mother in her world to a greater extent may be regretted if Mother moves too easily from her assigned role of outside consultant to that of Five-Star General in the Baby Brigade.

The Power of Motherhood: A Newfound Limit-Setting Skill

What if you arrive home from the hospital with your husband and new baby to find that your Controlling Mother has not only laid out the baby's new clothes (a chore you asked her to oversee, knowing how suited she was to the task and believing it would keep her happily occupied) but also laid in a six-month supply of formula—in case breastfeeding "doesn't work out—and stocked the refrigerator with spinach, liver, and other healthy foods she is convinced will help you recover from your cesarean section? You remind yourself that you are, in a way, grateful for so much well-meant attention and concern. In fact, you, the mother, were looking forward to being mothered!

But before you know it, Mom has all but kidnapped your baby under your own roof, contending that you simply aren't up to so much as changing a diaper. You watch her coo and cluck over your child while treating you and your husband like mere accessories. With a sinking heart you realize that she has surreptitiously established herself in your guest room, having unpacked enough clothing to last a month. You may feel the urge to evict her unceremoniously on the spot, but hold on. It seems you *did* ask her if she could stay for a few days. It's clearly limit-setting time again.

As always, use your three basic skills. *Be realistic.* You do want some assistance from your mother right now, but her Maternal Style is such than when you ask her for an inch, she gives you a mile, like it or not. *Prioritize.* It's fine to let her do some of the bustling around for a few days. You're not feeling one hundred percent yourself yet, and your husband has to get back to the office. But you want her to know that you, your spouse, and your baby want to have some private time together. *Be generous.* Your child is, after all, Mother's grandchild, and you do want her to be part of the baby's life from the first. And now, be firm.

Set a time limit. Be gracious but very clear about what would be an appropriate number of days for your mother to stay. Let her know your husband needs time with his child even while his mother-in-law is still around. Set space liimits. Be specific about what would not be helpful to you. Yes, you'd be pleased to have Mother change the baby when you're napping, but you want to feed him by yourself—without assiduous coaching from the sidelines.

It should almost go without saying that you will experience resistances when it comes to defining and enforcing these limits. Virtually all new mothers since Eve have felt unsure of their maternal abilities to some degree, anxious and fearful that their potentially dreadful mistakes will land their child in the emergency room or, later, in the office of a child psychiatrist. Naturally, if your mother has one of those styles that routinely serves to infuse you with self-doubt, these feelings will be heightened. How can you ask your mother to leave now when you're feeling so helpless?

As always, one must give these resistances their due. It is frightening to face the enormous responsibility of motherhood, but, as we cannot repeat too often, feelings of helplessness do not mean you *are* helpless. Trust your instincts and the love you feel for your child to help you triumph over inexperience. Trust them also to help you enforce reasonable limits where your mother is concerned.

The happy truth is this: Just as pregnancy allowed you to exercise new limit-setting prerogatives, so does your status as a mother. Your newfound authority and responsibility gives you added weight in others' eyes. You may not even be aware of it at first, so involved are you in feeling like a child yourself as you embark on this unknown journey, but you have been empowered. When you need to set a limit, you may diplomatically remind your mother that you must deal with your child in a way that feels right for you. "Mother," you may say, "I am the mother."

Because this variety of power is unfamiliar to you, it may be difficult at first to recognize and utilize, but if you run it up the proverbial flagpole a few times, you'll be amazed at who will salute. Your very own mother, for one.

No matter how accustomed she may be to getting her own way, your mother may be among the many mothers who have been known to back down a bit in consideration of this natural pecking order. Though she—and you—may be reluctant to acknowledge it at first, when it comes to your child, you get to make the final call.

DO WE REALLY DISAGREE?

Make no mistake, however, power is a tricky thing. Just because you have it doesn't mean there won't be times when someone (such as your mother, for example) will try to take it from you. And just because you have it doesn't mean you should abuse it by lording it over someone else (such as your mother, for example). Where your child's welfare is at stake, however, it will always be important for you to know when and if you and your mother really disagree.

If you and your mother have always had a chafing relationship, chances are you will at least occasionally rub each other the wrong way when it comes to how to handle your growing child. Even in cases where the period of your baby's infancy has been a time of relative "truce" between you, heightened conflicts may reemerge as the years pass. You want to be careful about assessing those conflicts before they carry you away on familiar paths of the Mother Maze. Know when you and your mother are actually at odds over a specific issue versus when you are rehashing habitual skirmishes and using your child as a kind of excuse to do so.

Take this incident, for example, recounted by forty-four-year-old Denise:

One day I arrived home from work to find my mother, who was staying with us for a visit, lecturing my fourteen-year-old daughter Celia. It seems Celia had come in from a girlfriend's house with newly pierced ears. My mother thought she was too young for pierced ears.

Now, my mother has never presented her criticisms in a very palatable way, and she was really all over my daughter. She was yelling at Celia: "How dare you do such a thing without permission? Who do you think you are? Besides, you could get an infection letting your friend's older sister pierce your ears. Have you lost your mind?"

Celia was sulking, and I started fuming. I told my daughter to go to her room, and Mother and I had one of the most spirited arguments of our lives. I found myself defending Celia's right to have her ears pierced if she felt like it. This was really odd because if I had been the first one to discover what my daughter did, I probably would have yelled at her, too. So why was I championing the rights of a fourteen-year-old to take such a thing upon herself? It's not what I believed in at all.

In this case Denise and her mother found themselves in the throes of what communications expert Dr. Paul Watzlawick calls *pseudodisagreement*.[1] Basically, this is what occurs when two people agree on a *content level* but disagree on a *relationship level*.

Here, Denise and her mother actually shared the same point of view. They felt fourteen-year-old Celia should not have had her ears pierced, certainly not by an amateur, and definitely not without parental consent. But Denise's mother breached a boundary when she reprimanded her granddaughter. The real point of discord between Denise and her mother was *who was the rightful person to reprimand Celia*.

The irony in all of this, of course, was that despite their pseudodisagreement, both Denise and her mother dearly love Celia. Yet their quarreling with each other did not help the girl at all. In the immediate aftermath of this incident, she felt more confused than ever—and more rebellious. As is often the case, the child was the loser when the pseudodisagreement occurred.

Had Celia's mother been more in touch with her power of motherhood, she might have been able to short-circuit this disagreement. She could have diplomatically informed her mother, "I'll take it from here," and spoken with her daughter in private. While sparing her daughter the more flamboyant aspects of her grandmother's Hypercritical Style, she nevertheless could have made her disapproval clear and clarified ground rules for the future.

Once Denise engaged in a battle with her mother instead, she was faced with two awkward problems: how to deal with Celia now that she had put herself in the position of defending her improper behavior, and how to reinstitute a reasonable degree of harmony between her and her mother, re-creating an atmosphere in which she could calmly and clearly delineate her own rights and the rights of her child. These goals could ultimately be accomplished, of course—few misunderstandings are irreparable—but in the aftermath of such a blow-up, doing so would prove more difficult than otherwise.

When grown daughters do learn to distinguish between genuine and bogus differences of opinion between them and their mothers, a child may be greatly benefitted, as shown by the following, recalled by thirty-four-year-old Louise:

My story is about something that happened to my son Gregory when he was just two and a half years old. He was playing in a sandbox when another little boy kicked over a little sand castle he was making. Gregory hit the boy, and I was just mortified. I admonished my son right then and there and made him apologize to the other boy immediately. Then I took him straight home.

I remember calling my mother shortly afterward and telling her, rather proudly, that I wasn't going to have an undisciplined child like some people. Gregory was going to learn early how to behave.

But Mother said, "You shouldn't have done that. Did you ever think you might have humiliated Gregory in front of the other children? You were too hard on him. You should have called him over to you and talked to him one-on-one."

Well, I was incensed. How dare my mother criticize me that way! I told her, "You don't understand the importance of nipping this kind of thing in the bud. I know what I'm doing. I don't want to hear this."

But later I thought about it and realized Mother had a point. I'm sure I could have handled my son in a way that spared him public embarrassment. I *was* very hard on him. Because of this realization I was able to talk with him about it so he felt a bit better, and I knew I would be more sensitive to his needs next time.

Here again, Louise and her mother did not really disagree. Neither believed it was okay for Gregory to hit another child, and neither wanted to damage the boy's self-esteem. Louise's mother simply had a more prudent plan of action in this particular instance. What prevented her daughter from assimilating it upon first hearing it rather than impulsively rejecting it was defiant habit.

If you are used to disagreeing with your mother, and especially if reaction formation is your primary modus operandi, you now have a new reason for curbing your knee-jerk reflexive tendencies: the well-being of your child. You do have the power to define bottom lines when it comes to your mothering, but you do not have to abuse that power by dismissing your mother's input *just because*.

THE GRANDMA-TERNAL STYLE: LEARNING TO ENLIST YOUR MOTHER AS AN ALLY

Remembering that the crucial common denominator between you and your mother is love for your child can help you implement yet another strategy when it comes to maintaining family harmony. Some women live in fear that the frustrating aspects of their mother's Maternal Style will be engendered in their own children as a result of her influence. Indeed, some-times they are. If that turns out to be your situation, you must learn to enlist your mother as an ally.

Let's say your mother has always been a Chronic Worrier. You couldn't participate in any activity without her rapid stac-cato of admonitions and anxieties getting in your way. As an adult you have learned to cope with the rat-a-tat-tat of her style, but now you find yourself wincing as your own children are subjected to it. Moreover, you find that your youngest daugher, Rachel, who is very close to Grandma, is showing signs of being overly cautious about getting hurt or sick. You have even begun to hear her express your mother's point of view when her siblings venture forth: "Billy, be careful. A boy with eyeglasses could get hurt on a bicycle!" There is little doubt about it. Grandma's Maternal Style has come home to roost.

You may well be tempted to fly into a frenzy and end up attacking your mother for injecting her unfounded fears into your would-be healthy home. But since you don't want to interfere with the positives of their love for one another, setting limits on her time with your daughter would be difficult and wanting as a strategy. The two are very attached, and because of this, Grandma's residual messages are powerful. Now it's time to recruit your mother for your own team.

This strategy requires *generosity* in the very beginning. For it to be effective you must acknowledge to your mother that she is important to your daughter and that your child loves her very much. Because their bond is so strong, you were hoping that she could be effective in turning a problem around.

What problem? your mother will probably ask. After all, from her perspective your daughter is being perfectly sensible.

Now here's where your *joining* and *mirroring* skills will serve you well. You must explain the problem in a way that will not offend your mother. You can't, therefore, blurt out: "She's just like you. She worries all the time over nothing. She's turning into an emotional wreck." Remember your mother's Maternal Style. She is a Worrier. She will feel comfortable, therefore, with another sort of communication, such as, "Mom, I'm worried about Rachel. She takes things too hard. It's not good for her. It could affect her whole future. You two are so close. I think you can help her with this by encouraging her to be a little bolder."

Your mother will be flattered by this approach, and you have said nothing untruthful. You *are* concerned about your daughter.

Now you must gently instruct your mother in how to help your child accept some of life's challenges with a bit more equanimity. You can let her in on the ways you have had to monitor the messages you give your daughter. Finally, acknowledge to your mother that what you are asking her to do may go against her grain a little but that you believe she can do it for the sake of the child you both love. By validating your mother in this way, you may well enable her to engage your daughter in a positive manner.

Likewise, let's say you have a Pseudoperfect Mother who habitually expresses her love by buying gifts. She has communicated her affection in this manner for as long as you can remember, and you never found it satisfying. Now your children rejoice at the news that Grandma is coming, but their comments—"I wonder what we're going to get this time! I can't wait. I told her about that new Nintendo game"—pain you. You already notice how their enthusiastic greeting of Grandma is followed by a retreat to their rooms where they play with their new toys and games, reemerging only to say good-bye and enumerate their requests for more booty. This won't do!

You don't want your children to equate money with love, quid pro quo. You don't want them to be shallow or spoiled. And you don't want them to "take advantage" of your mother. But your mother thinks everything is dandy. Remember, she's always been uncomfortable with intimacy. Though in her own way she dotes on your kids, it's fine with her if they focus more on their toys than on her. The more they enjoy her gifts, the more appreciated she feels.

Now you have a quandary. You can set gift limits, of course, and you should. You don't want your children growing accustomed to expensive things that are well beyond your means to provide even if you thought it was a good idea to provide them. But if you totally restrict your mother's ability to shower your kids with material goods, she will be emotionally at sea. Her comfort level around your kids needs to be maintained in order for a relationship to exist.

So be specific about the kinds of gifts that are acceptable. (As we've already mentioned, this is often key in setting gift limits without giving offense.) In doing so, try to enlist your mother as an ally. Once again, the key to getting her on your team means not challenging her style but joining and mirroring her instead.

Remember, your Pseudoperfect Mother is concerned about appearances, and therein lies your opening. "Mom," you can say, "it simply doesn't look right for the kids to have every $125 video game that comes out. The neighbor's kids get jealous and complain to their parents who can't afford that kind of thing. We don't want to look like the neighborhood troublemakers. Besides, Jimmy and Bobby are not getting enough exercise sitting in front of the TV so much. Why don't you bring them a basketball next time, and we'll put up a hoop. You don't want out-of-shape grandchildren, do you?"

Your mother can relate to this. She doesn't want you to look bad in front of your neighbors, and she doesn't want her grandchildren to look less than handsomely slim and trim. Now Mother is a team player, and it's all because you thought things through. You've exercised your maternal prerogative well, and everyone gains.

When Your Mother's a "Super-Grandma"

Before we leave the topic of grandmothers, there is one more issue we must address. What happens if your experience is like that of so many women who find their mother treating her grandchildren not the same way she treated her but differently. And by differently we mean better.

How many times have you heard people say that their mothers are better grandmothers than they were parents—meaning more easygoing and self-assured, less demanding. This is no great shock. It's easy to see why loving, once removed from day-to-day responsibility, is a simpler, more relaxed affair. As such it can inspire many grandmothers to experience their finest hours, interacting with their grandchildren from a flow of emotional generosity that comes straight from the heart and bypassing many of their all-too-familiar stylistic quirks as it springs forth.

Sounds wonderful, doesn't it? But suppose you find yourself in conversations with your mother where she jumps right over what is going on with you, reserving her rapturous attention for descriptions of the things little Debbie is doing in her playpen. Suppose every time Mother comes over she seems to make an instant empathic connection with your child that makes you wonder if there is some karmic bond between their souls.

A part of you will probably delight in your mother's interest. After all, you, too, think everything little Debbie does merits front-page headlines, and part of you is thrilled to see your mother respond to your child without being Hypercritical, Competitive, Controlling, or otherwise infuriating. But part of you is—you hate to admit it—a little resentful. When your mother and child bask in mutual adoration, when your child seems to get the unconditional approval you never got or the loving kisses you never felt, you are left wondering, "Hey! How come Mom was never like that with me?"

Your mother's seemingly newfound abilities may dredge up a longing from deep within that you have not felt for many years. How come your mother wasn't able to give you what you needed in the way you needed it? The question seems more poignant than ever now that you know what it feels like to have a child.

Alas, there are women for whom this question is never adequately answered. Though they are, on an intellectual level, well aware that love once-removed is sometimes more freely given, they remain caught up in pining for opportunities lost, for the aspects of their mother's love that eluded them during childhood.

The act of letting go of this longing is no small task, and it will seem more difficult than ever to relinquish "the myth of the ideal mother" when you see your mother behaving pretty close to ideally with your child. But the same principles we have stressed throughout this book apply. Without coming to terms with the reality of what transpired between you and your mother in the unalterable past, you will not be able to alter the patterns between you in the future.

So acknowledge your sadness and loss, and know that you cannot reinvent the past. Acknowledge your joy as well. Happy consequences can result when you learn to interpret your mother's love and approval of your child as tacit acceptance of you as a mother and approval of your ability to raise a wonderful, worthy person.

It is time to let go of the dream of all-encompassing mother-child love that ideally comes during childhood. Enjoy the contemporary company of this woman who cherishes your child as you do, and together you will blaze new trails in your relationship. Your mother may at last feel the esteem she always wished from you, and you from her, as you learn to value each other in this refreshing way.

CAN I TRULY BE DIFFERENT FROM MY MOTHER?

So far this chapter has been devoted to dealing with one's real-life mother when you become a mother yourself, but you've probably already anticipated this concluding section. It concerns the Mother Within. She is, of course, a powerful force that shapes our own parenting tendencies.

As we've said, some of you may be very comfortable with mothering more or less the way your mother did. If synchronicity is your way, you will feel relatively unperturbed when messages from your Internal Mother seem to dictate the way you respond to your child. But let's be real here. We said *relatively* unperturbed. Isn't there some part of you that has always wanted to be a better mother than her? It goes without saying that if your relationship with your mother was conflictful, you may wish to overturn nearly every maternal edict she has handed down. Either way, remember, all mothers frustrate their children's needs and desires sometimes. It simply comes with the territory of motherhood. Our introjects come with the territory, too.

In chapter six we offered various strategies to help you modify and modulate the internal maternal voice that sometimes seems to direct your actions and attitudes even when you wish it would be silent. As you practice those strategies they will become second nature to you and help you change course when you find yourself veering toward danger points.

But be prepared. We have also cautioned that no matter how highly evolved your sense of self-awareness has grown, no matter how skilled you have become at identifying *subtle signals* and activating *circuit breakers*, someone may occasionally press a button that will activate a spillover of the most frustrating aspects of your Mother Within. Don't be shocked if, more often than not, that "someone" is your child.

Emotional Generosity and Rational Anger

Let us say you are a genuinely warm, caring, not to mention psychologically sophisticated mother. You are skilled in providing emotional generosity, offering abundant praise and affirmation, focusing overwhelmingly on the positive so that your child feels competent and appreciated. You wisely allow yourself to feel all your feelings—including anger when it's appropriate—but are devoted to the ideal of rational anger. You allow a ten-second lag between any annoying incident and your expression of irritation, and you attach your anger to a specific event rather than a character trait in your child.

But every once in a while your daughter or son manages to do the very thing that sets you off. The muddy footprints decorating the new beige wall-to-wall carpet, the perfectly enunciated four-letter word dramatically uttered in the midst of a family gathering, the flagrant disobeying of an oft-repeated "one hour of television" rule ignite your fuse. Now you feel like exploding!

Instead of opting for a rational anger communication such as, "You're way past your TV watching hour. I've told you twice already it's homework time, and now I'm getting mad," you hear yourself impugning, "Turn that off, or you'll never watch TV again as long as you live. How did I get such a lazy child! They must have switched babies at the hospital!"

Sound familiar?

There isn't a mother in the world who doesn't get angry at a noncooperative child at times. But often the most distressing aspect of a woman's anger at her child is that it reminds her of her mother's anger toward her. We may still flinch when we recall the times our own mother yelled at us, yet we find ourselves yelling at our kids in a manner reminiscent of hers. Does that make us awful people?

No, indeed. In fact, if your idealistic aspiration has been to never, ever lose your temper with your children, then you are headed for disappointment and self-recrimination. Rational anger is a wonderful tool that we recommend highly, and enough can't be said about the benefits of emotional generosity. But you should expect there to be times when such estimable parenting skills will fall briefly by the wayside.

The Art of Apology

These are times to employ the art of apology. When we last wrote about introject spills, we mentioned how important it was to exercise some damage containment by simply saying "I'm sorry." This is true whenever you lose your head, but it is never more important than when you are dealing with a child.

It simply isn't possible to be the type of parent who never makes a mistake, but it is possible to be the type of parent who accepts her mistakes and owns up to them.

Of course we are not saying that any mistake you make will be attributable to your mother's "wiring." Far from it. We are certain you are capable of making mistakes entirely on your own. But many women tend to feel especially hopeless when they re-create a maternal pattern in a way they swore never to do. This very helplessness may upset them so that they forget to take appropriate reparative measures.

So you've done it. You've *overdone* it in a way your mother might have. Now you feel like a failure. Well, that is just a feeling. You are not a failure at all. And by apologizing ("Mommy was wrong. It makes me frustrated when you don't mind what I say, and sometimes I go overboard") you do not "lose face." Rather, you mark yourself as human and accessible. You also model a life skill that will stand your children in good stead. Finally, you come away feeling clear, unsullied by your outburst. Your child's forgiveness—and you will be amazed how easily that forgiveness comes—can itself be a healing elixir. And now you can both relax.

Know Thyself: A Conduit Toward Better Parenting

We have talked a great deal in this book about the myth of motherly perfection, but in light of how many women seem to have unrealistic expectations about themselves in this area, there is something we must clarify.

Love, as a feeling, *is* a perfect thing when it allows for all the collateral feelings that arise when we love someone. It is when we expect our day-to-day execution and expression of that love to be perfect that we set the stage for disillusionment. With a healthy dose of humility we must acknowledge limitations on our most well-meant aspirations. Somewhat paradoxically, the more accepting we are of our individual idosyncrasies, the more open we are to the purity and the power of love itself.

And so we must be honest with ourselves as we approach the joys and responsibilities of motherhood. Who are we? What are we really like? Are there, for example, parts of our personalities that are genuinely like our mothers, parts that, even if problematical, cannot be switched off or denied? Of course there are. As Rollo May has put it, "We were not born alone but in partnership with our mothers."[2] That partnership imprints us forevermore. Literally so, for we carry within us Mother's genes, after all, so we had best learn to observe and accept any such genuine similarities and work with them as best we can.

Knowing in what ways you genuinely resemble your mother can be helpful as early as the planning stage of your own parenthood. We know one woman, for example, the last of four children of a high-strung mother, whose acceptance of the fact that she was also high-strung was instrumental in her and her husband's decision to have a smaller family. "I felt that, like my mother, I had a propensity to get very irritable when too many demands were made on me and when I had no time to myself. It was better for me to be a calmer, more available mother of one," she said, "than the overburdened mother of four."

Self-knowledge will not always result in such carefully orchestrated before-the-fact strategies for mothering, but having the faculty to distinguish between what you can and cannot revamp about your personality will always serve you well when it comes to child-rearing.

But let's get one thing clear. In your quest for self-knowledge and self-acceptance, you need to be tolerant of more than just the parts of you that, for better or worse, resemble your mother. You need to come to terms with the parts of you that, for better or worse, are like your father or your grandparents or your great-uncle Elmo. And, or course, the parts of you that are simply unique.

Maybe, for any number of reasons or for no clearly discernible reason at all, you are a temperamental person, a competitive person, a person who craves order, or one who hates restrictions. And maybe that's something that is never going to disappear. So be it. If you insist on denying it, that's when your troubles can begin because denying who you are is antithetical to loving yourself. If you say instead, "That's who I am," you are being open—to truth, to life, and to love.

That's a fine thing. For the more open we are to love, the more open we will be to our children and the more open we will be to our mothers, who may well have loved us perfectly but expressed that love imperfectly.

CHAPTER 9

꩜

A MOTHER'S RITES OF PASSAGE

Seeing Mother divested of the symbiotic glamour she once held for us means she becomes another person, someone else, outside of us. Which means we have separated at last."
Nancy Friday, *My Mother, My Self*

We have devoted a great many pages to your rites of passage, to the ebbs and flows of your personal evolution as a woman, but just as your life is a journey across the thresholds of change and challenge, so, too, is your mother's. Just because she is your mother does not exempt her from life's vicissitudes. This chapter is devoted, therefore, to dealing with your mother's rites of passage. The better you are able to manage your response to your mother's changing needs and circumstances as she ages, the better your relationship with her will evolve and endure.

As adolescents and even as adults we often long for one thing above all else: that our mothers see us clearly for who we are, give us our due ration of respect, and acknowledge that the passage of years has indeed transformed us from pigeon-toed toddlers into graceful, mature adults. Possibly, with the help of the preceding eight chapters, you have already made strides toward achieving this goal by, among other things, listening to your mother and validating her, by setting appropriate limits, by being realistic and generous, by remembering the power of laughter and of silence, and by understanding your larger family context—the filigree in which you and she interweave. If you are consistently putting into practice the strategies we have outlined, you have likely enabled your mother to at least begin to form a more finely tuned picture of you as an autonomous being, someone who fulfills other roles in life besides the role of her darling daughter.

Now it is your turn. Now *you* must live up to the standards you have long hoped your mother would meet. Now *you* must provide *emancipation with support*. As both your lives march on, you must let your mother be who she is and grapple with her watershed events in her own way, even as you offer encouragement and empathy. This will definitely require broadening your view of your mother, for she is a woman who fufills many other roles in her life besides her maternal role. And, believe it or not, she has many concerns other than you. Those roles and concerns will shift as she ages, just as your roles and concerns will shift in your later years. As your mother's daughter, it will be your responsibility and your privilege to nurture her in ways that will help her addresss her shifting circumstances and priorities.

Now this may seem like a rather stiff requirement. After all, you have plenty going on as your own procession through life advances. More than plenty! Must you participate in your mother's transitions as well?

Indeed you must if you are determined to see this program through to its most satisfying conclusion. Remember, your mother's rites of passage may be different from yours at the moment, but you might as well begin contemplating them now. First, because doing so will enable you to be helpful to her as she faces life's trials, and second, because doing so will enable you to gain strength for yourself and to know yourself better. One day you, too, will be dealing with many of the same challenges your mother is dealing with now or may be dealing with in the near future. And you may well have to do it without her by your side.

IS IT TIME TO MOTHER YOUR MOTHER?

What are these changes, these rites of passage that loom so
large in our mothers' middle and later years? What kinds of
responses to them must you be prepared to manage?

There are some inevitabilities. As your mother grows older,
for example, she will have to contend with the physical changes
engendered by menopause and aging. You will have to contend
with watching your mother forfeit some of her youthful beauty,
some of her stamina. Ultimately, of course, you will both have
to come to terms with her mortality. But beyond this, there
are few absolute certainties.

Your mother may spend many, many years as a senior
citizen. She may live to be eighty, ninety, even one hundred.
Perhaps during those years she will face crises: illness, widowhood, financial reversals. If so, you may have to contend
with her increased dependency on you. But one never knows.
Perhaps she will go back to school, get a real estate license or
a pilot's license. Perhaps she will remarry or play the field.
Perhaps she will take up the cello or the tango. If so, for all
your joy and pride in her resilience, you may have to contend
with your own feelings of abandonment as you realize that
she is not needful of you in ways you may have anticipated.
At any rate, the time most probably will arrive when you must
mother your mother. While you may be intellectually prepared,
even logistically and financially prepared, to care for your
mother, you must ask yourself: Am I emotionally prepared?

Granted, it's hard to be completely prepared when events
are so unpredictable and not much can be counted on, but
count on this: As your mother advances toward her later years,
you will have to relinquish some of your fixed ideas where she
is concerned. The more able you are to observe facets of her
that are not necessarily congruent with your predetermined
view, the more nurturing you can provide.

The fact is that the best way to mother your mother in a
valid emotional sense and the best way to help her navigate

through her elder years with dignity and equanimity is not to infantilize her and "take over" her life. It is, rather, to do what all "good-enough" mothers should strive to do: Give up the idea of insisting that the person you love and care for should be *all one way*.

When it comes to dealing with you, your mother may continue to behave somewhat redundantly. Indeed, we have said many times that your new skills will result in increased harmony and synergy between the two of you only if you are realistic enough to accept that this might not *always* be the case. But expand the frame through which you perceive your mother, and you will see that the mere act of confronting, adjusting to, and enduring life's surprises, hardships, rewards, and disappointments have enriched and expanded her over time. Even a woman who clings tenaciously to aspects of her Maternal Style, remaining, for example, overly fretful, overly intrusive, or overly dictatorial in interactions with her daughter, is not some cardboard character. She is a multidimensional human being who means many things to many people. She holds dear many people and many aspects of herself. The trials and triumphs of life's later years may expose parts of her that have been long dormant and that were perhaps "back-burnered" while she devoted so much of her attention and energy to being a parent. The time has come to accept those sides because they are often liable to emerge prolifically as she faces the changes of aging.

How would you respond to your mother if she had to face life without your father? Or if she chose a new partner? Or if she had to approach the end of her life with a serious health problem? What shocks to your family system might such scenarios ignite? How could you use the skills you've acquired to light her way, to help and comfort her—as well as to help and comfort yourself—in the face of such events? How might your relationship with her progress and how might it prosper?

It would be impossible in what remains of this book to explore every possible contingency, to suggest specific courses of action for every conceivable combination of circumstances that might befall your mother in her middle and later years, but we are going to relate the stories of three grown daughters with elderly mothers. We will tell you what they told us— how they helped their mothers adjust to their rites of passage and how, at the same time, they managed their own responses to their mothers' changing lives.

We believe these vignettes will be helpful to you because they reflect events that are happening or that may happen in your own mother's life and also because they teach some valuable overall lessons. They teach that weathering your mother's rites of passage in a way that enhances both of you requires a willingness and a readiness to draw upon your entire repertoire of emotionally mature skills and strategies. They teach that the ability to empathize—to walk a mile in your mother's shoes—is key to "mothering" her in the fullest, kindest way. And, perhaps most of all, they teach that one must expect the unexpected in your mother's senior years. Though one cannot always plan ahead with certainty, one can be consistent in the determination to remain observant, caring, flexible, and self-aware, no matter what life brings.

WIDOWHOOD: THE STORY OF RUTH AND ANNABELLE

Our first story is that of Ruth, a fifty-two-year-old office manager, wife, mother, and daughter. It is also the story of her mother, Annabelle, who became widowed at the age of seventy-two. Here is how Ruth recalls the event surrounding her father's death and her mother's widowhood:

> I had always adored my father. Toward me he was loving and attentive. Yet I felt chronically torn between my parents. Mom and Dad had a tough time of it. I saw how he dominated her and how she was often hurt and angered by him.
>
> I felt Mom took out many of her frustrations on me. Although she gave me a great amount of responsibility—I was the oldest

child and often put in charge of the younger kids—she always criticized me for the way I handled things, much as Dad criticized her. If she couldn't tell him what to do, she sure could tell me.

From Mom I got the sense that I should always be doing better, always striving to improve, but from Dad I got the sense that I was just right. When he died, my world blew to pieces. Honestly, part of me was resentful that she survived and he had gone first. Then, of course, I was dreadfully guilty for having those feelings, and I was confused. I felt there was no time to deal with my sorrow. My own grief over Dad became quickly overshadowed by the pressing need to attend to my mother who, I was surprised to learn, knew little about tending to certain nuts-and-bolts details of everyday life.

I was immediately thrown into dealing with the years of dependency my father's domination had engendered in my mother. She wasn't sure how to handle things like banking or taxes or taking care of her car. And she did not make it easy for me to help her because she was now becoming quite reliant on me—not the way she was when I was the child who could help take care of my two younger sisters but in a very personal way. She was always on the phone, always calling with problems and questions, always wanting me to spend more time with her. But even as she seemed to be seeking more and more intimacy with me, she continued to criticize me. Whatever I did, she implied I wasn't doing it correctly—"the way Dad would have." I started to feel furious.

Like many grown daughters, Ruth found the immediate implications of her mother's widowhood extremely unsettling. It's easy to get thrown off balance in such situations because children are not always fully cognizant of the kinds of emotional pacts their mothers and fathers struck to keep the marital boat afloat.

Ruth was unaware that her mother had been, in some ways, quite comfortable with her Volatile Dad's domineering approach. Annabelle did not want to have to think about things such as money and cars. As far as she was concerned, who needed that aggravation? But the death of her husband left a void. Someone had to take care of these matters, and it seemed natural that her eldest daughter be handed the baton.

As the Parentified Child who had always been expected to conduct herself in an adultlike manner, Ruth was accustomed to tackling responsibility. Under ordinary circumstances being asked to oversee her mother's financial and mechanical affairs might not have disconcerted her. But these were far from ordinary circumstances. Ruth was flooded with sadness at the loss of her father and overwhelmed by her mother's ever-growing emotional proximity.

In recent years Ruth had settled into a place of "optimum distance" from which she dealt with her mother in a way that minimized friction. Now she felt crowded. Her mother was too close for comfort. Furthermore, Ruth had never realized the pivotal role her father had played in helping to curtail their mother-daughter border skirmishes. With him out of the picture, she no longer had to cope with a Hypercritical Mother whose dependency needs were focused on her husband; instead, she had to cope with a Hypercritical Mother who was for the first time also displaying aspects of a Merged Style toward her daughter. There is nothing like being called on the carpet by someone who is clinging to you more tightly each day! No wonder Ruth was getting angry.

But then something happened. A seemingly small incident allowed Ruth to shift her perspective and to become more tolerant and flexible as a result of that shift. As she remembers:

It had become clear that to make ends meet my mother would have to sell the house she and my father had shared. She was going to move to a smaller condominium and had to get rid of some things, including my father's golf equipment. One afternoon, she was cleaning out Dad's bedroom closet while I was packing books in the study. I went in to ask her a question, and I saw her just standing there. One of Dad's golf caps was perched on her head. She was holding a bag with a set of clubs in it, just staring at it. And then I saw that she was crying, really sobbing but without making a sound. I started to cry, too, and I went over and put my arms around her. I knew in that moment the suffering she felt. She had lost a husband, a partner she had been with for close to fifty years. Her grief was as genuine, as important as my own. Its magnitude was something we had in common, and yet I realized she was mourning a loss different from mine because the loss of a husband is different from the loss of a father. No one could replace what he was to her, and I wouldn't try.

From that moment on, Ruth determined she would attempt to help her mother get her needs met *without completely taking over as her father would have.* She had been frustrated by trying to step into his shoes and then being told they didn't fit. Now she realized they would never fit. That knowledge set her free—free to use her skills in managing her response to her mother and her mother's new situation. And here is what she did.

First, Ruth decided to take more time to *listen* to her mother. Whatever the nature of her parents' relationship had been (and Ruth now understood there were aspects of it to which she was never fully attuned), her mother had a right to her grief and to that grief's contingent feelings as well. In their initial interactions after her father's passing, Ruth had zeroed in on her mother's criticisms and judgment calls. Now she heard that a great deal more was being said. Her mother was lonely and anxious about what the future held. On top of that, she, too, was angry—angry at her husband for leaving her. Once she learned to appreciate her mother's feelings, Ruth could genuinely echo and mirror them. She, too, felt grief-stricken and anxious, albeit for somewhat different reasons. She, too, was mad at her father for abandoning her. Employing her heightened level of understanding, Ruth was able to expand on the nature of dialogue between her and her mother, often managing to veer off a collision course toward a course of commiseration. Beneath it all, her mother had been pleading for enriched emotional attention. Her daughter was now equipped to give that attention and, in the bargain, was able to receive.

Second, Ruth decided she would begin both to diminish the negative aspects of her entanglement with her mother and to facilitate Annabelle's self-sufficiency by *setting some rea-*

sonable limits. Rather than simply taking charge, she began to explain to her mother, slowly but surely, how to do things such as balance a checkbook and get her car serviced.

Third, Ruth marshaled the forces of her *sibling axis.* Since she had long been labeled the Parentified Child, no one in the family, including Ruth herself, was accustomed to her asking for help from her two younger sisters. But she did ask. She called her siblings, Emma and Jane, and asked if they would be willing to become more involved with Mother even though they lived at a greater distance, and to relieve her of some of her responsibilities. Somewhat to her surprise, they readily agreed, Indeed, they had felt somewhat ignored, daunted by what they perceived as the growing exclusivity of Ruth and Annabelle's bond. What Ruth came to realize as she requested and received a helping hand from her sisters was that under the powerful pressures of time and circumstance, the family filigree was shifting. Happily, labels that had long stuck like glue could suddenly be peeled away to reveal hidden potential.

At times, especially when she was under some special stress, Ruth's mother still approached her eldest daughter in a demanding and guilt-invoking manner. But now, instead of allowing her mother's persistent requests and recriminations to rattle her, Ruth had conversations that went something like this:

MOTHER: I've been calling you all morning. Why didn't you have your answering machine on? My car broke down in the driveway, and I couldn't get to that widow's support meeting you told me to go to. Your father could always look under the hood and know exactly what to do.

DAUGHTER: I remember how Daddy used to be able to do that. He was amazing. I know things like this remind you how much you miss him. So what did you do? (She joins her mother's underlying communication—"I feel helpless without my husband"—thus validating her mother and showing support. But she does not accept blame.)

MOTHER: Nothing! I couldn't get you on the phone. I thought you were always home on Friday afternoons. Where did you go?

DAUGHTER: I'm not always home. I wish I had been able to help. (She sets an information limit by not volunteering her minute-by-minute whereabouts, yet she generously and sincerely expresses a wish to assist.) Maybe we should discuss how you can get help in case this happens again and I'm unavailable. In fact, I'll tell you how you can go ahead and take care of this right now since I'll be tied up for the rest of the day. (She offers to teach her mother the skills she needs—much as she might make such an offer to her own growing children—rather than perpetuate an unhealthy level of dependence.)

MOTHER: I can't think of what to do! I have no idea about cars.

DAUGHTER: I know, Mom, and I can relate. I often have problems with the station wagon, and they always seem to happen when John is out of town. (She mirrors her mother, for she really can relate!) First, you call a local towing company to come and jump-start the motor. I'll give you the number. Then, if they think it's necessary, you drive the car straight to Taglet's Motors on Route 9. I use them, and they're really nice guys. If they have to keep the car for repairs, ask someone there to drive you home. (While emancipating herself from being her mother's chauffeur, she emancipates her mother to achieve more autonomy.)

MOTHER: But how will I get the car back? I need it, or I'll be trapped here. What will I do?

DAUGHTER: Did you forget? Jane is driving down tomorrow to visit for the weekend. I'm sure she'll take you over to Taglet's to pick it up. (The sibling axis to the rescue!)

With the implementation of all her skills, Ruth helped her mother weather a dramatic and difficult rite of passage. She also helped herself and her sisters. The framework of any family is rocked by the death of a father. All members feel the impact, and, for a time everything is in flux. Usually, the children— even if they are well into adulthood themselves—are startled and confused by the imbalance. They see their mother alone and in pain, and that is hard.

We don't want our parents to appear weak, uncertain, or bereft. As Julia Phillips has put it, "All children think their parents are the three omnis: present, potent, scient."[1] But, of course, part of the art of growing up is realizing that no parent, no mother, is really all these things. That's why making the transition from awestruck child to nurturing adult where your mother is concerned is so important. And that's why mothering your mother involves accepting and integrating the new roles and relationships that surface with the advent of widowhood.

REMARRIAGE: THE STORY OF IRENE AND BETTY

We've all read or heard about scientific data that assures us a woman will likely outlive a mate of the same age by an average of seven years. All things being equal, then, there is a significant probability that your mother will find herself swept from the bonds of matrimony into the maelstrom of widowhood and that you will be there to witness this upheaval. As we have just seen, much psychic readjustment and realignment may be in order but sooner or later things tend to settle down. Life for you without your father and for your mother without her mate establishes a flow of its own. The new patterns of interaction that have taken hold become second nature.

But sometimes, just when a daughter thinks it's safe to be back in the Mother Maze, things change again. Mother has a beau, and she's going to marry him! Talk about a shock to the system.

No matter how old you are, the thought of your mother remarrying "at her age" to a man who is "not my father" is a shake-up for which few grown daughters are adequately primed. No matter how open-minded you consider yourself to be and regardless of how many times you have voiced the wish that your mother would "get out and date a little," you may not be prepared for the *fact* of her dating, let alone her growing intimate with a new man. Hence the apocalyptic feeling that often occurs when she announces her plans to wed.

Here's how Irene, a thirty-seven-year-old music professor, an only child, and a relatively new bride herself, explains her response when her mother, Betty, announced that she was remarrying at the age of sixty-two.

Both my mother and my father had always doted on me—a bit too much, I'd always thought. I guess you'd call my mother a Worrier where I was concerned, and my father basically followed her lead. It made for a somewhat claustrophobic upbringing, but I loved them both dearly. They were such good people, such a good team. They were both teachers and inspired many of their students, but they took their job as parents most seriously of all, working hard their whole lives to keep a nice house, send me to good schools, give me piano lessons.

I guess you could say they were a bit sober. They planned ahead to the penny and often deprived themselves of what they called "extravagances" so they could set money aside for my college education. About three years ago, my father died suddenly, just as he was on the verge of retirement at last. It was an awful blow. I wished so badly he'd had a chance to sit back and enjoy life.

After the first wave of sadness and mourning subsided, I began to encourage my mother to "live a little." I did not want to see life pass her by, and I did not want her main focus to continue to be me—or so I thought. At the time I was happily in love and engaged to be married to the man who's now my husband. I tried to persuade Mom to seek some male companionship, too. "You're still vibrant and attractive," I told her. "Find a nice man to spend time with."

I guess the applicable phrase here is, "Be careful what you wish for," because when she did what I suggested, I was thrown for a loop. She went on a cruise and met Harold, a handsome, well-to-do widower who became entranced with her. Yes, *with my mother!* Harold was full of a zest for living, and he simply swept her off her feet. He took her to places she'd never been before. He took her ballooning and horseback riding. Half the time I didn't know what she was up to, and I started being the Worrier, reminding her to check in and to be careful. I think I started to drive my husband a bit crazy, I got so obsessed with her whereabouts.

My mother seemed very cheerful and light-hearted, sort of modern and "with it." Even her wardrobe was getting more colorful—sexier! Part of me was glad, of course, put part of me thought, Hey, she is becoming selfish. She didn't visit as much and didn't come to as many of the orchestra concerts I conducted at school. She didn't ask a thousand questions about my life anymore and didn't confide all her many worries to me as she once did. She'd still call me with tidbits of motherly advice, but the "take your umbrella" missives were wedged betwen ecstatic descriptions of the fun she and Harold had on their dude ranch vacation. Being happy for her was my intellectual response, but emotionally *I wanted my old mother back.*

When Mom and Harold announced their engagement and their plans for a fancy wedding party, I was hard-pressed to appear thrilled. My husband teased me that I was becoming the "drudge" in the family. Oh, boy, I thought, how did I get here? And what am I going to do about it?

As it happened, Irene was able to do something about it, but her efforts required much skill and self-discipline as well as caring and empathy. After all, the thoughts and feelings she was experiencing were powerful and not uncommon under the circumstances. Imagine living under the watchful gaze of a mother with a Chronically Worried Style and suddenly finding she seems not to be worried about much at all, least of all you. What gives? You have come to expect those 7 A.M. phone calls with the long-range weather report and those little envelopes filled with clippings about the benefits of yearly mammography.

Despite Irene's resistance to change and her longing to reinstate the status quo in her relationship with her mother, she
knew there was really no alternative but to reconcile herself
to this new set of circumstances. As a somewhat overprotected
daughter, Irene had had spats on occasion with her mother
when she expounded on her right to *live her own life without
someone breathing down her neck*. Now, turnabout seemed fair
play. Didn't Betty have a right to live her life unencumbered
by her daughter's incessant misgivings?

Obviously, she did, so Irene had to manage her response
to her mother's reinvention of her life. First, she had to remember that although Betty was her mother, she was also
many other things. She was a veteran teacher who had influenced countless lives. She was the surviving spouse of a long
marriage who had known the rewards of a solid relationship
and the pain of its conclusion. She was a friend to many.
And, of course, she was a daughter herself. But first and
foremost, she was a woman. Irene thought how *she* might feel
if someone denied her her womanliness just because she had
borne children and lived a long time! In other words, she *put
herself in her mother's shoes and walked a mile*.

Second, Irene *gave herself permission to feel all her feelings
fully*. She got in touch with her need to mourn the loss of the
mother of the past and thus made room for the mother of the
present. She also dealt with the need to reconcile her feelings
about her "betrayed" father, the dear, hardworking soul supplanted by Harold the bon vivant. She told herself that though
Harold might not have made the ideal life mate for her mother
to raise a family with, he was an excellent companion for life's
later years--a time when those who are lucky enough can enjoy
diminished responsibility and more time for themselves.

Third, Irene *resolved to come to terms with her Chronically
Worried maternal introject*, for she realized that a large part
of her excessive concern with her mother's well-being was
being manifested at its behest. By activating her anxious feelings of foreboding, she was, in effect, hanging on to her mother
of yore. She did a Believe-It-or-Not Checkup and asked herself:

Are Harold's diversions really likely to cause my mother harm? Well, probably not. She had read that ballooning was actually quite safe, and as for horseback riding, well, she suddenly seemed to recall that her mother was raised around horses. Funny how she had repressed that information. In fact, much of her vigilance suddenly struck her as somewhat funny, and *she enjoyed a hearty and healthy chuckle at her own expense,* which certainly didn't hurt. As soon as she saw the humor in the situation, much of her tension was dissolved and she was able to enjoy more pleasant, jocular exchanges with her mother. When Betty waxed eloquent about her courtship, Irene was able to convert her formerly embarrassed and guarded reactions to playful, enthusiastic rejoinders such as:

MOTHER: And then we went dancing. Everyone was look-
            ing at us like we were young lovers! Harold didn't
            care, though. He just kept nibbling my ear as
            we danced. He's so free and wonderful.

DAUGHTER: (Taking a crucial moment to silence her scan-
            dalized Mother Within) You know, you two
            should be careful, or some jealous soul will turn
            you two in to the vice squad.

Soon enough, however, it was time for Irene to face the prospect of her mother's actual wedding day, and that very public aspect of this rite of passage raised some fresh anxieties. She wanted to be there for her mother in all the right ways, but she recognized ahead of time that she would have to discipline herself to focus on her mother's joy instead of her own apprehension. Consciously employing the art of *anticipation,* which, you'll recall, is a mature defense against anxiety, she resolved to concentrate on the many positive things this union would engender. A happy marriage would be good for her mother's mental and physical state. She'd probably live longer. Her financial prospects were certainly improved. And Harold was, well, kind of a hoot. Her husband really admired his vivaciousness, and that meant they could have some fun as a foursome. Besides, she wanted children herself, and she bet he would be an enthusiastic step-grandfather. On top of this, Irene visualized herself at the wedding reception, looking gorgeous, acting gracious. By doing this she felt more in control of herself, making it easier to face the big day.

And indeed the day was great. Everyone, including Irene and her husband, had a fine time at the wedding of Harold and Betty. There was, Irene remembers, one moment of profound emotion. When Harold put a ring on her mother's finger, this grown daughter felt she might give in to a few tears of self-pity. Things would never really be quite the same, after all. She would no longer be the Confidante who routinely provided a sounding board for Mother's worries. She and Betty would have to forge new roles and new ways of relating, and who knew exactly what those would be! In the midst of what seemed like an emotional rebirth, her mother was no longer so predictable. But Irene pulled herself together. She knew the future would have ample opportunity to reveal itself. She would have to take things one day at time. For now, she would celebrate. As for the rest, she'd think about it tomorrow.

FACING ILLNESS: THE STORY OF DINAH AND JOYCE

The foregoing story contained a somewhat startling feature. In Betty, we saw a mother whose prevalent style of mothering, her Chronically Worried approach, mellowed dramatically. We have said many times thoughout this book not to harbor false expectations that your mother's Maternal Style will miraculously shift gears. We stand by that. One mustn't *expect* anything, but one must remain open to the new. If anything has the potential to at least soften your mother's Maternal Style, remarriage to a man quite different from your father *could* be just the very thing. By the same token, if there is one thing that can underscore your mother's style, it might be the onset of illness.

Illness is, of course, exceedingly stressful, and a mother who is physically debilitated may unwittingly overcompensate by clinging more tenaciously to familiar ways of interacting with her daughter, even if those familiar interactions have long been a source of frustration. If such is the case, a grown daughter may find herself in a quandary. How will she contend with the intensification of what might be the most exasperating aspects of her relationship with her mother even as she struggles to come to terms with Mother's physical frailty and its frightening ramifications?

On top of this, another quandary commonly exists when a mother falls ill. How can a grown daughter summon up the wherewithal to take care of business on her mother's behalf, if that's what's required, when by the sight of her mother's condition part of her feels reduced to the state of a helpless little girl?

Here is how Dinah, a forty-eight-year-old librarian, navigated her way through some extremely taxing emotional dilemmas when her mother, Joyce, underwent heart surgery at the age of seventy-four:

For much of my life it has seemed as though my mother and I faced an uphill road. My mother's style could be called Controlling, with a dose of Competitive thrown in for good measure. I was enamored of my father, though. He was a very dynamic, successful man, and he was my Not-So-Secret-Admirer, as I was his. I was the only girl in the family, sandwiched in between two sons. Mom seemed more comfortable with the boys, while Dad and I were truly in sync. Over the years, however, I became aware of the ways in which my bond with my father cut me off from certain possibilities with Mom.

Then the birth of my first child seemed to draw us together. I entered the universe of motherhood where she already dwelt. This was one place we could be together where my father and brothers could not follow. We became better friends, albeit still strained at times in our attempts to communicate.

Perhaps the fact that the two of us were on a sounder footing than ever caused me to ignore the first signs of her illness. I suspect I did not want to allow for the possibility that something might interfere with our newly budding, but still precarious camaraderie. Slowly, though, the symptoms of Mother's increasing discomfort became undeniably evident. As we walked she'd stop frequently to catch her breath. She'd complain of "indigestion" pains in her chest. My father and I insisted she see a doctor, who told us he was amazed at how long and how well she'd managed to conceal from everyone the extent of her problem. Mother's heart was weak. Medication and restriction were deemed mandatory. Coronary bypass surgery was strongly recommended. Her life was in danger.

My first reaction? I was outraged that Mother had not taken better care of herself. How could she have been so irresponsible, so cavalier about her health? Then that rage subsided a bit. I knew her desire not to be seen as incapacitated was part and parcel of her character. It was no use to wish it hadn't existed. It simply had—and did. This is a woman who does not want to appear to be in less than full control. It was a matter of dignity, and I realized she was entitled to live her life as she chose.

The next phase of my reaction was even more difficult for me to handle. Mom had the surgery and, thank goodness, it was successful. But as I drove to the hospital for the eighth time in four days, I became aware of feelings for my mother that I had not fully experienced since I was a small child. I began to cry for her and for me. Here I was an adult woman who was playing the grown-up to the hilt. I was dealing with the logistics of my mother's hospital stay, consulting with doctors, filling out forms, planning for convalescent care, disseminating information to relatives far and wide—who had all seemed to decide en masse that I be the one to call to find out what was going on. But the little girl in me was crying out for her mother's protection and love. The very idea of her mortality flooded me with fear, sorrow, and longing. I thought I had reached a place of acceptance when it came to my mother. I had come to terms with the fact that we might never be really close but that we could be friends. Now I found myself weeping in the parking lot and thinking, I want my Mommy. The Mommy who would give me everything I ever wanted: unconditional approval, boundless affection.

After a while I calmed down, mopped up my tears, and marched into the hospital ready, I thought, to do whatever needed to be done. What I found was that my mother had recovered enough to start complaining about everything and ordering everyone around, including me. She seemed full of anger and contempt for all the people that were there to help her. Now I didn't know quite how to feel. I was irritated, and felt guilty for being so.

On top of this I was starting to feel resentful for having to take on so much in the course of this crisis. A great many of the chores that went along with Mother's recovery seemed to be falling to me. My "dynamic" father seemed somehow befuddled and extremely reliant on my judgment. And my brothers seemed too preoccupied with their jobs and their own families to take on much of this burden—never mind that I had a job, a marriage, and two teenagers at home. I thought of that old saying: "A son is a son till he marries a wife; a daughter's a daughter the rest of her life." It rang true. My life was the one getting rearranged, and for all of this, I knew I would never get what the little girl in me pined for.

Somewhat ironically, for Dinah it was the realization that her particular sibling axis would not offer her immediate deliverance from her intense involvement with her mother during this time that ultimately helped her help herself. For in Dinah's family, as in many others where there is a single female child, the reality was that the men tended to defer to her when it came to hands-on matters of coping with Mother's illness.

While Joyce's recuperation continued, first at the hospital and later at home, Dinah tried to puzzle out why this was, and she began to note the very real distinctions between her brothers and herself. As the daughter, she was the only member of this family besides Mother with a female perspective on the body and its changes. On an emotional level, she was able to commiserate more emphatically with her mother than anyone else about the physical toll of her mother's condition. On a purely practical level, she was able to perform more delicate tasks than her brothers without embarrassment. If her mother needed aid going to the bathroom or bathing or "putting on a face" for visitors, Dinah was the designated helper. Though in the vast majority of areas anatomy is certainly not destiny, Dinah came to feel that perhaps women caring for women is part of the natural order of things.

By the same token, however, Dinah recognized the value of men bonding with other men. It occurred to her there was, in fact, a necessary emotional task her brothers might be willing and able to perform. She asked them to spend more time with their father.

Faced with the stress of Joyce's risky and complicated operation, and the possibility of losing his wife, Dad was also in need of extra attention. In the early phases of this family trauma, her father's reliance on Dinah above everyone else had brought his daughter some degree of satisfaction. Remember, while she was growing up, Dad had been Dinah's Not-So-Secret-Admirer. So she readily lent him her ear, even though ministering to Dad meant taking even more time from her job and family. But the concerns confided by Dad in the hospital cafeteria in the aftermath of Mom's surgery began to have the familiar ring of secrets—secrets that Dinah had resolved some years ago to give up keeping with her father. She did not feel it was her place to hear the intimate details of his marriage that were being offered, and she resolved to get *generational boundaries* clear once more. She encouraged him to raise his concerns directly with his wife.

It was time for Dad to disengage from her and to take his mind off his troubles for a while. At Dinah's request her brothers pitched in and organized a campaign to get Dad out of the house a bit more. They took him to ball games with their own kids and challenged him to tennis matches, which he thoroughly enjoyed. They also began to involve members of the extended family in their activities, inviting Dad's brothers and cousins along on occasion. A fortuitous side benefit of this strategy was that Dinah was, to some degree, relieved of her duty as hub of the family communication network. More avenues of communication had been opened, and people were talking to one another without having to filter every question and concern through her.

Still, many difficult tasks remained ahead. Dinah was learning to be of assistance and comfort to her mother without getting riled by her continuing bossy attitude and redundant complaints. At first, going to see her mother after her surgery had felt like walking into a lion's den. Part of Dinah was tempted to yell, "Be nice. Be cooperative. Be different!" Another part was tempted to misrepresent the facts of the situation to her mother, minimizing its severity so that Joyce would be less frightened and less inclined to gripe. But neither of these approaches was really fair to her mother, she realized. Mothering her mother did not consist of demanding that she undergo a personality bypass in addition to her heart bypass, or of treating her like a child. Gradually, she began to calm Joyce and temper her irritable stance by *joining* and *mirroring* her so that mother-daughter exchanges began to take a somewhat different turn:

MOTHER: Those idiot nurses. Could you imagine them telling me not to sit up? How am I supposed to get better if I lie here like a wet noodle? The doctor didn't say anything about not sitting up. Don't these people talk to one another? The left hand doesn't know what the right hand is doing.

DAUGHTER: I know, Mom. It's so frustrating to be in a hospital. I remember when I gave birth to Sam. After the cesarean nobody seemed to give me a straight answer about what to expect or do. I appreciate how hard it is for you. It's hard to feel you don't have control of your own body, let alone the things around you. Why don't I get the doctor to clarify the timetable here?

As Joyce continued to recover, Dinah continued to show respect for her feelings and her frustrations and to share with her whatever she learned about her mother's prognosis. She came to understand that her mother's complaints and stubborn insistences that she was "one hundred percent okay" were coping mechanisms consistent with her character. Just as it had been a matter of dignity for Joyce to conceal her condition for so long before the operation, pride now contributed to her overexerting herself at times when she still needed to take things slowly. Dinah was conscious of limiting her own reprimands and recriminations. Her tough-minded mother had never been docile, and it didn't look as if she was going to turn from a lion to a pussycat now, no matter what.

As the months passed, the importance of relinquishing old resentments toward her mother crystallized. The truth was, there was no more hoping that "someday" all would be perfect between them. Joyce might survive for years, but not forever, and this mother-daughter relationship would never be perfect. But love, as we know, is itself perfect. Dinah could express that love the best she knew how, with an awareness of all her feelings toward her mother along with a willingness to transcend the ones that had, in the past, sometimes compelled her to quarrel pointlessly, to withhold affection, or to cast blame.

The time for compassion and generosity had clearly arrived, and with every act of mature love this grown daughter displayed toward her mother, she felt stronger and more sanguine about the time they had left. No longer caught up in waiting for her mother's boundless comfort to come to her, she felt nestled in the warmth of the comfort she gave her mother.

SAYING GOOD-BYE

The scale by which we measure the aging of our mothers is almost infinitely incremental. Each notch denotes a tiny, almost imperceptible change. Bit by bit, her hair grays and her gait slows. One day she may be squinting at the newspaper, soon the squint becomes a habit, and then bifocals appear perched atop her nose. One day she may seem a little absentminded about where she left the grocery list, and soon there are lists everywhere. Little self-adhesive paper squares adorn the refrigerator and the bathroom mirror, reminding her of all the things she can't seem to keep track of anymore.

These anomalies drift into a mother's life and alter her in such subtle ways that a daughter may neglect to register them for a while. Sometimes there are small moments of revelation—"Mom, when did you start wearing those glasses?" But even so, it often takes until symptoms associated with aging figure prominently in Mother's life that the balance of the scale is tipped and one begins to think of her as "getting old."

In Dinah's case, as in many others, a dramatic change in the form of a major illness was required to bring about this perception full force. But sooner or later the indisputable reality dawns on every daughter: Mother is growing older, and she will not be around forever.

Coming to terms with the mortality of one's mother is never easy. Along the way, complicated issues can arise, and many tough decisions may have to be made. In some cases a daughter may find herself living under the same roof with her mother, having to renegotiate old ground in new ways. In other cases, if she finds herself too uncomfortably sandwiched between the demands of her own children and spouse and the demands of her aging mother, a daughter may be forced to compromise and delegate the daily care of her mother to others. Few things in her life may be harder than making such a choice or helping her mother to understand and accept it. But with love and generosity, and with respect for oneself as well as for one's mother, all things are possible, though they may not be pleasant.

Whatever transpires in your family as your mother ages

and moves toward her mortal end, that end will prove less heartbreaking if one steadfastly clings to love even as life slips away.

Like Dinah, all of us must resolve to ease the pain of our mother's passing, for ourselves as well as for her, by being our best, most gracious selves, by accessing our positive feelings toward her, and by tolerating yet transcending our negative feelings. No matter what the exact nature of your maternal bond, you will inevitably have both positive and negative feelings toward your mother as she faces her own death—positive because she gave you life, held you, and cared for you to the best of her ability; negative because she is not going to be able to hold you and care for you, at least in a literal sense, any longer.

So allow yourself your anger, your grief, your fear, but allow yourself your loving memories as well. For even as your mother leaves you, she stays with you. In many ways she *is* you and lives through you, and if you've let yourself see all or even some of the many aspects that defined her as a woman, you will see that she does so not only in the form of an "introject" but in a sacred essence that goes beyond such things. In the wisps of a long-ago lullaby, in the recall of a caress, in the tilt of your chin or the curve of your daughter's nose, she lives on, just as she lives on, perhaps, in your fiery passion for life, in your facile intellect, in your tendency to cry at sad movies, or in the sound of your laughter.

In her novel, *At the Bottom of the River*, Jamaica Kincaid has written, "The shadow of my mother danced around the room to a tune that my shadow sang." It is not only a poignant image but an especially apt one because it conveys the knowledge that the unyielding bond between mother and daughter spans the distance from the earthly to the ethereal. And that's a knowledge we carry in our bones.

Your mother created a thread between you and the generations of women that preceded you. You are the thread to the future. Through your work, through your love, through your own children, you can embroider and embellish the family legacy. So whatever you do, whatever choices you make in your life, carry with you your mother's gifts and the strengths you have gained from learning to manage well the most potent, the most unforgettable relationship known to humankind.

SOURCE NOTES

CHAPTER 1

1. *Newsweek* (July 16, 1990), pp. 48–54.
2. Polster, Erving, Ph.D., and Miriam, Ph.D. *Gestalt Therapy Integrated* (New York: Vintage, 1974).

CHAPTER 2

1. Mahler, Margaret S. *Selected Papers, Volume 2* (New York: Jason Aronson, 1979).
2. Deutsch, Helene. *Neuroses and Character Types* (New York: International Universities Press, 1965).

Sources consulted for analysis of the Demeter and Persephone myth included Manuela Dunn Mascetti's *The Song of Eve* (New York: Fireside, 1990) and Paul Hamlyn's *Greek Mythology* (London: Drury House, 1963).

CHAPTER 3

Information on seed dispersal is detailed in *Elements of Ecology, Second Edition* by Robert Lee Smith (New York: Harper & Row, 1986).

CHAPTER 4

1. *Webster's New Collegiate Dictionary* (Springfield, Mass.: J. & C. Merriam Co., 1975).

CHAPTER 5

1. Ackerman, Nathan W. *The Psychodynamics of Family Life.* (New York: Basic Books, 1958).

2. Rhodes, Sonya, D.S.W., and Wilson, Josleen. *Surviving Family Life*. (New York: G.P. Putnam & Sons, 1981).
3. Kaplan, Louise J. *Oneness & Separateness*. (New York: Simon & Schuster, 1978).
4. Rhodes, *Surviving Family Life*.
5. Lasky, Judith, and Mulliken, Susan F. "Sibling Relationships and Mature Love," in *Love: Psychoanalytic Perspectives*, edited by Judith F. Lasky and Helen Silberman (New York: New York University Press, 1988).
6. Rhodes. *Surviving Family Life*.

CHAPTER 8

1. Watzlawick, Paul, Ph.D., Beavin, Janet, A.B., Jackson, Don, M.D. *Pragmatics of Human Communication*. (New York: Norton, 1967).
2. May, Rollo. *The Cry for Myth*. (New York: Norton, 1991).

CHAPTER 9

1. Phillips, Julia. *You'll Never Eat Lunch in This Town Again*. (New York: Random House, 1991).

INDEX

About the Authors

Nancy Wasserman Cocola, M.S.W., C.S.W., is a psycho-therapist who, for the past twelve years, has had a private practice in Manhattan. As the supervising social worker and administrator on adult and geriatric psychiatric units at New York Hospital-Westchester Division, she taught a required family therapy seminar for M.D.s completing their psychiatric residencies at New York Hospital. She now lives in Pawling, N.Y., with her husband and son. This is her first book.

Arlene Modica Matthews is a psychotherapist in private practice in New York City. She is the author of several books, including *Why Did I Marry You, Anyway?*, and of articles in such publications as *Lear's*, *Money*, and the *San Francisco Chronicle*. She has frequently appeared on national television shows, including "Oprah" and "Today."